DALITS AND HUMAN DEVELOPMENT
Contemporary Issues and Emerging Patterns

Other Books of Related Interest...

Economic Development and Dalit Agricultural Workers
L.C. Mallaiah and L. Ratna Kumari
23 cm Cloth 160 pp 2007 Rs. 480
ISBN 978-81-89886-17-2

The Relevance of B.R. Ambedkar's Views on Indian Agricultural Development
L.C. Mallaiah
23 cm Cloth 224pp 2006 Rs. 580
ISBN 81-88683-08-6

Behind the Veil: Dalit Women in Panchayati Raj
Sunita Dhaka & Rajbir S. Dhaka
23 cm Cloth 160 pp 2007 Rs. 480
ISBN 978-81-89886-17-2

SC/ST Students' Access to Education: Challenges and Opportunities
Mahendra Kumar Seth
23 cm Cloth 288 pp 2006 Rs. 850
ISBN 81-888683-94-9

DALITS AND HUMAN DEVELOPMENT

Contemporary Issues and Emerging Patterns

Edited by:

L.C. Mallaiah
K.B. Ratna Kumari

ABHIJEET PUBLICATIONS
DELHI 110 094

ABHIJEET PUBLICATIONS
2/46 Tukhmeerpur Extension
Delhi-110 094
Phone: 011-22960492, 65698474
E-mail: abhijeetpublication@gmail.com

DALITS AND HUMAN DEVELOPMENT: CONTEMPORARY ISSUES AND EMERGING PATTERNS

First Published 2008

ISBN 978-81-89886-39-4
(Price: Rs. 750/- INR)

PRINTED IN INDIA

Published by J.K. Singh for Abhijeet Publications, Delhi-110 094, Lasertypeset by Gaurav Graphices, New Delhi and Printed at Himanshu Printers, Delhi.

Acknowledgements

At the very outset we are very much thankful to Prof. Hunumaiah, Vice–Chancellor, Babasaheb Bhimrao Ambedkar Central University, Lucknow, for encouraging young academicians like us in the University and showing right path in difficult situations and trying for the betterment of the University.

We are very much indebted to Prof. G. Nancharaiah, Ex-Vice-Chancellor, Babasaheb Bhimrao Ambedkar University, and Lucknow, who guided, helped and encouraged us at all stages of our carrier with great care and patience.

We are also thankful to the participants who had taken the trouble and of writing and presenting these well-researched papers in the National Seminar organized by Centre for Ambedkar Studies, B.B. Ambedkar University, Lucknow.

We are thankful to the Vice–Chancellor, Registrar, Finance Officer and other functionaries of Babasaheb Bhimrao Ambedkar University, Lucknow, for extending their full co-operation in organizing the seminar and publishing these papers in book volume.

We would like to express my sincere thanks to Prof. B. Kamaiah who was always there in times of need, showed us right path in difficult times, guided and encouraged us in all stage of our research work. I am also thankful to Prof. L. Karunyakara, for his moral support and encouragement.

We would love to give this share of happiness as a token of love to our sweet little daughter Meghana Lakkineni (Sweety) and son Akash Lakkineni (Chintoo).

Our special thanks are to Abhijeet Publications for publishing this work.

Dr. L.C. Mallaiah
Dr. K.B. Ratna Kumari

Contents

Introduction

Human Development is the process of enlarging people's choices—not just choices among different detergents, television channels or car models but the choices that are created by expanding human capabilities and functioning—what people do and can do in their lives. At all levels of development a few capabilities are essential for human development, without which many choices in life would not be available

Dalits remained for centuries economically deprived and socially depressed under the influence of the Hindu society and its orthodox laws. After independence the policy of protective discrimination was initiated. But the package of protective discrimination have been failed to improve the human development of dalits even after sixty years of independence. Moreover, a debate is going on at national level on the issue of creamy layer among the Dalits. Now the question is that whether the human development of Dalits is increasing or decreasing.

Human Development indicates the socio-economic, political and cultural development of the people. According to UNDP reports Human Development Index has been improved in India. But the Human Development Report of 1996 noted that the globalization causing greatly for the rise of levels of inequality and widening the gap between rich and poor particularly in the field of social services like education and health. Privatization of education has been the role model for all successive governments, which required to be understood in the context of globalization. The theme and sub themes are aimed to address the development of dalits not only based on the human development index but emphasis on new dimensions of Dalit development in the context of globalization.

Human development is a process of enlarging people's choices, as well as raising the level of well being in terms of Economic, Social, Political and Cultural Status of the people in the society. One of the most significant factors, which decide the human development of the people, is the Economic condition. It went far beyond narrowly defined economic development to cover the full flourishing of all human choices. It emphasized the need to put people—their needs, their aspirations and their capabilities—at the center of the development effort. And there is a need to assert the unacceptability of any biases or discrimination, whether by class, gender, race, nationality, religion, community or generation. Human development had arrived. Depressed economic conditions lead to illiteracy, social immobility, and loss of personal freedom and eventually affect the growth of human personality. This is particularly so in the case of the backward and deprived sections of the society like Dalits who have been virtually denied all the choices even after the commitment made by successive governments. However the position appears to have changed thanks to the affirmative actions. It has been urged and realized that the improvement in the economic conditions of the Dalits is a prerequisite for their emancipation from traditional bondage to the caste Hindu and bitter status in the society. Keeping this in mind Government has undertaken various steps under five year plans to improve the human development of Dalits by improving the socio economic, political and cultural conditions. Further the government embarked upon a package of programmes to improve the socio economic, political and cultural conditions of the Dalits. New Economic Policy brought dramatic changes in the attitude of Government affecting the socio economic welfare of the Dalits by withdrawal from the role of providing education, health, employment and food security and equality with social justice.

A two-day national seminar on the theme "Dalits and

Human Development: Contemporary Issues and Emerging Patterns" was organized by the Dr. Ambedkar Studies Centre, Babasaheb Bhimrao Ambedkar University, Lucknow on 29th & 30th November 2006, with the objective of discussing the contemporary issues and emerging patterns of dalit human development and the role of the state to enhance the human development of dalits and need for a separate dalit human development index in India. However, the issues like state withdrawal, role of NGO's in the developmental field and affirmative actions in the private sector are to be addressed in these deliberations.

The seminar was divided in four sessions. First session was the inaugural session, which comprised welcome speech by Prof. L. Karunyakara and keynote address by Prof A.K Sing and presidential address by Prof G. Nancharaiah. The remaining three sessions were academic sessions, in which three themes of the seminar—Economic Development, Social Development and Cultural Development were dealt with. On the theme of Economic Development, different scholars presented papers on different sub themes like Agricultural Sector, Non Farming Sector and Food Security. On the theme of Social development, the eminent scholars presented papers on sub themes like Education including Primary, Secondary higher, technical and Vocational, affirmative action and Gender Dimension. And on last theme on Cultural Development, scholars presented papers on sub-themes like Dalits Traditions and Customs, Cultural Identity. The abstract of the papers are as follows.

I

Poverty means nothing but dalits. In this paper Dr. L.C. Mallaiah attempts to examine the dimension of poverty among scheduled castes vis-a-vis others in rural India during 1970s to 2000. He found that despite the achievement of near self-sufficiency in food grains in terms of increasing the purchasing power of the poor by raising the employment and wage, the impact has been extremely limited among the SCs. Even though the number of schemes launched in sixth and seventh plans did not benefit the SCs significantly. But confined only to rich farmers and developed regions as noted by many studies, because the SCs are asset less, low literacy rates, low income levels and lack of social security. They possessed only one asset, labour power, but this too is highly insecure owing to high infant mortality. Poor people have a right to be consulted on decisions that affect their lives. This requires processes that expand political space to give voice to poor people and their advocates, including NGOs, free media and workers associations. As UNDP's Poverty Report 2000 points out, "holding governments accountable is a bottom-line requirement for good governance." This requires that people be organized, informed and able to claim political space. It also calls for devolution of authority to local governments and transparency in use of public funds.

II

Since 1950 the Government of India had been implementing several rural development programs to eradicate the poverty among dalits. But Integrated Rural Development Program is special and very comprehensive program to help for the poor particularly dalits. Here Dr. Mallaiah and Dr. Ratna kumari made an attempt to study the impact of IRDP on lives of Dalits. It says that IRDP conceived as anti poverty programme aimed at helping the small and marginal farmers, landless labourers and artisans. It was thought by planners that these people were poor because they possessed neither any productive assets nor any special skill. Therefore the IRDP was designed to help the poor by creating new assets for them. The IRDP is continued to be an important self-employment program for the rural poor during 9th plan. Therefore, it is suggested to redesign the program as a credit based self-employment programme with an element of subsidy rather than a programme based on the provision of subsidy and supplemented by bank credit. In this effort the financial institutions would have to participate more actively by mobilizing and disbursing enhanced flows of credit to the beneficiary. Other programmes for development of the SC/STs should work as an integral part of IRDP. The Program Evaluation Organisation of the planning commission, the

Reserve Bank of India, the NABARD and the Institute for Financial Management evaluated the performance of the IRDP at different points of the time. They concluded that the program was not very effective as poverty alleviation measure. However it has now been restructured and renamed as Swarnajayanti Gram Swarozgar Yojana (SGSY). Further more, the initiatives taken in respect of credit flows through self help would have to be suitably strengthened. In this effort, voluntary organizations and Panchayat Raj Institutions (PRI) would have to play a predominant role in empowering the poor through advocacy, awareness of generation and social mobilization. As social animators and rural organizers they would help the poor to form these self-help groups in order to take advantage of the policies and programs of the government for their socio-economic betterment.

III

Prof. Diwakar has made an exercise towards understanding and exploring the possibility of human development by acquiring sustainable basic needs through access to land resources. He primarily intended to examine as to how far access to land has been instrumental in facilitating basic needs for human development on sustainable basis. Primary data for this purpose have been collected from 1126 households through census survey in ten villages—one from each sample block spread over five districts namely, Chandauli, Gorakhpur, Rai Bareli, Muzaffar Nagar and Hamirpur representing different regions and climatic zones of Uttar Pradesh. Households with different size of land holdings and with different operational status have been considered for this examination. Distribution and possessions of ceiling surplus (CS) and gram samaj (GS) land and the impact of land reforms on basic needs and social development in Uttar Pradesh (UP). This paper is divided into four parts: Part one deals with agrarian structure, whereas part two discusses agrarian reforms, part three analyses access to land towards fulfilment of basic needs and social development followed by part four as an attempt to consolidate the findings along with policy advocacy forwarded by the rural households. Summarising the analysis and discussions in order to arrive at conclusions regarding access to land for sustainable basic needs in Uttar Pradesh he tried to understand the process of land reforms and various initiatives taken-up by the governments, particularly after independence with special reference to Uttar Pradesh. He found that in order to overcome the shortcomings of UPZALRA, ceiling on land-holdings was imposed and surplus lands were acquired. However this process was also not free from manipulative syndrome. Exemption on various categories of land and sub-judice status on sizable ceiling surplus land provided a significant cover to and in favour of land-owning castes and class. More than 8 per cent of declared ceiling surplus land (i.e. 30,391 acres) is yet to be taken in possession. Moreover, all the land distributed to the peasants is not fertile and irrigated and therefore all the beneficiaries of ceiling surplus land did not cultivate land themselves.

Land vested in Gram Sabha (GS) is leased to poor peasants of different social groups i.e., SC/ST, OBC and army men, since 1975-76 in Uttar Pradesh for residence, cultivation, plantation, fishing and pottery. About 26,52,263 acres land has been distributed among SCs (54.8%), BCs (25.9%), and other castes (19.2%) and remaining land to STs and army personnel. However, mere allotment of land did not serve the purpose. Possession over allotted land remained a difficult task. Non-possession was reported on account of influence and control of big farmers. Landless households were still waiting for possessions. Under possession in terms of area was also found in case of marginal holdings, SCs and Muslims. Over possessions were found with OMC, MRG and SML households. Status of possession became explicit in case of purpose-wise segregated details. Even medium-cum-big farm holdings could manage land allotment reflecting procedural lapses of the scheme. A sizeable non-deserving beneficiary household were selected at the cost of genuine potential households, because of lapses in procedure, bribery, lack of awareness and sensitive implementing agencies.

Even political powers with this given superstructures remain ineffective. Despite ruling of effective implementation with a declared deadline by the state government land reforms remained on the same ground with a marginal difference, as superstructure did not correspond because of their anti-dalit and anti-poor attitude. This suggests that unless superstructure is radically transformed in favour of poor and landless peasants mere usurpation of political power does not empower in real sense to implement the agenda of poor, may be land reforms or basic needs. Vicious nexus of land owning social groups and class embedded with their bureaucratic connivance because of their common interest, all sorts of manipulations of record have been done to foil the efforts of implementation of land reforms. Majority of functionaries from village to secretariats are represented and controlled by the landowning class and its natural allies in politics. Indifferent attitude towards implementation of land reforms and to ensure possession has been quite obvious. Now the land reforms have been pushed to back seat.

Despite the fact that there has been obvious indifference in implementation of redistribution of land and limited implementation, land reforms measures could bring positive and visible results. To the extent of limited implementation, land redistribution could create space for economic security, reduced landlessness, and initiated income generation. Indications of liberation from bondage on account of ownership of residential land were found. Poor could erect houses and enjoy relatively comfortable living elevating their social status. In case of the beneficiary households of cultivable land, production of food grain increased which placed them relatively comfortable at food front. Land as collateral security provided access to public institutional network and credit. These could reduce their dependence on exploitative usury network of moneylenders. Allied activities such as cattle rearing to supplement their income became possible. However, due to lack of comprehensive follow-up package much is left to be desired. Findings also suggest that there were considerable differences in terms of indicators of social development, particularly in the areas of health and schooling. It is sad on the part of implementation that land reforms measures, which have enormous potential for fulfilling sustainable basic needs for human development, have become victim of neglect of ruling class and its natural allies. There is an urgent demand of reorienting policies through effective mobilization of poor so that the policy makers and implementing functionary do not have any excuse and option but to work in favour of deprived masses. But unfortunately advocacy and policy for corporate farming has been accepted which prove a drag on accessibility of land for sustainable basic needs for poor.

He suggested the following measures for effective implementation of land reforms: (1) There is need of ensuring effective possession of redistributed land through direct accountability of concerned functionaries. A land management committee at village level with proper representation of poor peasants should be formed to verify the implementation status. Undistributed scattered land parcels should be consolidated and redistributed through co-operative ownership. Poor peasants co-operative should be formed and follow up packages, access to credit, etc. should be rooted through co-operative. Pending cases on sub-judiced land should be disposed off on the priority basis and a separate legal committee should be constituted for technical support of the poor peasants. Poor peasant committee should be provided legal support to identify benami transfer of land. The benami land should be declared surplus and those surplus lands should be redistributed among poor households on the recommendation of poor peasant land management committee. Wasteland should be acquired and transferred to landless through their co-operative ownership and follow up assistance should be rooted through co-operative in reference. Assured irrigation co-operatives of landless peasants should be formed to provide irrigation on distributed and other lands. Effective insurance cover on crops should be extended through micro-finance co-operative of land beneficiaries. Ban on individual purchase of redistributed land should be executed effectively. A provision for direct institutional loan on land should be extended to the beneficiary of land directly on producing kisan passbook. Subsidised inputs should be provided to the beneficiaries of land. Indifference and negligence in implementation of land redistribution and possession by functionaries should be treated as cognisable non-bailable offence. Administration and Policy implementing agencies should be made accountable directly for non-possession and should be punished in terms of career of service. Best implementing functionaries should be given incentives. Minimum wages should be implemented effectively. Poor households should be organised and proper support should be extended to safeguard the interest of the beneficiary of land. Participation of poor in co-operatives, PRI and land management committee should be ensured. Illegal possessions of redistributed land by influential persons should be liberated on priority basis. Pro-poor social activists should be involved in organizing poor. Effective flood control measures should be initiated. Rural industrialisation, functional education and women participation should be encouraged. Micro-financial credit groups should be formed and self-help women cooperatives should be promoted. PRI should be empowered to form women co-operatives and Functional Education Groups. Technical support should be ensured to promote women participation. Land Records should be computerized, updated and easy access to the records should be ensured for information. Above all unless poor friendly environment is ensured any amount of attempts or initiatives with pious intention can hardly make substantial dent towards saturating basic needs on sustainable basis.

IV

Professor K. Nageswar Rao has studied the pattern of land distribution for dalits in the state of Andhra Pradesh. He proved that the scheduled caste and scheduled tribe people failed to get their due share in land distribution even after fifty nine years of independence In India the average distribution of land to all weaker sections in 1996 works out to 1.018 acres per household. It is clear form the data that per household land distribution to scheduled castes and scheduled tribes is less than the All India average while it exceeded this average for the household groups belonging to other castes.

The introduction of land reforms changed the distribution of land holdings in Andhra Pradesh state during the last three decades. It is showing positively skewed distribution of land holdings in favor of large and medium size landholders.

Similarly, the structure of distribution of land holdings among different categories of scheduled tribes remained unchanged during 1995-2001. There are no females controlling large holdings among the scheduled castes and scheduled tribes in Anantapur district.

V

Dr. Sridevi examined the Intra household allocation of food. Her analysis shows that consequences of getting less food are more serious in households within sufficient food entitlements. Female members of the household have more food insecurity when compared to male members of the household. Any change in distribution of food will effect the intra- household allocation of food. The changing cropping pattern number of days of available employment has declined over the years for agricultural labour (during early 1990's it used to be nearly 9 months of employment but now 6-7 months) which intern impacted the purchasing power at the household level. Men and women play roughly an equal role in the labour inputs to agricultural production, but women are paid less for it, as their daily wage rates are lower by 50 to 60 percent of men's daily wages.

Given the existing patterns of consumption, ensuring adequate food security for the poor is possible by raising their purchasing power. Within the households, female members generally go hungry when available food quantity is low. First priority is given to the adult male and male children of the family. About 60 percent of female households said they do not get sufficient food when they eat. Distribution of food grains plays an important role in providing the food security at household level. Poor households with no ration card are at the higher risk of food insecurity compared to Households with white cards. With the targeting of PDS exclusion errors increased which had a negative effect on consumption at household level. From the analysis it clearly comes out that although there is an improvement in the income levels of the households during 2002, while malnourishment and hunger increased over this period. Based on official poverty line nearly 50 percent of the households are below poverty line but based on BMI 71.2 percent of the female children and 57.5 percent of adult female are under nourished. Our analysis clearly shows that food security did not deteriorate exclusively on the account of non-availability of food but more so due to distributional bottlenecks and administrative lapses resulting into the poor remaining out of the safety nets. The targeting errors are clear indicator of this fact. An adequate quantity of grain needs to be distributed to make a sizeable contribution to household food security. Major improvements are needed in the administration of PDS to ensure a non-corrupt and efficient delivery system. Decentralisation can improve the working of the delivery system.

VI

Water is the major source for human development. Dr. Sanatan Nayak made an attempt to assess the trend of groundwater irrigation across regions in the state. He also studied the extent of groundwater depletion and the factors held responsible for its consequence across the regions in the state and to estimate the level of inequity in accessing various types of groundwater and minor surface irrigation sources in the state. This may be attributed here that over exploitation and depletion of groundwater resources is progressing in the state. The inequity in the accessibility of groundwater irrigation sources among various farm size operation holdings is significant, in which the farmers of marginal and small-holdings are not in a position to access the resource and are the first victims of the externalities arising in the process of resource depletion. As a result of water depletion, majority of farmers of marginal and small holdings lose access to water. In other words, they are denied their genuine share of common pool resources. At present, legislation does not guarantee equity in access to groundwater resources to all section of the community, irrespective of their land ownership. Moreover, there is no legislation that supports the sharing of groundwater equitable. Therefore, there is string case of internalizing these externalities in a systematic fashion. One way of minimizing the externalities is to strengthen the resource base that is replenishing groundwater through rainwater harvesting. This calls for policy changes towards prioritization of minor surface irrigation in the fragile regions as well as supporting cheaper access to technology. The following policies need immediate attention. For example, investment on community basis rather than individual basis would be more preferable. Similarly, integration of groundwater development/exploitation with surface water bodies like tanks is a precondition for sustainable water resource management. In addition, economic approaches need to be integrated with institutional arrangements in order to make the policies effective. Community involvement is required to make groundwater a common pool resource in the true sense.

VII

Prof. Karunyakara has explained the social exclusion and inclusion in Ambedkar perspective. Indian understanding on social exclusion, without Ambedkarian approach becomes a borrowed concept from European realities. He concludes that the Amedkarian perspective invalidates the idea of poverty as the cause of social discrimination in Indian society and finds Caste as the cause of discrimination. It also finds the divine sanction of social discrimination in India as religious scriptures of Hinduism support it. The remedy is Buddhism as Ambedkar felt Buddhist India means non-existence of social discrimination.

VIII

An attempt is made here to analyse the Process of Globalisation and impact on Dalits livelihoods confining Employment, Education Land and Labor and Health in the state of Andhra Pradesh. Globalisation-driven economic reforms and the facts indicate a declining livelihood status among Andhra Pradesh Dalits across key socio-economic rights. Caste discrimination remains a key factor that continues to deny Dalits access to resource and opportunities for socio-economic development, leading to their lower levels of livelihood capitals as compared to other social groups. Therefore, bearing in mind that equality in dignity and rights implies an absence of poverty and discrimination, which is the key goal of most livelihood development strategies. It is essential that those involved in livelihood development processes understand the need and begins to analyze globalisation-induced projects and programmes from a Dalit perspective. This applies to the Andhra Pradesh Government through its Vision 2020 and other economic policies, to international development cooperation agencies, international funding agencies, human rights and other organisations working to secure sustainable livelihoods.

A Dalit perspective to livelihoods entails factoring in social exclusion through caste discrimination into assessment of the potential impacts of policies, programmes and projects on particularly Dalits and lower caste-class groups. This factor has been missing from most attempts so far to assess the impact of globalisation driven projects on livelihoods. A more holistic picture of livelihoods in a caste society emerges if one examines caste predication of access to benefits and opportunities, which pinpoints where greater emphasis needs to be laid to bring these communities into the process of development.

They found that as of the year 2001, the 10.529 million Dalits in the state, constituting 15.93 percent of the state's population, lag behind the general Andhra Pradesh population on almost every development indicator, their precarious livelihood status is borne out by 50.4 percent being below the poverty line as compared to 32.0 percent for the general population. With around 80 percent of Dalits found in rural Andhra Pradesh, available data up to 1993-94 indicates increasing proportion of Dalit rural household engaged in labour work and particularly agricultural labour work. Twice the proportion of rural Dalit households is engaged in agricultural labour as compared to non-Dalit households. The agricultural wages, an important determinant of rural poverty in an agrarian economy, have not risen to meet inflation and rising costs of living in the state. The result can be observed in the vastly different monthly per capita consumption expenditure levels of Dalits as compared to non-Dalits. While the average monthly per capita consumption expenditure in 1999-2000 across Andhra Pradesh was Rs.

453.61, the expenditure level for Dalits stood at a mere Rs. 381.82 as compared to Rs. 564.50 for non-Dalits. Further accentuating the gap between Dalits and the rest of the working population, both agricultural and non-agricultural enterprise ownership by Dalits in 1990 accounted for only 6.3 percent of total enterprise ownership, while non-Dalits owned 88.8 percent of enterprises. Moreover, in terms of establishments, this disparity was greater, with Dalits owning only 2.0 percent of establishments as compared to 97.3 percent for non-Dalits. Between 1998 and 1994 there was an overall growth rate of around 2 percent in public sector employment for Dalits, while the trend for non-Dalits saw declining public sector involvement . The significance of these divergent trends is that with public sector reforms introduced by the State Government in the late 1990s signaling increasing disinvestment and privatisation of public sector enterprises, this alternative avenue of employment for Dalits is slowly being curtailed.

He concludes that the role of state has to be not only economic and also protective to enables dalits to overcome the problems of poverty and social discrimination and access to livelihoods. Their skills are to be improved through expansion of educational facilities. Effective implementation of land reform is essential, given the skewed distribution of land, to reduce the inequalities.

IX

Education is the only route for the empowerment of dalits. Babasaheb Bhim Rao Ambedkar was instrumental in opening the gates of the education to the common people. He was of the firm view that education is not only the birthright of every human being but also a weapon of social change. Prof. Karunyakara made an attempt to explore Ambedkar's educational background, his role to establish various important educational institutions and his ideas on the importance of education for the development of dalits. Ambedkar's educational philosophy is not just for backward classes, indeed it meant for all sections of the society. He wanted to make education to be within the reach of everyone and particularly higher education to be made as cheap to the poorer classes as it can possibly be made. Ambedkar urged Government employees, "Those who are employed in government services, it is their duty that they should contribute willingly 20th part of their salary to the cause. Then only the society will progress. Otherwise only one family will improve. The boy who is educating in a village, the entire society has expectation from him. One educated social worker can prove a boon for them. There is no exaggeration in my statement. What have the Shudras (OBCs) or the Untouchables (SCs) gained? As soon as the wife of a brahmin man conceives, she thinks of the High Court whether any post of a judge has fallen vacant but when our woman becomes pregnant, she cannot think of anything better than a sweeper's post under the municipal Committee. This deplorable situation exists only because Hinduism has inculcated this kind of ambitions to the latter. No change in our status can be expected if we continue to be slaves of Hinduism. If we have any hope it is by renouncing the Hinduism.

X

Dr. Chinnarao made an attempt in this paper to study the rise and growth of elementary education in India with special reference to Dalits, especially in the context of ongoing mega project of Sarva Shiksha Abhiyan (SSA). First part of this paper deals with the rise and growth of elementary education in India since Independence and some of the major initiatives taken by the government with a special thrust on elementary education; Second part deals with the initiation and idea behind the whole project of EFA and its implementation modalities and the finally, perhaps more importantly the last part will discuss the problems and the prospects of Dalits' elementary education in India will be discussed. He remarked that there has been large scale funding and assistance for elementary education since the 1990s, following commitments made by the international community at the Jomitien Conference and Dakar framework for Action. Large scale programmes of 'Education forAll' emerged in the form of District Primary Education Programmes. These EFA programmes were spread to cover almost half the country along with mass literacy campaigns. Although there has been a substantial increase in the primary and middle schools in India since the fifties, i.e., around three times increase till the nineties it, the entire population of the country has no adequate access to the facilities for basic schooling, more so in case of Dalits.

A major concern to consider is the level of success achieved in reaching communities such as dalits and tribals, whose children have been traditionally excluded from schools. Although the national statistics show very positive changes, the figures may not represent the field situation accurately. Provision of early childhood care for such groups may be of vital importance due to severe social and economic conditions, and this remains an area that this not adequately addressed by our national policy. For instance, when the SSA adopted the Dakar Framework for Action (which is originally international character), when it got imported to India, they continue to use certain concepts like "vulnerable sections", "disadvantaged children", "ethnic minorities", etc., which are problematic in visualization of the programme in the Indian context. Crucially, nowhere in its allocation of funding, concentration of a locality where the target communities habitate is given a special thrust in their policy making. Unless and until the policy makes special provisions for targeted groups such as Dalits, and tribals, these groups continued to remain at bay, without any progress. As a result this SSA programme also will remain defunct, at least it will not be of any use to Dalits, as one of many centrally sponsored programmes and schemes that have been winding up. So also the programme, unlike its earlier precedents, needs to recognize the specific needs of the communities and in the process restore their dignity not treating them as objects of reform. This can be possible by ensuring quality education, ensuring access to nutrition, maintenance and motivation of the children belonging to the target communities. However, given the history of state intervention, the SSA is most like to be no different from earlier programmes and will simply be statistical exercise without any change in the lives of various communities who are to be benefited by the SSA.

XI

Dr. Srinivas has analysed the role of education in social and economic mobility among dalits with special reference to middle class dalits. Education is the means for achieving social and economic mobility and middle class status in general. The education profile of the respondents of the present study also reflects these claims. Higher the educational qualification of an individual, higher is his/her social status among the Dalits. Dalit men were better placed in modern occupations compared to Dalit women. The education, occupation and income levels of the middle class Dalits are higher compared to their paternal families. There is a visible upward mobility in the case of respondents, especially; occupation and monthly income of male respondents were more than their spouse in comparison to female respondents. The educational profile of the respondents' parents and grandparents suggested that majority of the respondents were first generation educated. In few instances, wherein either the parents and/or the grandparents were educated, the respondents' had benefited in terms of resources and guidance with respect to their education and career. Second or third generation educated respondents were highly educated in comparison to the first generation educated respondents. This indicated that Dalits had access to education only in recent times. Apart from that, Dalit men had the privilege of being highly educated in comparison to Dalit women. The educational profile of the respondents' fathers, mothers and grandparents showed that the majority among all the three categories was predominantly illiterate. The pattern of occupation too corresponded with that of education, placing fathers over mothers and grandparents. Similarly, Dalit men were better placed in modern occupations compared to Dalit women.

XII

In this paper Dr. Ravi kumar and Mr. Ravi examined the implementation process of Participatory Forest Management (PFM) and assessed its performance in terms of governance and livelihoods.

To analyze the impact of PFM on Dalits' livelihoods in Andhra Pradesh, this paper is organized into four sections: First section deals with introduction, analytical frame work and methodology. Second section analyses how the SC/STs were excluded in the decision making process related to forest governance. Third section shows how the SC/STs livelihoods were effected after implementation of PFM and final section documents some broad summary and conclusions. This paper reveals that the envisaged objective of peoples' centric orientation to participatory forest management has not been achieved due to multiple social and political inequalities on the one hand and unequal power relations between forest department and communities on the other. The institutional and structural changes introduced for inclusive development of forest dependent communities were jeopardized by the indifferent attitude of government to implement reform hurtfully. Unless Participatory Forest Management in Andhra Pradesh go beyond temporary arrangements to comprehensive structural changes focusing on long term and short terms strategies emancipation of the marginalized communities would continued to be remained as distinct dream.

XIII

Christianity in India cannot be separated from the Indian Christians. Ambedkar's writings reveal his own interpretations of why Christianity had no appeal for the Brahmans. He blames the lack of Philosophy in it for them. In this paper Dr. Ninadavid has analysed the Ambedkar perception on Christianity in India. She says that Ambedkar failed to amalgamate/recognize Indian Christians in Indian Nationalism of his times only holding their religion against them. The Missionaries, elevated to a recognizable status finally winning the approbation of Ambedkar, rescued the neglected class. Here it is noteworthy that he accepted the deprived status of the Indian Christians while overlooking their Imperialist connection. Social Justice was necessary for them too, like the rest. If they had being dependent on government help, they would have to 'mobilize, to agitate, to organize' for effective political action.

Ambedkar always spoke in favour of the deprived classes irrespective of the religion they belonged to. Ambedkar went on to give explanations for the failure of Dalit Christians to found a movement. He blamed educated Christians for not taking up cudgels on their behalf, because of class divisions. Dalit Christians were hence leaderless (today Udit Raj takes the lead). Then, their mental make-up does not let them break away from the past. Lastly, he blames the teachings of the Christian church which promises forgiveness of sins on conversion.

The two questions that Ambedkar raised forty years ago have more relevance today than earlier. 'The mentality of the convert has not changed and neither has it discarded Caste. There are Brahman Christians and Non-Brahman Christians.' The social condition of the coverts is unchanged. Even now, they want 'safeguard of their civil liberties and ways and means for their economic uplift'. The Missionaries had highlighted that the Caste-system was an insult to human dignity. The egalitarian ideas spread by them, had encouraged the lower castes to raise themselves.

XIV

Human development and Human rights are closely inter-related. The development of human being cannot be accomplished if all the aspects of human rights, such as civil, political, socio-economic and culture rights are recognised and protected. In the contemporary human right discourse, the importance of human development cannot be overlooked. Human rights are inalienable and it consists of civil-political, socio-economic and cultural rights of human being as a individual or group. The individual need a conducive environment for complete development of self.

Here Mr. Shashi Kumar attempted to study the human development of dalits in human rights perspective. He has analyzed the nature of discrimination and exploitation pertaining to dalit community in India. It discusses the various constitutional safeguards and measures provided by the state in ameliorating the condition of the dalits.

From the human rights point of view the Hindu Social system has conflicting relation with universal human rights norms. In the Hindu social order the life of human being is regulated by religion. The Hindu social system of social and religious governance is found not on the principle of liberty, equality and fraternity and the democratic values, which formed the basis of universal human rights, but the principle of inequality in every sphere of life. Even after the sixty years of independence in the contemporary Indian society, these disparities and inequalities in the context of dalits are still prevailing. The unjust social order of Hindu society obstructs in the fulfilment of universal respect for human rights.

Though the dalit word is not reflected in the Constitution of India. But the reference of Scheduled Caste and Scheduled Tribe connotes its synonym. Under the Article 14, in Indian Constitution, all the citizens of our country are equal before law and they are treated equal irrespective of their difference on caste, creed, language and regions. Under the Article 17 the untouchability has been abolished. To provide effect to this article, the Untouchability (Offences) Act, 1955 and later this act was made more stringent through amendment and also renamed as the Protection of Civil Rights Act, 1955. The PCR Act provides for penalties for refusing admission to hospitals, educational institutions, hostels, or temples etc., for refusing to sell goods or vendor services, for preventing the exercise. Article 330 provides for reservation of seats for SC/STs in the Lok Sabha. Article 332 provides for reservation of seats for SC/STs in the State Vidhan Sabhas (Legislative Assemblies). Despite of the constitutional safeguards protection and promotion of human rights of dalits couldn't be materialised without a sensitisation of the society. There is greater need for effective state intervention in the form of rigorous implementation of various legislative and development measures for the dalits.

1

Rural Poverty and Dalits

Dr. L.C. Mallaïah

Human Development Report 1997, on poverty, defined it as deprivation in the valuable things that a person can do or be. The term human poverty was coined to distinguish this broad deprivation from the narrower income poverty, a more conventional definition limited to deprivation in income or consumption.

Poverty for generations has been a permanent feature in Indian life. It is as old as caste. If caste was divisive, poverty was distressing. They account for almost all the miseries of Indians. Their contributions proved formidable against all attempts at redemption.

The poor in India is often identified with cultivators' agricultural laborers, artisan, craftsman, slum dwellers, coolies, scavengers, sweepers, weavers and other low and menial occupations in towns, cities and villages, SCs, STs, and other backward classes. They have been termed as weaker sections in the society. This paper attempts to examine the dimension of poverty among scheduled castes vis-a-vis others in rural India during 1970s to 2000.

Poverty: Definition and Measurement

Human Development Report 1997, on poverty, defined it as deprivation in the valuable things that a person can do or be. The term human poverty was coined to distinguish this broad deprivation from the narrower income poverty, a more conventional definition limited to deprivation in income or consumption. Poverty is often viewed as a state when an individual cannot secure enough to extensively perform productive tasks. Extreme poverty is absolute and in principle, individual specific, as the needs of individuals change with age, sex and life conditions. The nutrition experts have tried to quantify this in terms of calorie intake equivalent to daily energy requirements. There is considerable disagreement on the issue of what is adequate calorie intake for an average India (Sukhatme 1965). Irrespective of the inconclusive nature of the debate, the narrow definition of Poverty in terms of minimum daily dietary requirements of an individual has been accepted by the Planning Commission and many other researchers as the norm for the measurement of poverty.

The issue of minimum level of living expressed in terms of daily food requirements found place perhaps for the first time in a study entitled a perspective of Development: 1961-1976, "Implications of Planning for a Minimum Level of Living" (1962),[1] prepared by the perspective planning division of the Planning Commission. It advocated a minimum consumption level of Rs. 20 per capita per month at 1960-61 prices (Rs. 25 per capita per month for urban areas). A norm of 2,250 calories was used by (Dandekar and Rath 1971), the monetary equivalent of this calorie norm is used as the 'poverty line' to distinguish between the poor from the non-poor. The 'Task force' (Planning Commission 1979) has presented this at 2,435 calories intake per day/per head for rural areas rounded off to 2,400 and 2,100 calories for urban areas. Such definition does not clearly consider the need for having a minimum norm for clothing housing, medical and educational facilities.

The method of converting the minimum adequate calorie intake into its cost equivalent is also not agreed to unanimously. There is considerable disagreement on the consumption basket (Panikkar) and the relevant price indices that have been used in the estimation of poverty (Jain & Minhas) India being a vast country with varied consumption habit it has been impossible to have a single representative consumption basket and have over the years witnessed wide variations in different parts of the country. The present official procedure for updating the poverty line takes care of only price changes while the consumption basket has been kept constant. Hence, a number of estimates were given Rs. 18.26 (FAO) Rs. 15.71 (Sukhatme), Rs. 14.0 (Bardhan) Rs. 16.67, (Minhas), Rs. 18.0 (Ohja), Rs. 16.63 (Rudra) and Rs. 14.2 (Dandekar and Rath) all at 1960-61 prices. The Planning Commission used a norm, which is close to Rs. 20, and its calorie is equivalent till a force in the Planning Commission estimated the poverty line at Rs.49.09 per capita per month for rural areas and Rs.56.64 per capita per month for urban areas at 1973-74 prices. Since then this figure has been updated taking into account the changes in price levels.

Current consumption is generally regarded as a better measure of living standard than current income, since it reflects house-holds ability to better their standard of living through saving and borrowing, despite income fluctuation. A consumption-based poverty line reflects the expenditure necessary to buy the minimum standard of calories as prescribed in the poverty norm. The household consumption surveys undertaken by the National Sample survey Organization (NSSO) in India is the only source material that could be used for making such poverty estimates at national and regional level.

Incidence of Poverty Among Scheduled Castes

From Table 1.1 it is noted that incidence of poverty in case of SCs was 64.6% and 72.4% in case of the total population at all India level. It declined by 1987-88 among all social groups in rural areas. In 1987-88 the incidence of poverty among SC was 44.7% and 52.6% in case of STs, while it was only 33.4% in case of total population. But poverty remains to be high in case of SC/STs. From Table 1.2 it is noted that incidence of poverty in case of SCs and STs in urban areas was high with 40.4% and 39.9 respectively in 1983-84. In 2000 the poverty is 36.25 percent in rural SC and 38.47 in urban areas. But in case of ST it is 45.86 percent in rural areas and 34.75 percent in urban areas.

From tables 1.3 and 1.4 it is found that there was some improvement in the monthly per capita expenditure at all social groups during 1983 to 1987-88 in both rural and urban areas at all India level. However there is a significant gap between the per capita consumption levels of SC/ST and others and it has widened during 1983-1987. At all India rural level compared to the MPCE of Rs. 112/- the corresponding amount are Rs. 99/-, Rs. 87/- and Rs. 120/- respectively for SC, ST and others during 1983 and among all groups it increased compared to the MPCE of Rs.123.71, the corresponding amount are Rs. 133.35/-, Rs. 123.04 and Rs. 169.23/- respectively for SC, ST and others during 1987-88 (Table 1.3).

The relative position of the three groups of population with respect to their MPCE in the urban areas, as may be observed from Table 1.4, is not much different from that of the rural, the only opponent difference is that the level of MPCE is marginally higher for ST and both for SC and ST the MPCE is less than 80% that others in 1983 and 1987.

Table 1.5 and 1.6 gives the average MPCE (Rs) for the different groups of households for the rural and urban areas state wise during 1983 to 1987-88. In the states of Sikkim, Punjab, Himachal Pradesh and Haryana the MPCE was higher among all households. In almost all the states there is a significant gap between the per capita consumption levels of SC/ST and others and it has widened during 1983-1987. In the urban areas (Table 1.6) similar trend was observed.

Agricultural Growth and Rural Poverty

It is fruitful to examine the trends in the agrarian economy, which have a bearing on the direction of change in the incidence of rural poverty. Even though no firm relationship has been established between the rate of growth of agricultural production and reduction in rural poverty, higher over all rates of growth with perceptible margins above the rates of growth of rural population should be expected to set the pace for sustained reduction in poverty. High rates of growth also help through their favourable affect on prices paid by the poor for food and also through employment linkage effects between agriculture and non-agriculture.

The results of the analysis of data of 32nd Round (1977-

78), 38th (1983-84) and 43rd (1987-88) on rural poverty indicates a reduction in the percentage of poor from 51.2% to 33.4% for SCs. Among the major states, almost all states showed a decline of poverty among SCs and STs. (Hanumantha Rao 1985), (Vaidyanathan 1986) study show that the rate of growth of food grain production could be expected to reduce the incidence of rural poverty. But the decline in the incidence of poverty across the states does show a pattern which can be meaningfully related to growth rate of agricultural production. The agriculturally developed states such as Punjab and Haryana where the growth rates were at 3.80% and 4.52% in 1981-82 and 1991-92 respectively the incidence of poverty recorded low where MPCE was Rs. 270.30 and Rs. 251.37 respectively in 1987-88. (Ahulwalia 1985) study highlights the condition, his study on rural poverty show the growth of agricultural output per head. The regions experiencing a faster rate of out put growth (GNF) has shown a reduction in the proportion of people below the poverty line. Whereas, the agriculturally backward areas such as Bihar (71.1%), Orissa (54.9%), Maharashtra (55.9%) are marked with high incidence of poverty in 1983-84 among SCs. Even though the higher rate of growth agriculture showed a decline in the incidence of poverty. There was a wide gap between the Scheduled Castes (53.1%) and non SC/ST (40.4%) during 1983-84. (Radhakrishna 1985) study shows that the agricultural growth has benefited only the big farmers, the losers well the small farmers and the backward people.

Even those who recognize the positive role of agricultural development in eradicating poverty think in terms of 'trickle down' effects of agricultural growth. The very term implies scanty benefits flowing to the poor from agricultural growth among the small farmers and share croppers, increase in cropping intensity of rise in agricultural wages and employment as necessary mechanism through which agricultural development can make a significant impact on rural poverty and equality. Studies by (Parthasarathy, 1971), (Srinivas, 1979), (Hanumantha Rao, 1977) shows the situation.

Unemployment Situation of the SCs

The trends in real wages of the rural poor together with trends in employment provide the basic information to judge whether condition are being created for the incomes of the poorest section in rural society.

There are number of studies (Bardhan, 1984), (Brahmananda, 1982), (Visaria, 1980), (Krishna Murthy, 1984), on the trends for the fifties and sixties.

The SCs constitute a significant section of the poor in India. A look at some of the variables of economic level of living brings out the fact clearly. The occupational distribution and the access to land highlights that the economic level of living among SCs is very low compared to other.

The high incidence of landlessness and near landlessness among SC population creates an enormously high proportion of large labor among them. The information generated by successive rural Labour inquires throw additional light on the incidence of wage labour among SCs in rural areas. In 1987-88 of the total SC, rural households, this proportion was quite high compared to 51.16% among others. This indicates that nearly 63% of SC households have to resort to wage employment to earn major part of their income (Table 1.7).

As the wage earnings position and real agricultural wages were not available for the SCs separately to understand the wage earnings, the percentage of wage earners to total earners in rural labour household presented in Table 1.8 are used. From the table both the male and female wage earners to total earners declined since 1974-75 to 1987-88. The decline is very much higher among the females; similar trend was observed in all the states.

Table 1.9 shows that the real agricultural wages have raised both for male and female during 1964-65 to 1987-88. The growth rates remained to be stagnated in the rural India (Table 1.10). The state level real wages too remained stagnant during 1983 to 1987-88, both among men and women, even though the agricultural growth recorded 3.43% during 1980s.

The economic well-being would depend on the employment opportunities both in farm and rural non-farm sectors. Table 1.11 presents the picture on persons usually employed and usually co-employed for rural and urban areas during 1977-78 to 1987-88. As per the NSS survey the persons engaged in any gainful activity are considered "employed" and persons who, owing to lack of work, had not worked but either express their willingness or availability for work under the prevailing conditions of work and remuneration are considered "unemployed". It is noted that among all groups the unemployed persons are raising since 1977-78 among SCs both in rural and urban areas compared to STs and others. The rate also seems to be much higher at 12.71% in 1987-88 for SCs in rural areas among male, whereas it was only 8.60% for STs and 6.09% for others. Let us view this unemployment trends separately in Table 1.12 it presents the unemployment rates for SC, ST and others for the year 1977-78, 1983-84 and 1987-88. In the case of unemployment rate based on usual status there is no significant difference in the unemployment rate between the SCs and others. In fact, the unemployment rate of SCs is slightly lower than others. This has been the case in earlier years as well. The NSS treats a person to be usually employed if he or she worked for more than 180 days, in a year. Since SC workers have limited alternative other than wage employment their participation in the work would be certainly higher (i.e., more than 180 days) than others. Now sooner we move on to the unemployment rate based on current weekly status and current daily status the picture changes completely. The unemployment rate for SCs is much higher than the other group. For instance, in 1977-78 and 1983-84 the unemployment rate of SC male workers were higher at 3.90% and 4.03% for others respectively. Similar gap exists for female too. The same was observed for the year 1987-88.

Table 1.13 and 1.14 presents the state wise analysis of the usually employed and unemployed in rural India for the years 1983 and 1987-88. Factors noted from the tables are the unemployment rates among the agriculturally developed states are higher for SCs than others and STs in 1987-88. In Punjab, 13.89% of male SCs where unemployment where as it is only 11.07% for STs and 6.50% for others and in Haryana 13.37 of male SCs where unemployed, whereas females. Same situation prevailed in 1983. Whereas in the states with low agricultural growth the percentage of unemployed was higher among the SCs compared to others. The unemployed increased in all states among SCs except Tamil Nadu where the unemployed decreased from 22.20% to 13.47% during 1983 to 1987-88 among males. The female unemployed too increased in all states. The unemployed where very high among SCs both in male and female compared to STs and others.

The distress economic situation of scheduled caste workers is reflected in the unemployment rate, which is not allowing them to come out of the grip of poverty. Since there has been a decline in the growth rate of employment in rural non-farm sector and urban informal sector in public sector and near stagnation in the growth rate of employment in organised private sector, must have affected more seriously the employment of scheduled caste as they mainly depend on wage paid or employment.

Table 1.15 the percentage of non-form male workers for general population declined from 25.5% in 1987-88 to 24.40% in 1992 and for female from 15.30% to 13.80% respectively. About 25% of SC males and 17.39% of SC females in 1987-88 were employed in rural non-form activities. The percentage of SC male and female workers in rural non-form sector declined from 23.40% to 15.60% respectively in 1992-93. The decline in rural non-farm and urban sector was the outcome of curtailment in the government expenditure. It is well known that growing public expenditure was in part mainly responsible for rapid employment growth in the rural non-form sector in 1980s.18

Regarding the trends in employment of SCs in Government service and public sector undertakings Table 1.16 and 1.17 provides the details. It is observed that since the beginning of the reservation in these sectors, there has been an improvement between 1970 and 1990. However the representation varied across services. The representation of SCs was much below the required quota in grade 'A' and 'B' services. There was a high concentration of SC employees in C and D grade jobs. This can be due to the low educational status of SCs.

Education is an important component of development index. Education not only improves the skills of people leading to increase in the level of productivity but also acts as an agent of social change. Education particularly technical and vocational education helps the people in securing employment in increasingly their level of income and consumption and living standards and social and economic status of people. The literacy rates (Table 1.18) in an important indicator of educational development. As per the 1991 census, the literacy rate was 37.4% for SCs, 29.6% among STs and 57.7% among others. Even though there was improvement in literacy rates. In 1981 the literacy rates were 21.38%, 16.35% and 36.23% for SC, ST and others respectively. Kerala recorded the highest literacy rate for (79.7%), for SCs / STs (57.2%) and 91.3 for others in 1991. In 2001 it is little improved among all sections. The lowest literacy rate was noted in Bihar at 19.9% for SCs, 26.8% for STs and 43.1% for others in 1991. In the case of STs Manipur had a literacy rate of 53.6% while Andhra Pradesh had only 17.2% as per 1991 census.

It is also noted that a large number of SC and ST children discontinue their studies prematurely before completing the level for which they were enrolled. The reports of commission for SC and ST show that there was some improvement in the higher education among the dalits.

Even though it is noted in Table 17 that the literacy rates have increased from 1981 to 1991. We find that there is a wide gap between the dalits and others regarding the educational levels. The low level of educational development was mostly because of poverty and also due to social stigma like untouchability as found by many studies. (Nancharaiah, Hanumantha Rao, G) This deficiency is making them to depend on agricultural sector as agricultural laborers.

Despite the achievement of near self-sufficiency in food grains in terms of increasing the purchasing power of the poor by raising the employment and wage, the impact has been extremely limited among the SCs. Even though the number of schemes launched in sixth and seventh plans did not benefit the SCs significantly. But confined only to rich farmers and developed regions as noted by many studies because the SCs are asset less, low literacy rates, low income levels and lack of social security. They possessed only one asset, labour power, but this too is highly insecure owing to high infant mortality. Poor people have a right to be consulted on decisions that affect their lives. This requires processes that expand political space—to give voice to poor people and their advocates, including NGOs, free media and workers associations. As UNDP's Poverty Report 2000 points out, "holding governments accountable is a bottom-line requirement for good governance." This requires that people be organized, informed and able to claim political space. It also calls for devolution of authority to local governments and transparency in use of public funds.

REFERENCES

1. Planning Commission (1962), 'Perspective of Development 1961-1976: Implications of Planning for a Minimum Level of Living. A Decade of Development', Perspective Planning Division, reproduced in *Poverty and Income Distribution in India,* edited by T.N. Srinivasan & P.K. Bardhan (1974).
2. Dandekar, V.M. & N. Rath (1971): *Poverty in India* (Poona, Indian School of Political Economy).
3. Planning Commission (1979) , "Report of the Task Force on Projections of Minimum Needs and Effective Consumption", Government of India.
4. Panikkar, P.G.K. (1972), "Economies of Nutrition", *EPW,* Annual Number, 1972.
5. Jain, L.R. & B.S. Minhas (1991). "Rural and Urban Consumer Price indices by commodity Groups (States and all India: 1970-71 to 1983)", *Sarvekshana,* Vol. XV, No. 1, July-Sept. 1991, (Issue No. 49).
6. Sudip Kumar Mohapatra (1997): "Poverty alleviation Anathema of the Indian experience". *Reserve Bank of India Occasional papers,* Vol. 18, Nos. 2 & 3, special issue (June and Sept.)
7. Hanumantha Rao, C.H. (1985); "Agricultural Growth and Rural Poverty: Some lessons from past Experience", *EPW,* Vol. XII, Nos.33 & 34, Special Number, August.
8. Vaidyanathan (1986), Agricultural Development of Rural Poverty, Institute of Development Studies, Madras (Mimeo).
9. Ahluwalia, M. (1978), "Rural Poverty & agricultural

Performance in India", *Journal of Development Studies*, Vol. 14, April 1978, pp. 298-323.

10. Radhakrishna, R., S.A.R. Sastry and S. Sudhakar Reddy (1983): "Determinants and Dimensions of Rural Poverty, some Implications for Development". CESS, Hyderabad, Nov. 1983.
11. Parthasarthay, G. (1987): Changes in the Incidence of Rural Poverty and Recent Trends in some aspects of Agrarian Economy, *Indian Journal of Agricultural Economics*, Vol. 42, No. 1, Jan.-March: 1987.
12. Srinivasan, T.N. (1979): "Trends in Agriculture in India 1949-50 to 1977-78", *EPW*, Vol. XIV, Nos. 30, 31 and 32. Special Number, August 1979.
13. Hanumantha Rao, G. (1977): *Caste and Poverty: A Case Study of SC in A Delta Village*, Savitri Publications, Malikipuram.
14. Bardhan, P.K. (1984): *Land, Labour and Rural Poverty: Essays in Development Economics*, Oxford University Press, Delhi: 1984.
15. Brahmananda, P.R. (1982): *Productivity in the Indian Economy*, Himalaya Publishing House, Bombay 1982.
16. Visaria, P. (1980): 'Poverty and Unemployment in India', *Indian Journal of Agricultural Economics*, Vol. XXXV, No. 3, July.-Sept.
17. Krishnamurthy, J. (1984: "Changes in the Indian Work Force", *EPW*, Vol. XIX, No. 50, Dec. 15.
18. Thorat, S.K. (1996): "The impact of New Economic Policy on the Scheduled Castes". *The Fourth World Journal of the Marginalised People*, NISWASS.
19. Nancharaiah, G. (1988): *Land & Caste*, New Himalaya Publishers, Bombay.
20. Hanumantha Rao, G. (1985), *Op. Cit.*

Table 1.1: Incidence of Poverty Among Social Groups in Rural Areas

In Percentages

Year	*Total Population*	*Scheduled Castes*	*Scheduled Tribes*
1977-78	51.2	64.6	72.4
1983-84	40.4	53.1	58.4
1987-88	33.4	44.7	52.6

Source: Govt. of India VIII Five Year Plan, p. 420.

Table 1.2: Poverty Among Scheduled Castes and Scheduled Tribes

In percentages

Year	1977-78		1983-84	
	S.C.	S.T.	S.C.	S.T.
Rural	64.6	72.4	53.1	58.4
Urban	63.2	52.6	40.4	39.9

Source: Standard of living of Indian People (CMIE) 1988.

Table 1.2: (Contd...): Poverty among Scheduled Castes and Scheduled Tribes

Year	Scheduled Caste		Scheduled Tribe		Others
	Rural	Urban	Rural	Urban	
1987-88	55.22		59.92		39.45
1993-94	48.11	49.48	51.94	41.14	32.96
1999-2000	36.25	38.47	45.86	34.75	24.4

Source: Rural Development Statistics NIRD, 2004.

Table 1.3: Average Monthly Per Capita Expenditure by Social Groups at all India Level (Rural)-Value (Rs.) of total Consumption Per Person Per 30 Days

Year	S.C.s	S.T.s	Others	All
1983	94.31	87.15	120.42	112.31
1987	133.35	123.04	169.23	213.71

Source: Sarvekshana, Oct.–Dec., 1993, Vol. XVII, No. 2.

Table 1.4: Average Monthly Per Capita Expenditure by Social Groups at all India Level: (Urban)-Value (Rs.) of Total Consumption Per Person Per 30 Days

Year	S.C.s	S.T.s	Others	All
1983	128.95	133.11	172.11	165.80
1987	185.03	201.79	258.50	245.72

Source: Sarvekshana, Oct.–Dec., 1993, p. 41-42, Vol. XVII, No. 2.

Table 1.5: Average Monthly Per Capita Consumer Expenditure by Social Groups-Statewise Rural (Value (Rs.) of total consumption per person for 30 days)

Year	*S.C.*		*S.T.*		*Others*		*All household*	
	83-84	87-88	83-84	87-88	83-84	87-88	83-84	87-88
Andhra Pradesh	97.84	132.32	94.29	120.79	121.83	169.06	115.58	220.47
Assam	111.07	166.00	108.80	145.12	114.17	160.80	113.03	203.91
Bihar	76.02	114.54	80.68	122.98	99.49	141.96	93.73	150.85
Gujarat	103.47	144.01	87.50	131.73	131.04	172.52	119.25	210.45
Haryana	113.64	168.24	--	195.20	160.39	239.88	149.14	251.37
Himachal Pradesh	125.69	179.93	--	212.13	159.70	217.00	150.05	282.82
Jammu & Kashmir	112.96	179.00	--	176.58	129.79	198.96	128.11	282.64
Karnataka	94.61	112.07	87.84	130.48	125.14	159.45	118.12	228.81
Kerala	105.07	163.39	--	186.69	150.74	215.53	145.24	317.08
Madhya Pradesh	87.47	124.98	79.43	106.49	119.02	159.66	101.78	181.39
Maharashtra	93.60	130.80	90.01	129.78	116.75	168.36	110.98	231.62
Manipur	--	--	122.28	167.58	137.97	192.66	131.45	187.32
Meghalaya	--	202.15	--	167.51	--	192.10	--	222.22
Nagaland	--	--	--	--	--	--	--	--
Orissa	87.30	117.63	72.73	93.72	110.63	144.96	97.48	185.00
Punjab	132.05	178.91	--	--	186.30	273.58	170.30	270.30
Rajasthan	110.17	160.01	90.11	125.26	140.01	190.08	127.52	208.93
Sikkim	--	145.57	--	152.82	--	159.78	--	206.51
Tamil Nadu	87.53	118.13	--	151.95	119.74	169.50	112.19	239.43
Tripura	--	158.55	--	155.01	--	205.09	--	232.56
Uttar Pradesh	88.57	124.72	--	132.90	108.82	158.33	104.25	193.36
West Bengal	94.99	137.28	85.29	127.18	110.95	161.43	104.60	208.05
Andaman & Nicobar	151.45	--	146.07	252.44	159.56	265.59	156.75	339.28
Arunachal Pradesh	--	--	--	202.12	--	184.94	--	222.47
Chandigarh	116.60	--	--	--	220.77	274.01	199.41	--
Dadra & Nagar Haveli	--	--	82.36	111.73	179.81	204.56	93.33	220.32
Delhi	22.85	--	129.09	--	208.02	369.59	208.81	368.70
Goa, Daman and Diu	--	--	124.12	159.94	172.37	188.40	169.12	224.90
Lakshadweep	--	--	--	232.02	--	--	--	275.60
Mizoram	--	216.30	119.21	243.21	131.17	204.63	119.81	268.62
Pondicherry	69.80	127.24	--	--	109.62	199.46	96.02	240.79

Source: Sarvekshna, Vol. XVII, No.2, Oct-Dec, 1993, Issue No. 57.
Sarvekshna, Vol. XII, No. 3, Issue No. 38, Jan-March, 1989.

Table 1.6: Average Monthly Per Capita Consumer Expenditure by Social Groups-Statewise Urban

India/States	*S.C.*		*S.T.*		*Others*		*All household*	
	83-84	87-88	83-84	87-88	83-84	87-88	83-84	87-88
Andhra Pradesh	139.62	176.20	--	174.21	162.91	236.19	159.55	228.07
Assam	113.82	206.60	--	278.25	167.18	262.82	160.48	256.15
Bihar	121.17	149.96	--	170.19	142.34	193.88	139.58	187.21
Gujarat	146.29	189.96	--	186.95	168.92	244.66	164.06	234.32
Haryana	144.21	184.73	--	--	191.80	269.51	189.97	253.46
Himachal Pradesh	186.85	252.53	--	--	274.30	361.86	257.09	326.98
Jammu & Kashmir	--	199.91	--	--	155.90	268.50	155.19	265.39
Karnataka	132.41	178.19	--	169.56	173.81	230.49	168.11	223.50
Kerala	133.99	182.39	--	--	181.90	267.27	178.31	261.70
Madhya Pradesh	113.09	173.86	136.55	171.41	155.30	247.27	148.39	232.98
Maharashtra	125.08	190.32	--	194.81	195.78	289.26	187.50	273.10
Manipur	--	--	114.98	207.61	142.16	201.51	138.20	202.47
Meghalaya	--	252.16	--	316.12	--	391.19	--	337.26
Nagaland	--	--	185.56	390.36	213.76	402.81	196.43	391.60
Orissa	115.74	179.59	111.79	174.59	164.44	233.86	151.35	222.01
Punjab	145.99	220.61	--	255.94	196.39	289.52	184.38	275.67
Rajasthan	136.71	207.83	--	272.39	164.39	252.13	159.96	245.11
Sikkim	203.90	275.15	268.01	277.43	216.14	283.06	222.81	281.24
Tamil Nadu	113.50	179.96	--	192.05	170.30	254.17	164.15	245.19
Tripura	--	200.23	--	--	--	264.51	--	261.25
Uttar Pradesh	117.14	167.84	--	174.89	140.68	221.13	137.84	214.00
West Bengal	133.44	175.52	--	207.77	177.04	259.97	169.94	248.00
Andaman & Nicobar	--	--	162.21	--	249.10	413.29	240.79	403.61
Arunachal Pradesh	--	--	--	260.17	--	261.98	--	264.56
Chandigarh	195.14	293.88	--	--	308.43	453.31	289.55	422.01
Dadra & Nagar Haveli	--	--	--	--	--	--	--	--
Delhi	138.59	230.78	--	363.46	259.62	474.95	230.43	428.86
Goa, Daman and Diu	--	--	--	--	226.66	301.44	222.91	798.81
Lakshadweep	--	--	--	214.30	--	283.94	--	222.38
Mizoram	--	--	190.71	348.09	304.31	--	192.31	349.13
Pondicherry	88.49	144.39	--	--	168.34	210.45	160.34	179.15
All India	128.95	185.03	133.11	201.79	172.11	256.50	165.80	245.72

Source: Sarvekshana, Vol. XII, No.3, Issue No. 138; Jan-March, 1989.

Sarvekshana, Vol. XVII, No.2, Oct-Dec. 1993, Issue No. 57.

Table 1.7: Some Features of Rural Labour Households in India

Category & Year	*% of Rural Labour Households*	*% of Rural Labour Households with land*	*% of Rural Labour Households with land*	*Total*
1. Scheduled Caste				
1964-65	--	42.3	57.7	100.00
1974-75	57.41	44.4	55.6	100.00
1977-78	63.18	42.6	57.4	100.00
1983	62.55	37.77	62.23	100.00
1987-88	63.14	75.54	24.46	100.00
2. Scheduled Tribe				
1964-65	--	46.2	53.8	100.00
1974-75	31.03	51.3	48.7	100.00
1977-78	43.11	52.7	47.3	100.00
1983	44.05	56.04	49.96	100.00
1987-88	49.60	53.09	16.91	100.00
3. Non SC/ST				
1964-65	--	44.30	55.70	100.00
1974-75	26.65	52.27	47.73	100.00
1977-78	28.88	53.17	46.83	100.00
1983	29.14	46.33	53.67	100.00
1987-88	31.16	80.92	19.08	100.00

Source: Government of India (1994): Rural Labour Enquiry (1987-88)
Government of India (1981): Rural Labour Enquiry (1974-75)
Government of India (1973): Rural Labour Enquiry (1964-65)

Table 1.8: Percentage of Wage Earners to Total Earners in Rural Labour Households (All Ages)

States	*1964-65*		*1974-75*		*1977-78*		*1983*		*1987-88*	
	M	*F*	*M*	*F*	*M*	*F*	*M*	*F*	*M*	*F*
India	96.1	92.7	96.3	87.5	81.6	81.1	90.5	89.3	79.5	42.2
Andhra Pradesh	93.1	100.00	96.2	97.4	86.4	92.0	89.1	92.1	74.2	45.2
Bihar	93.5	90.4	96.9	84.6	88.9	89.6	93.6	92.7	88.5	59.5
Gujarat	97.9	98.9	98.6	97.4	85.6	83.6	92.4	88.7	82.8	36.7
Haryana	--	--	94.2	72.2	84.9	70.1	90.8	90.6	83.5	12.0
Karnataka	91.3	93.4	95.6	93.3	--	--	87.1	92.3	74.8	49.0
Kerala	94.6	90.4	95.4	90.1	84.3	88.4	88.4	86.2	70.0	53.6

Madhya Pradesh	96.8	97.9	99.3	99.1	91.2	92.8	90.9	92.1	80.6	51.6
Maharashtra	96.1	97.2	95.2	97.7	86.6	93.0	90.7	93.0	78.7	34.3
Orissa	97.6	94.9	99.2	96.1	91.0	92.6	92.5	90.9	84.5	39.6
Punjab	97.3	83.8	92.2	51.0	85.0	53.1	88.7	68.7	74.8	12.0
Rajasthan	89.5	79.8	94.3	88.6	78.8	66.4	84.9	71.2	70.3	18.4
Tamil Nadu	96.5	97.9	93.7	95.4	86.7	88.9	92.2	91.3	75.4	55.0
Uttar Pradesh	92.0	78.3	95.6	78.9	85.8	75.5	85.8	77.3	82.3	23.9
West Bengal	97.7	96.9	98.6	84.0	91.5	89.2	93.1	90.6	79.2	37.5

Sources: Government of India (1994) Rural Labour Enquiry 1987-88 Report on employment and unemployment of Rural Labour Households, Labour, Bureau, Department of Labour, Ministry of Labour and Rehabilitation, Chandigarh.

Government of India (1984), national sample survey: 32 round 1977-78, Report 301/2, wages and Earnings of Rural Labour Households, NSSO, Department of statistics, Ministry of Planning, New Delhi.

Government of India (1984) Rural Labour Enquiry 1974-75, Final Report on Income, Consumption, Expenditure Labour Bureau, Department of Labour, Ministry of Labour & Rehabilitation, Chandigarh.

Table 1.9: Real Agricultural Wage Earnings in Rural Labour Households at 1960-61 Prices

States	*1964-65*		*1974-75*		*1977-78*		*1983*		*1987-88*	
	M	*F*	*M*	*F*	*M*	*F*	*M*	*F*	*M*	*F*
India	1.0	0.6	0.9	0.6	1.2	0.8	1.0	0.7	1.4	11
Andhra Pradesh	0.9	0.4	0.8	0.6	1.2	0.8	1.1	0.8	1.6	1.1
Bihar	0.9	0.8	0.8	0.2	1.0	0.9	0.9	0.7	1.3	1.2
Gujarat	1.1	0.9	1.0	0.8	1.4	1.3	1.2	1.0	1.6	1.5
Haryana	--	--	1.4	1.1	1.7	1.5	1.2	0.9	1.5	1.1
Karnataka	0.8	0.5	0.8	0.5	1.0	0.7	0.8	0.7	1.4	1.0
Kerala	1.6	0.9	1.6	1.1	2.2	1.5	2.0	1.6	2.6	1.9
Madhya Pradesh	0.8	0.6	0.6	0.4	0.8	0.6	0.7	0.6	1.2	1.0
Maharashtra	1.0	0.5	0.7	0.4	1.0	0.6	0.9	0.6	1.4	0.9
Orissa	0.9	0.6	0.7	0.5	0.9	0.7	0.6	0.5	1.1	0.8
Punjab	1.5	1.0	1.9	1.0	2.2	1.4	1.8	0.9	2.3	0.9
Rajasthan	1.2	0.8	1.0	0.7	1.4	1.0	1.1	0.6	1.5	1.4
Tamil Nadu	1.0	0.6	0.9	0.6	1.3	0.8	1.0	0.7	1.5	1.0
Uttar Pradesh	0.7	0.6	0.8	0.6	1.1	0.8	0.8	0.5	1.3	1.0
West Bengal	1.3	1.0	1.0	0.8	1.3	1.2	0.9	0.9	1.8	1.6

Sources: Government of India (1994) National Sample Survey, 32 Round 1977-78. Report No. 30 employment and unemployment of Rural Labour Households, Labour, Bureau, Department of Labour, Ministry of Labour and Rehabilitation, Chandigarh.

Government of India (1994), Rural Labour Enquiry, 1987-88, Report on Employment and Unemployment of Rural Labour Households, Labour Bureau, Department of Labour, Ministry of Labour and Rehabilitation, Chandigarh.

Government of India (1981) Rural Labour Enquiry 1974-75, Final Report on Employment and Unemployment of Rural Labour Households, Labour, Bureau, Department of Labour, Ministry of Labour and Rehabilitation, Chandigarh.

Govt. of India (1973): Rural Labour Enquiry, 1963-65, Final Report, Labour Bureau, Department of Labour, Ministry of Labour and Rehabilitation, Chandigarh.

Table 1.10: Growth Rates of Real Agricultural Wage Earnings in Rural Labour Households

States	*1964-65 to 1974-75*		*1974-75 to 1977-78*		*1977-78 to 1983*		*1983 to 1987-88*	
	M	*F*	*M*	*F*	*M*	*F*	*M*	*F*
All India	-0.1	0	-0.3	0.33	-0.16	-0.12	0.4	0.57
Andhra Pradesh	-0.1	0.5	0.5	0.33	-0.08	0	0.45	0.37
Bihar	-0.2	-0.12	0.25	0.28	-0.1	-8.3	0.44	0.71
Gujarat	-0.12	-0.12	0.4	0.62	-0.14	-0.23	0.33	0.5
Haryana	--	--	0.21	0.36	-0.29	-0.4	0.25	0.22
Karnataka	0	0	0.25	0.4	-0.2	0	0.75	0.42
Kerala	0	0.22	0.85	0.36	-0.09	0.06	0.3	0.18
Madhya Pradesh	-0.25	-0.33	0.33	0.5	-0.12	0	0.71	0.66
Maharashtra	-0.3	-0.2	0.42	0.5	-0.1	0	0.55	0.5
Orissa	-0.22	-0.16	0.28	0.4	-0.33	-0.28	0.83	0.6
Punjab	0.26	0	0.15	0.4	-0.18	-0.35	0.27	0
Rajasthan	-0.16	-0.12	0.4	0.42	-0.21	-0.4	0.36	1.3
Tamil Nadu	-0.1	0	0.44	0.33	-0.23	-0.12	0.5	0.42
Uttar Pradesh	0.14	0	0.37	0.33	0.27	-0.37	0.62	1
West Bengal	-0.23	-0.2	0.5	0.5	-0.30	-0.25	1	0.77

Sources: Calculated from Table 8.

Table 1.11: Number of Persons 'Usually Employed and Usually Unemployed' Per 1000 Persons (WPR) by Sex and Principal Status of each Household Groups

Category/Round/ year	*Rural*				*Urban*			
	Employed		*Unemployed*		*Employed*		*Unemployed*	
	Male	*Female*	*Male*	*Female*	*Male*	*Female*	*Male*	*Female*
STs 43 (1987-88)	547	368	8	8	494	184	24	6
	(86.23)	(68.33)	(8.60	(20.00)	(91.71)	(75.76)	(4.52)	(7.61)
38 (1983)	577	409	4	2	489	223	26	4
	(90.96)	(75.94)	(4.30)	(5.00)	(91.71)	(75.76)	(4.90)	(15.07)

32 (1977-78)	590	420	4	10	494	283	22	17
	(93.00)	(77.98)	(4.30)	(25.00)	(91.71)	(96.12)	(4.15)	(21.55)
SC 43 (1987-88)	518	275	13	14	481	166	35	11
	(81.70)	(66.22)	(12.71)	(38.22)	(91.12)	(82.60)	(7.15)	(8.29)
38 (1993)	534	281	10	4	477	164	32	8
	(84.22)	(67.66)	(9.78)	(10.92)	(90.36)	(81.61)	(6.54)	(6.03)
32 (1977-78)	547	284	11	22	496	190	34	34
	(86.27)	(68.28)	(10.76)	(60.06)	(93.96)	(94.55)	(6.95)	(25.63)
Others 43 (1987-88)	512	219	17	8	498	108	32	12
	(89.76)	(74.43)	(6.09)	(10.3)	(93.13)	(82.47)	(3.54)	(5.01)
38 (1983)	520	217	13	4	503	110	31	9
	(91.16)	(73.75)	(4.66)	(5.15)	(94.07)	(84.00)	(3.43)	(3.76)
32 (1977-78)	527	215	14	13	496	112	33	26
	(92.38)	(73.07)	(5.02)	(16.74)	(94.07)	(85.53)	(3.65)	(10.86)

Source: Sarvekshana, Oct-Dec. 1991, Vol. XV, No. 12, Issue No. 49, (PP. 58 & 59) Figures in brackets refer to percentages.

Note: 'WRP' Work participation rates (Percentage of persons, employed to total persons).

Table 1.12: Unemployment Rate: Percentage of Unemployed (Age 5 Years and Above) According to Usual, Current Weekly and Daily Status: Rural

Category	*Year*	*Usual Principal Status*		*Usual Status*		*Current Weekly*		*Current Daily*	
		M	*F*	*M*	*F*	*M*	*F*	*M*	*F*
Scheduled Caste	1987-88	1.30	1.40	0.90	1.10	--	--	--	--
	1883	1.14	0.50	0.76	0.23	3.22	2.16	7.16	4.23
	1977-98	1.23	2.58	--	--	2.93	1.90	6.73	4.09
Scheduled Tribes	1987-88	0.80	0.80	0.40	0.60	--	--	--	--
	1983	0.49	0.18	0.34	0.80	1.47	1.21	3.29	2.57
	1977-98	0.52	1.22	--	--	1.57	1.22	3.31	2.37
Others	1987-88	1.70	0.48	1.10	0.70	--	--	--	--
	1983	--	--	--	--	--	--	--	--
	1977-78	--	--	--	--	--	--	--	--
Non SC/ST	1983	1.49	0.43	1.03	0.29	2.15	0.91	4.04	1.72
	1977-78	1.57	1.53	--	--	2.15	0.97	3.90	0.92

Source: Employment Survey, NSS, 1991.

Table 1.13: Percentage Distribution of Person Days of 'Usually Employed and Usually Unemployed' (Age 5 Years and Above) in the Principal Status (Rural India State-Wise 1983, 38th Round)

India/State	Scheduled Tribe				Scheduled Caste				Others			
	Employed		*Unemployed*		*Employed*		*Unemployed*		*Employed*		*Unemployed*	
	M	*F*	*M*	*F*	*M*	*F*	*M*	*F*	*M*	*F*	*M*	*F*
India	90.96	75.94	04.30	05.00	84.22	67.66	09.78	10.97	91.16	73.75	04.66	05.15
Andhra Pradesh	85.40	66.49	4.70	5.36	80.57	62.52	9.75	13.67	88.65	72.23	5.56	6.34
Assam	98.35	90.52	0.13	0.87	96.24	80.81	2.20	1.18	95.81	90.21	1.10	3.11
Bihar	95.23	84.23	2.61	12.75	84.68	65.97	11.40	16.45	93.37	77.43	4.20	8.08
Gujarat	91.00	72.58	5.12	6.58	85.92	70.08	8.26	6.21	92.41	70.64	3.36	1.64
Haryana	--	--	--	--	87.15	80.23	7.82	0.44	96.12	63.93	2.78	1.33
Himachal Pradesh	97.60	78.13	--	--	95.52	67.10	0.58	--	97.91	73.53	0.13	--
Karnataka	83.94	73.47	8.89	6.10	79.59	67.20	10.03	9.49	89.52	77.36	4.22	5.74
Kerala	72.90	45.66	18.45	24.53	65.18	56.44	27.39	23.97	78.78	65.80	12.83	13.46
Madhya Pradesh	93.74	79.29	1.56	19.73	90.85	74.82	3.07	2.83	94.08	78.91	1.32	1.02
Maharashtra	85.34	67.31	5.89	6.93	81.57	72.71	8.84	7.28	89.87	68.06	4.14	4.68
Orissa	88.60	67.91	7.04	9.64	87.62	70.82	8.12	11.90	92.03	68.56	4.84	6.95
Punjab	91.36	100.0	4.53	--	84.02	76.32	10.27	4.44	94.55	71.56	2.00	0.31
Rajasthan	95.76	90.11	2.12	0.65	90.56	82.54	4.58	3.21	95.37	87.76	2.25	0.92
Tamil Nadu	80.69	72.43	8.46	11.42	70.84	55.86	22.00	22.00	82.00	67.41	11.66	11.76
Uttar Pradesh	94.64	80.49	2.34	--	89.70	74.10	5.17	4.28	95.35	81.08	1.87	0.98
West Bengal	82.60	64.61	13.20	25.07	81.35	68.13	13.62	19.15	86.96	78.76	9.36	9.30

Source: Serveksliana, July-Sept. 1989.
Vol. XIII, No. 1, Issue No. 40, (pp. 24 and 27).

Table 1.14: Percentage Distribution of Person-Days of 'Usually Employed and Usually Unemployed' (Age 5 Years and Above) in the Principal Status (Rural India State-Wise 1987-88 (43rd Round)

India/State	Scheduled Tribe				Scheduled Caste				Others			
	Employed		*Unemployed*		*Employed*		*Unemployed*		*Employed*		*Unemployed*	
	M	*F*	*M*	*F*	*M*	*F*	*M*	*F*	*M*	*F*	*M*	*F*
India	86.23	68.33	8.60	20.00	81.70	66.22	12.71	38.22	89.76	72.23	6.09	10.30
Andhra Pradesh	93.95	92.84	8.37	29.34	88.32	--	11.70	47.65	--	--	6.00	15.54
Assam	76.30	7.79	7.38	9.37	78.70	13.24	13.42	11.28	84.32	22.70	6.17	5.05
Bihar	84.49	44.01	8.79	20.21	78.54	52.25	12.49	28.54	82.39	29.48	5.25	3.81
Gujarat	89.23	79.66	9.33	21.90	82.17	76.33	12.63	28.78	91.86	82.36	6.17	7.15
Haryana	70.46	25.62	--	--	71.61	26.04	13.37	19.34	78.18	37.62	6.71	6.00
Himachal Pradesh	87.81	66.10	--	--	82.01	89.09	9.82	27.85	83.62	--	5.97	11.92
Karnataka	86.39	64.62	8.39	26.19	85.80	93.18	12.47	48.81	97.64	97.95	6.04	14.47
Kerala	83.71	44.92	9.52	12.28	75.70	76.33	--	57.09	81.53	53.21	5.97	11.53
Madhya Pradesh	87.65	75.38	8.60	17.50	84.06	91.74	13.74	42.82	91.33	99.90	5.73	9.82
Maharashtra	83.39	82.99	8.49	23.91	82.64	--	11.78	42.82	90.62	--	6.00	10.96
Orissa	95.68	71.12	8.26	16.60	87.85	60.44	12.20	35.91	92.91	45.75	5.91	5.62
Punjab	77.09	--	11.07	13.91	81.22	84.03	13.89	21.64	96.24	24.39	6.50	4.48
Rajasthan	84.97	96.18	7.6	24.67	76.49	84.05	11.86	53.41	84.50	--	5.71	11.53
Tamil Nadu	90.17	90.61	9.60	26.73	87.06	--	13.47	61.44	100.98	--	6.76	17.70
Uttar Pradesh	80.87	42.89	8.54	7.93	79.80	54.18	13.47	29.70	86.77	49.14	5.84	5.72
West Bengal	84.65	47.90	9.48	19.34	82.33	27.90	13.39	23.94	88.76	25.42	6.40	8.01

Source: Servekshana, Oct-Dec., 1991, Vol. No. 2, Issue No. 49, (pp. 59 and 60).

Table 1.15: Employment in Rural Non-Farm Sector Percentage of Rural Non-farm workers to total Rural Workers

Category	*1977-78*	*1983*	*1987-88*	*1992-93*
General:				
Male	19.3	22.20	25.5	24.30
Female	11.80	12.20	15.30	13.80
SC				
Male	--	--	24.56	23.40
Female	--	--	17.36	15.66

Source: S.K. Thorat, No. 5, (April, 1997) *The Fourth World.*

Table 1.16: Representation of Scheduled Caste in Government Jobs

Year	*No. of SCs*	*Percentage*
1960	228497	12.42
1965	311425	13.28
1970	291874	13.09
1975	408879	13.84
1980	490592	15.64
1985	567356	16.32
1990	590108	16.97

Source*

Table 1.17: Representation of Scheduled Caste in Public Sector Undertakings

Year	*No. of SCs*	*Percentage*
1970	40640	7.24
1975	236810	17.25
1680	318204	17.08
1985	395622	18.94
1990	432890	19.54

Source: "The impact of New Economic Policy on the Scheduled Castes" S.K. Thorat, *The Fourth World, Journal of the Marginalized People,* No. 5, (April–1977).

Table 1.18: Literacy Rates 1991 and 1981

States	*Scheduled Caste*		*Scheduled Tribes*		*Others*	
	1981	*1991*	*1981*	*1991*	*1981*	*1991*
India	21.38	37.40	16.35	29.60	36.23	57.7
Andhra Pradesh	17.65	31.60	7.82	17.20	29.94	39.0
Arunachal Pradesh	--	--	--	34.4	--	53.7
Assam	--	53.9	--	49.2	--	53.9
Bihar	40.40	19.90	7.82	26.80	26.20	43.10
Goa	--	58.7	--	--	--	75.90
Gujarat	39.79	61.10	21.14	36.40	43.70	65.9
Haryana	20.15	39.2	--	--	--	59.8
Himachal Pradesh	31.50	53.2	25.90	47.1	42.48	68.0
Karnataka	20.59	38.1	20.14	36.0	38.46	60.5
Kerala	55.96	79.7	31.79	57.2	40.42	91.3
Madhya Pradesh	18.97	35.1	10.68	21.5	27.87	54.5
Maharashtra	35.55	56.5	22.29	36.8	47.18	69.2
Manipur	33.63	56.4	39.74	53.6	41.35	63.4
Meghalaya	25.78	--	31.55	46.7	34.08	62.9
Mizoram	--	--	--	82.7	--	75.2
Nagaland	--	--	40.32	60.6	42.57	69.0
Orissa	22.41	36.8	13.96	22.3	34.23	61.6
Punjab	--	41.1	33.13	--	40.86	65.1
Rajasthan	14.4	23.3	--	19.4	24.34	44.8
Sikkim	28.6	51.0	10.22	59.0	34.05	56.8
Tamil Nadu	29.67	46.7	20.46	27.9	46.76	66.80
Tripura	33.87	56.7	23.07	40.4	42.12	72.8
Uttar Pradesh	14.96	26.8	20.45	35.7	27.16	45.9
West Bengal	24.37	42.2	13.21	27.8	40.94	65.0

Source: Census of India 1981.

Census of India 1991.

Table 1.18 (Contd..): Literacy Rates of SCs and STs Sex Wise All India in 2001

Social Group	*Rural*			*Urban*		
	Males	*Females*	*Persons*	*Males*	*Females*	*Persons*
S.T	53.8	30.1	42.2	78.1	61.2	70.0
S.C	58.8	33.6	46.6	76.0	55.7	66.2
O.B.C	67.8	41.1	54.8	83.5	66.4	75.3
Others	78.1	56.7	67.7	91.4	81.0	86.5
All	67.1	43.4	56.0	86.5	72.3	79.8

Sources: Servekshana, Vol. XXIV, No. 2 & 3 85th issue, 2000 Oct.-March 2001.

2

Rural Development Programmes and Dalits

Dr. L.C. Mallaiah
Dr. K.B. Ratna Kumari

Directive Principles of State in Indian Constitution provide that India is a welfare state committed for the welfare and development of its people in general and of Dalit in particular. Hence the responsibility of planning and an implementation of welfare programmes rest with Central and State Governments of India. The programmes are directed to promote socio-economic and educational empowerment of Dalit who have been under deprivation and socio-economic discrimination for centuries in the pretext of manmade socioeconomic taboos. India is a welfare state committed to the welfare and development of its people in general and of weaker sections in particular. In this democratic country the responsibility of planning and implementation of welfare and poverty alleviation programme rest with both the central and state governments. The social welfare programs seek to serve development and rehabilitative needs of the vulnerable sections such as scheduled castes and Scheduled Tribes who have been under deprivation and socio-economic discriminations for centuries on the pretext of manmade socio-economic taboos. Hence, as a matter of strategy, the Indian government has resorted to plan development for minimizing inequality in income status and maximizing the opportunities for the people. This strategy is directed to secure distributive justice and utilization of economic resources to sub serve common goods.

The programmes are directed to promote educational and economic interest of weaker sections in general and that of SC's and ST's in particular to avoid injustice and exploitation. Hence, so many poverty alleviation programmes are being implemented with varying proportions of subsidies for various social and economic groups depending upon the degree of vulnerability (Chakrawarthi 1977).

Since Independence several programmes have been launched for the development of rural areas and rural people with a more focus on deprived sections of populations like SC's and ST's. Some of the programs like Community Development Programme (CDP) and National extension service made a general approach covering all aspects of rural development including eradication of rural poverty. But integrated Rural Development Programme is a major instrument for the alleviation of rural poverty. To gain some perspective it might be worthwhile to reiterate briefly the major landmarks in the evolution of rural development programmes in India since independence.

In the early fifties, the Community Development Programme, National Extension Service (NES), the first rural development programmes were initiated and implemented and the block administration was created as a centre for rural development activities. This programme failed as blocks were quite large and often unwieldy and mainly left the weaker sections untouched. Moreover, heavy reliance on bureaucracy hampered their effectiveness in delivery services. In order to fill the gap created by the CDP and NES, some popular institutions were created in the name of democratic decentralization popularly known as panchayati raj institutions. These institutions were closer to the rural society. Village panchayats, the first tier of panchayatraj system were constituted in a village or a group of villages which were usually within 4-5 Kms of each other. As the rural society has traditional culture, the elite belonging to higher social strata dominate these bodies. Added to this the panchayatraj institutions suffered from many structural and functional inadequacies. Due to these problems, these institutional devices also left untouched the rural poor. The early sixties witnessed an effort to promote rapid agricultural production, which culminated in Intensive Agricultural District Programme (IADP) the programme succeeded in increasing agricultural production. But the benefits accrued only to rich and progressive peasants; once again landless and agricultural labourers were left untouched (Tripathi, 1987).

The fourth five-year plan in the name of "Growth with social justice" initiated efforts towards uplifting the vulnerable sections of rural society. In this connection, a lot of special economic programs were launched. Programmes such as Small Farmers Development Agency (SFDA), Marginal Farmers and Agricultural Labourers Agencies (MFALA) Drought Prone Area Programmes (DPAP), Tribal Area Development Program (TADP) were introduced in the rural development scenario. These programmes addressed themselves for the upliftment of weaker sections of rural society and this new approach was called target group approach. These programs did succeed but only in limited areas. The basic problems were departmental administrations coupled with problems of coordination. Moreover these programs were implemented through the existing administrative apparatus at block and village level (Tripathi, 1987).

Hence a review of various on going programmes was taken up during the late seventies indicated the need for new comprehensive programmes for the development of rural areas. Though a number of programmes have been in operations for the development of rural poor, yet any significant improvement could not be achieved among the poorest of the people in rural areas. The programmes could not cover the all parts of the country, though a large number of blocks in the country had more than one of these programs operating simultaneously in the same area and for the same target group. This territorial combined with different findings patterns of those programmes not only created considerable difficulties in effective monitoring and accounting but blurred the programmes objectives. It was therefore that such multiplicity of programmes for rural poor operated through a multiplicity of agencies should be ended and should be replaced by one single integrated programme called Integrated Rural Development Programme (IRDP) which could operate throughout the country (Tripathi 1987).

IRDP conceived as anti poverty programme aimed at helping the small and marginal farmers, landless labourere and artisans it was thought by planners that these people were poor because they possessed neither any productive assets nor any special skill. Therefore the IRDP was designed to help the poor by creating new assets for them. These assets would include sources of irrigation, bullocks and implements beside inputs like seeds and fertilizers for farming animals for dairy and other animal husbandry activities and tools and training for cottage industries and handicrafts. The basic strategy was self-employment of the poor with the help of these assets so that they manage to earn enough to rise above the poverty line. IRDP is an important poverty alleviation programme, which was introduced in 1978 for self-employment generation in 2, 3000 blocks throughout the country. The programme was extended to cover all the blocks in the country with effect from 2nd October 1980. Earlier programmes such as SFDA, DPAP, CADP, NREP, MNP, NRLEGP, were merged in it. The main objective of the programme is to enable the identified poor families to augment their income and cross the poverty line though requisition of credit based productive assets, which provide self-employment on a sustained basis. It is mainly an economic programme supported by social development programmes, pertaining to health, nutrition and education and it concentrated on families below the poverty line.

The target groups under IRDP are small and marginal farmers, agricultural labor and rural artisans having income below the poverty line of Rs.11, 000 per annum. In the identified target group at least 50% of the assisted families should belong to SC's and ST's.

The work taken up by IRDP is income-generating activities in the primary, secondary and territory sectors of the rural economy. The criteria for allocation are down through a centrally sponsored scheme funded on 50:50 basis by the centre and states. Financial institutions such as commercial banks, cooperative banks and Regional rural banks provide institutional credit. The patterns of subsidy entitled to the target group is, for small farmers, 25 percent of project cost; marginal farmers agricultural labour and rural artisans 25 percent and SC/ST beneficiaries and physically handicapped persons 50 percent.

IRDP is implemented through DRDAs the governing body at the district level provides guidance and direction. At grass root level the block staff is responsible for implementation of the programme. The Ministry of Rural Development is responsible for release of central Share, policy formulation, overall guidance, monitoring and evaluation of programme.

The main thrust of the programme is on the poorest of the poor, consisting of small and marginal farmers, agricultural and non-Agricultural laborers, rural artisans and craftsmen, particularly SC's and ST's. It gives special priority to the SC/ST peoples, because, these people are very much below poverty line. Majority of rural poor belong to SC/ST category. At least 50 percent of the beneficiaries must be drawn from these categories and the subsidy earmarked to them is also 50 percent. In this connection this paper studies that to what extent the IRDP is helpful to the poorest of the poor i.e., SC's and ST's, in their socio-economic development during 50 years of independence.

Before going into examining the role of IRDP in socio-economic development in SC's/ST's, let us have a glance at some of the important studies on this area. The different views were expressed from different authors and investigators. The study of Harikumar (1984) from Ernakulam district of Kerala, says that only 20.6 per cent of the beneficiaries have crossed the poverty line and remaining of them still are below the poverty line even after taking the IRDP loans and the selection process of IRDP beneficiaries is not according to the guidelines of the programme. The study of Perumala Rao (1988) and Nataraja on "IRDP assistance in AP" proves that because of insufficient amount of loans these schemes have failed to generate employment opportunities. Rakha Upadaya (1984) found in his study "Integrated Rural Development in India" that in majority cases the amount of the loan and subsidy was not adequate to meet the cost of investment, as a result, the programme could not improve the socio-economic status of the poor and the poor families did not even cross the poverty line.

The study of Satyendra Tripathi (1987) "Development for

Rural Poor" shows that the benefits are not percolating to the really needy groups nor they are suited to the requirements of the needy people. Another study by Kattar on Rural Development IRDP in Mahendragarh district of Haryana indicates that the socio economic conditions of beneficiaries have improved after taking the IRDP financial assistance and the IRDP have made a significant change in the income, consumptions and employment on the whole. Here the IRDP has shown positive impact on beneficiaries. This positive impact is also supported by Prakash Mehata and Bharadwaja in their study aimed to see the changes in cropping pattern income and employment generation. This is a case study in Himachal Pradesh (Prakash Mehata, 1987) By reviewing the major studies on IRDP, it is clear that majority of these studies shows that the programme has failed to achieve desired ends. Because of wrong identification of beneficiaries, lack of service facilities, ineffective administration, and low participation of people and lack of coordination among the implementation agencies etc. Intensive observations of these studies show that none of the studies focused on the impact of the programme exclusively on the weaker sections of the society, especially on SC's/ST's since independence. In view of the above gap, the present study aimed to study the impact of IRDP on socio-economic conditions of SC's and ST's.

The SC's are specified in accordance with article 341 of the constitution according to which certain communities, suffering from the social disabilities including unsociability have been specified in the states and union territories as SC. Population wise the SC/ST and OBC together constitute more than 60 per cent of India's population, 16.48 per cent of the country's population belong to SC's: they are treated as untouchables by large number of castes Hindus. They occupy a low position in the caste hierarchy. They are socially and economically subjected by dominant castes. According to the population census 1991, the population of the country excluding Jammu and Kashmir was 838.58 million of which 138.22 millions are SC's. According to the latest estimation of incidence of poverty in 1987-88, the incidence of poverty among SC's is 44.7 percent, while it is only 33.4 percent in case of total population.

The ST's constitute 8.08 percent (67.76 million) out of total population. The incidence of poverty in ST's is 52.6 percent. These people are divided into two tribal categories viz., frontiers and non frontiers tribes. The frontiers tribes are those who inhibit the northeast frontier states of Arunachal Pradesh, Assam, Meghalaya, Manipur, Mizoram, Nagaland and Tripura. The rest of ST's are distributed over eastern and central India particularly Bihar, Orissa, West Bengal, Madhya Pradesh Gujarat and Maharashtra.

The SC community is the worst suffers in all walks of life. They are at the bottom of Hindu caste hierarchy; also they were equally at the bottom of economic hierarchy having no hand of their own and relegated to menial dirty and ill paid jobs. They developed a kind of resigned attitude towards the life. The problem of economic poverty, illiteracy, ignorance, fear and resultant inability to asset themselves have kept the SC's and ST's down. The main cause for the socio-economic backwardness of these people is the age old practice of untouchability due to which they have been deprived of economic opportunities in the society. Even today, these people are depending upon Hindu dominated caste people for their daily life. Because of lack of economic support and base to that deprived section of people. They have no alternative in rural villages. In spite of sincere efforts by the government there has been very insignificant change in their lives. The task of their socio-economic development is therefore, gigantic.

Hence, the IRDP was introduced to bring socio-economic changes of SC's/ST's through providing financial assistance and support. The percentage coverage of beneficiaries among SC/ST's under this programme which is implemented in all the states and union territories is analyzed below. The details of coverage of SC/ST beneficiaries under IRDP are presented in the Table 2.1. In this table it is clear that SC/ST together constitute less than the prescribed norm of 50 percent as per the guidelines of IRDP, in all the years except 1991-92 and 1993-94 years. In this two years the IRDP has succeeded in achieving the target covering 50 percent of SC/ST population.

Regarding their physical targets and achievements of IRDP since 1985 to 1997, Table.2.2 shows that more than targeted families are given assistance under this programme. But the target has decreased from 1986 onwards 24.71 lakhs families are supposed to be given assistance in 1985-86 but in 1996-97 it is only 7.79 lakhs families. In remaining years it shows trends in coverage of families.

Table 2.3 gives the details of state wise coverage of SC's/ST's under IRDP, since 1985 to 1997 in all states and union territories. In this table, the highest percentage coverage of SC families can be seen in Punjab (50.84 in 1997-98) followed by Uttar Pradesh (50.47), Tamil Nadu (46.81) and Haryana (46.851). The same trend is observed since 1985. But in case of ST families' cent per cent achievement is reported in Arunachal Pradesh, Mizoram, Nagaland and Lakshadweep. In Meghalaya, it is very near to cent per cent. The percentage achievement is less than national average (10.95%) is reported in Andhra Pradesh, Himachal Pradesh, Karnataka, Kerala, Tamil Nadu, Uttar Pradesh and West Bengal. The above data clearly indicates that less per cent of SC/ST's are getting really benefited through IRDP. Except in few states, the IRDP is not reaching the aimed target. The SC/ST beneficiaries constitute less than the prescribed norm of 50% as per the guidelines of IRDP in almost all the states in case of SC/ST population.

In spite of the integrated programme, several other poverty alleviation programmes have been functioning in the country. Table 2.4 shows the number of SC/ST households assisted under various poverty alleviation programmes. State wise details of SC/ST families assisted in crossing poverty line are documented in this table. Except in Karnataka which shows increasing trend, In all most all the states the SC/ST families assisted in crossing poverty line is showing decreasing trend. From the above information, it is clear that majority of SC/ST families are still below poverty line. It is proved with empirical evidence from Table 2.5, which gives the incidence of poverty of SC/ST and others since 1977-78 to 2000 in rural areas. Even though poverty declined by 1987-88 among all social groups in all rural areas, the incidence of poverty among SC's and ST's is high. In case of SC's it is 44.7 percent and 52.6 percent in case of ST's, while it was only 33.4 percent in case of total population. Hence it is clear that even though, one side, the IRDP has been helping the SC/ST families to cross poverty line, the poverty of SC/ST's remains to be high comparatively on the other side.

Hence, it can be said that the programme has failed to achieve the estimated target. As highlighted by many micro-level studies on the programme in the country, the major reasons for failure of this programme are the following i.e., (1) Improper utilization of the loan by the beneficiaries, (2) Lack of effective monitoring, (3) insufficient amount of the loans to complete the schemes, (4) corruptions and mismanagement on the part of the bureaucrats, and (5) effective planning which results in non-suitability of the schemes to the requirement of the beneficiaries and conditions of the areas.

On the other hand, awareness of the programme is a pre-requisite for its success. In spite of massive media build-up and working of governmental and non-governmental agencies to make the rural people aware of the developmental programmes, there is still a wide spread ignorance about the developmental schemes launched by the government to uplift the SC's/ST's. Since the literacy rate is the major factor in making people aware of the government programmes. As is known more the education greater the awareness of socio-economic development. As shown in Table-2.6, as per 1991 population census the literacy rates are very low among SC's/ST's. i.e., 37.40 per cent is for SC's and 29.60 per cent for STs. But in case of others, it is nearly 57.7% of literacy. Hence, it indicates that illiteracy is the main cause of non-awareness of developmental programmes and schemes. This is also proved by Hari Kumar in his study (Harikumar, 1984).

It is known that most of the developmental works in rural areas have become place for corruption. The developmental agencies, the beneficiaries and the mediators are collaborating to share the developmental bounty which has been specially designed to help the rural poor particularly SC/ST's. The sanctions of loans are also time consuming process the time lag occurs not only because of procedural formalities but also because of ample opportunities available for the concerned authorities to extort money from the borrowers. Time lag caused more expensive in getting loans under the programmes. Thus the SC/ST beneficiaries are not satisfied with IRDP, because of insufficient amount of financial assistance, non-availability of the scheme of their choice and non-availability of loans at the right time. This situation was also highlighted in a micro-level study by Chiranjeevi (Chiranjeevi, 1992).

On the side of beneficiaries, it is found that the SC/ST beneficiaries are not utilising the loans for the given purposes. They are diverting the money for some other purposes such as family expenses and debt repayments etc. This is one of the main causes for the failure of the government efforts to uplift the poor particularly SC/ST people. Most of the beneficiaries are spending the amount, which they got by disposing their schemes for socio-economic needs. If there is no help from IRDP the socio-economic conditions of these SC/ST people would have been perhaps worse. In this extent, the IRDP has positive impact on the socio-economic conditions of these people.

The IRDP loans have to be repaid by the beneficiaries within the prescribed time. The main reasons for not paying the loan in time are inadequate generation of income, obligation to meet the family expenses, diversion of income towards settlements of old private debts and lack of money with the beneficiaries because of domestic financial crisis. Though the IRDP was expected to improve the income and employment generation of the poor, its actual impact on living conditions of the poor especially the SC's/ST's is very negligible.

Thus the above analysis reveals that there is not much improvement in the income levels of SC/ST's. Further the schemes did not enable them to cross poverty line. So the major anti-poverty programme has not been successful in enabling the poor particularly SC/STs to cross the poverty line. The Programme Evaluation Organisation of the planning commission, the Reserve Bank of India, the NABARD and the Institute for Financial Management evaluated the performance of the IRDP at different points of the time. They concluded that the programme was not very effective as poverty alleviation measure. However it has now been restructured and renamed as Swarnajayanti Gram Swarozgar Yojana (SGSY).

The IRDP is continued to be an important self-employment programme for the rural poor during 9th plan. Therefore, it is suggested to redesign the programme as a credit based self-employment programme with an element of subsidy rather than a programme based on the provision of subsidy and supplemented by bank credit. In this effort the financial institutions would have to participate more actively by mobilizing and disbursing enhanced flows of credit to the beneficiary. Other programmes for development of the SC/STs should work as an integral part of IRDP. The Programme Evaluation Organisation of the planning commission, the Reserve Bank of India, the NABARD and the Institute for Financial Management evaluated the performanceof the IRDP at different points of the time. They concluded that the programme was not very effective as poverty alleviation measure. However it has now been restructured and renamed as Swarnajayanti Gram Swarozgar Yojana (SGSY). Further more, the initiatives taken in respect of credit flows through self help would have to be suitably strengthened. In this effort, voluntary organizations and Panchayat Raj Institutions (PRI) would have to play a predominant role in empowering the poor through advocacy, awareness of generation and social mobilization. As social animators and rural organizers they would help the poor to form these self-help groups in order to take advantage of the policies and programmes of the government for their socio-economic betterment.

Table 2.1: Percentage of SC/ST Beneficiaries Under IRDP in India

Years	*S.C.*	*S.T.*
1985-86	32.05	13.04
1991-92	36.08	15.02
1992-93	35.96	13.35
1993-94	36.49	13.65
1994-95	34.01	15.76
1995-96	33.75	14.77
1996-97	34.01	11.38
1997-98 Upto Aug.97.	35.51	9.57

Source: Rural Development Statistics, 1998, 1993-94, 1990.

Table 2.2: Physical Targets and Achievements of IRDP

Year	*Families Target*	*Assisted (lakhs Achieved*	*Percentage of Achivement Target*	*SC/ST families assisted*
1985-86	24.71	30.60	124	43.23
1986-87	35.0	37.47	108	44.83
1987-88	39.64	42.47	108	44.83
1988-89	31.94	37.72	118	46.40
1989-90	29.08	33.51	115	46.10
1991-92	22.52	2525.37	112.66	51.10
1992-93	18.75	20.69	110.33	51.10
1993-94	25.70	25.38	97.13	50.00
1994-95	21.15	22.14	104.69	49.97
1995-96	20.45	20.89	102.15	48.52
1996-97	7.79	7.91	78.75	45.14

Source: Rural Development Statistics 1990, p. 99.
Rural Development Statistics 1998, p. 169.

Table 2.3: IRDP: Physical Performance Percentage of SC/ST Beneficiaries

Sl.		*1985-90*		*1991-92*		*1992-93*	
No.	*Status/U.T*	*SC*	*ST*	*SC*	*ST*	*SC*	*ST*
1.	Andhra Pradesh	38.07	11.42	39.53	10.40	37.79	10.21
2.	Arunachal Pradesh	00.00	95.39	00.00	100.00	00.00	100.00
3.	Assam	8.87	22.61	13.63	27.18	11.97	27.14
4.	Bihar	28.46	15.12	31.03	17.85	32.09	20.12
5.	Goa	3.17	0.57	1.30	0.00	0.82	0.00
6.	Gujarat	12.96	30.10	14.74	38.39	15.49	34.28
7.	Haryana	33.87	.00	48.55	0.00	46.89	.00
8.	Himachal Pradesh	52.48	9.50	42.36	9.95	38.84	14.37
9.	J & K	9.27	0.00	12.54	4.67	10.41	5.01
10.	Karnataka	23.98	2.85	36.09	4.60	30.83	6.55
11.	Kerala	30.63	2.90	42.88	3.76	42.31	2.98
12.	Madhya Pradesh	21.86	31.66	24.19	34.36	19.96	23.03
13.	Maharashtra	22.83	16.44	26.78	18.82	24.32	16.15
14.	Manipur	0.78	65.94	1.89	58.72	0.55	67.83
15.	Meghalaya	0.01	98.92	0.59	99.41	0.00	100.00
16.	Mizoram	0.00	99.39	0.00	100.00	0.00	100.00
17.	Nagaland	0.00	100.00	0.00	100.00	0.00	100.00
18.	Orissa	29.97	27.31	29.24	30.91	25.87	31.80
19.	Punjab	52.48	0.00	51.64	0.00	48.68	0.00
20.	Rajasthan	34.70	18.51	33.79	19.57	34.27	18.37
21.	Sikkim	5.49	30.19	8.51	32.92	4.53	42.83

22. Tamil Nadu	45.80	1.76	49.10	2.03	47.22	1.48
23. Tripura	13.31	34.69	16.25	30.31	13.73	33.85
24. U P	46.72	0.39	54.94	0.67	53.07	0.61
25. West Bengal	31.72	5.54	35.88	5.75	34.15	5.96
26. A&N Island	0.00	15.74	0.00	20.31	0.00	30.77
27. Chandigarh	25.25	0.00	0.00	0.00	0.00	0.00
28. D&N Haveli	4.18	9.3.07	0.32	99.04	5.00	93.57
29. Delhi	29.04	0.00	0.00	0.00	0.00	0.00
30. Daman & Diu	3.78	18.25	4.15	15.98	6.19	9.52
31. Lakshadweep	0.00	100.00	0.00	100.00	6.00	83.46
32. Pondicherry	28.40	0.01	38.72	0.00	28.04	6.07
All India	32.05	13.04	36.08	15.02	35.96	13.35

Table 2.4: SC & ST Families Assisted in Crossing Poverty Line

Sl. No.	*State*	*1985-90*		*1992-93*	
		SC	*ST*	*SC*	*ST*
1.	Andhra Pradesh	141.75	205.60	91.58	111
2.	Assam	62.24	31.70	37.61	33
3.	Bihar	108.71	117.08	54.40	107
4.	Goa	106.24	--	30.20	--
5.	Gujarat	105.24	125.42	98.33	116
6.	Haryana	119.04	--	76.48	--
7.	Himachal Pradesh	124.26	153.98	123.08	118
8.	Jammu and Kashmir	72.48	--	19.60	3
9.	Karnataka	98.03	122.24	104.23*	107
10.	Kerala	147.30	146.33	83.96	40
11.	Madhya Pradesh	103.80	122.03	88.24	106
12.	Maharashtra	126.03	126.03	91.00	100
13.	Manipur	96.10	114.40	90.83	49
14.	Orissa	148.80	140.69	83.01	124
15.	Punjab	134.88	--	82.15	--
16.	Rajasthan	108.38	115.19	100.15	111
17.	Sikkim	140.75	170.58	100.00	101
18.	Tamil Nadu	105.55	111.21	101.37	92
19.	Tripura	111.01	126.91	69.92	88
20.	Uttar Pradesh	115.85	129.51	78.93	97
21.	West Bengal	103.77	108.44	36.96	91
22.	Chandigarh	143.20	--	101.41	--
23.	Delhi	111.62	--	52.52	--
24.	Pondicherry	103.85	--	99.80	--
25.	Daman and Diu	56.05	136.54	--	95
26.	A & N Island	--	146.27	--	97
	TOTAL	115.05	127.27	79.60	99

Source: Rural Development Statistics, 193-94, pp. 230-231.

Table 2.3 (Contd..)

Sl. No.	Status/U.T	1993-94 SC	1993-94 ST	1994-95 SC	1994-95 ST	1995-96 SC	1995-96 ST	1996-97 SC	1996-97 ST	1997-98 SC	1997-98 ST
1.	A.P.	39.48	10.81	37.23	10.15	35.48	10.44	31.02	10.12	34.36	11.05
2.	Arunachal Pradesh	0.00	100.0	0.00	100.0	00.00	100.0	0.00	100.0	0.00	100.0
3.	Assam	13.76	22.07	15.10	24.44	15.07	24.06	12.83	24.62	11.52	26.06
4.	Bihar	33.83	21.57	32.58	21.68	30.90	17.74	31.26	15.69	28.54	17.90
5.	Goa	0.83	0.00	1.00	0.00	1.21	0.00	0.90	0.00	0.00	0.00
6.	Gujarat	15.50	34.96	15.89	34.94	17.76	27.27	15.29	24.85	16.12	23.33
7.	Haryana	46.26	0.00	48.02	0.00	48.91	0.00	46.70	0.00	43.64	0.00
8.	Himachal Pradesh	37.49	11.08	38.72	12.66	40.95	8.86	35.61	7.35	35.11	5.88
9.	J& K	13.56	15.62	15.18	12.06	13.41	10.32	1.55	1.99	0.00	0.00
10.	Karnataka	31,88	6.47	30.98	7.50	30.21	7.54	29.14	8.03	27.82	8.01
11.	Kerala	45.02	3.05	46.03	3.23	40.36	2.91	36.82	2.41	42.12	2.18
12.	Madhya Pradesh	24.34	32.37	4603	34.30	24.69	33.13	20.29	27.71	20.92	25.70
13.	Maharashtra	23.06	13.18	25.18	17.16	24.11	15.3	21.31	13.50	18.51	11.99
14.	Manipur	0.56	63.99	1.59	75.35	1.27	69.48	3.22	72.03	0.00	0.00
15.	Meghalaya	0.00	100.0	1.63	98.37	0.33	99.67	0.30	99.74	0.36	99.64

(Contd...)

Table 2.3 (Contd..)

16.	Mizoram	0.00	100.0	0.00	100.0	0.00	100.0	0.00	100.0	0.00	100.0
17.	Nagaland	0.00	100.0	0.00	100.0	0.00	100.0	0.00	100.0	0.00	0.00
18.	Orissa	28.13	31.92	25.81	29.74	25.54	29.70	25.29	26.71	24.11	20.50
19.	Punjab	51.03	0.00	52.87	0.00	53.34	0.00	50.51	0.00	50.30	0.00
20.	Rajasthan	33.98	18.56	35.33	19.56	32.67	20.20	29.07	22.77	23.35	30.16
21.	Sikkim	5.18	27.55	6.09	41.30	5.38	38.34	5.21	43.44	6.68	41.98
22.	T.N.	47.14	1.62	45.31	1.87	45.02	2.07	46.82	1.19	44.90	2.31
23.	Tripura	20.00	12.78	17.19	34.63	16.04	36.34	15.05	33.93	25.61	20.98
24.	U P	51.52	0.31	51.00	0.80	51.46	0.93	51.13	0.94	50.58	0.82
25.	West Bengal	40.20	4.45	34.27	6.78	34.37	6.06	32.35	5.99	31.54	6.12
26.	A&N Island	0.00	0.45	28.69	28.69	0.00	6.85	0.00	0.00	0.00	1.30
27.	D&N Haveli	8.43	86.52	6.29	88.41	1.82	9.72	22.22	77.78	0.00	0.00
28.	Daman & Diu	0.76	35.14	10.31	45.36	18.71	32.90	18.54	28.65	7.35	42.65
29.	Lakshad-weep	0.00	100.0	0.00	100.0	0.00	100.0	0.00	100.0	0.00	100.0
30.	Pondicherry	35.90	0.00	43.16	0.33	35.12	2.56	31.22	0.25	0.00	0.00
	All India	36.49	13.65	34.01	15.76	33.75	14.77	34.01	11.38	35.51	9.57

Source: Rural Development Statistics 1998, p. 159, 160, 161, 162.
Rural Development Statistics 1993-94, pp. 116, 117, 118.
Rural Development Statistics 1990, p. 100, 101.

Table 2.5: Incidence of Poverty Among Social Groups in Rural Areas

Year	*Total Population*	*Scheduled Caste*	*Scheduled Tribes %*
1977-78	51.2	64.6	72.4
1983-84	40.4	53.1	58.4
1987-88	33.4	44.7	52.6
1993-94	32.96	43.48	49.8

Source: Rural Development Statistics 2004.

Table 2.5: (Contd..): Poverty Among SCs and STs Rural and Urban in India

Year	*SC*		*ST*		*Others*
	Rural	*Urban*	*Rural*	*Urban*	
1987-88	55.22	....	59.92	.....	39.45
1993-94	48.11	49.48	51.94	41.14	32.96
1999-2000	36.25	38.47	45.86	34.75	

Source: Rural Development Statistics 2004.

Table 2.6: India: Literacy Rates 1991 and 1981

Year	*Scheduled Caste*	*Scheduled Tribes*	*Others. %*
1981	21.38	16.35	36.23
1991	37.40	29.60	57.7

Source: Census of India 1981 and 1991.

REFERENCES

1. Chakravarthy. B. (1977): Constitutional Safe Guards and Development Programmes for Weaker Sections , Planning and Management of Development Projects for SCs and STs, NIRD, Hyderabad.
2. Satyandra Tripathi (1987): *Development of Rural Poor,* Rawat Publications, Jaipur.
3. Satyandra Tripathi (1987): *Development of Rural Poor,* Rawat Publications, Jaipur.

4. Satyandra Tripathi (1987): *Development of Rural Poor,* Rawat Publications, Jaipur.
5. Harikumar (1984): "Has Integrated Rural Development Programme Succeeded", *Yojana,* Vol. 28, September 1-15, 1984.
6. Perumal Rao and Natarajan (1988): "Integrated Rural Development Programme Assistance in AndhraPradesh : An Evaluation", *Kurukshetra,* Vol. 36, No. 6, March 1988.
7. Rakesh Upadhyaya: *Integrated Rural Development in India: A Basic Approach in Policy,* Himalaya Publishing House, Bombay.
8. Satyandra Tripathi (1987): *Development of Rural Poor, Rawat Publications,* Jaipur.
9. Prakash Mehata and Bhardwaja (1987): *Integrated Rural Development Programme : A Case Study in Himachal Pradesh,* B.R. Publishing Corporation, Delhi.
10. Harikumar (1984): "Has Integrated Rural Development Programme Succeeded", *Yojana,* Vol. 28, September 1-15, 1984.
11. Chiranjeevi (1992): "Impact of Integrated Rural Development Programme on SCs and STs: A Case Study", Unpublished M.Phil. Dissertation submitted to University of Hyderabad.
12. *Rural Development Statistics Report 1998,* Published by NIRD, Hyderabad.
13. *Rural Development Statistics Report 1994 and 1995,* Published by NIRD, Hyderabad.
14. 8th Five Year Plan Documents, Planning Commission, Government of India.
15. Population Census Report 1981 & 1991, Directorate of Census, Hyderabad, Government of India,
16. *Rural Development Statistics Report 2003 and 2004,* published by NIRD, Hyderabad.

3

Agrarian Structure and Reforms Towards Sustainable Basic Needs and Human Development in Uttar Pradesh

D.M. Diwakar

Introduction

Generally the issues of basic needs have been focussed through crash programmes to ensure their fulfilment, such as, public distribution system (PDS) in general and now with focus on BPL target groups for food security, housing schemes—Nirbal Avas Yojana, Indira Awas Yojana, etc., for providing shelter and piecemeal package for intermittent employment opportunities for purchasing power to secure other basic needs. National Programme for Minimum Needs got such articulation in the Approach paper of the Fifth Five Year Plan. Approach Paper mentioned home-sites for rural landless under basic needs. Realisation was further deepened towards expansion of employment opportunities and minimum standard of living.

> "Even with expanded employment opportunities the poor will not be able, with their level of earnings, to buy themselves all the essential goods and services which should figure in their reasonable concept of a minimum standard of living. The measures for providing larger employment and incomes to the poorer sections will, therefore, have to be supplemented up to at least certain minimum standard, by social

consumption and investment in the form of education, health, nutrition, drinking water, housing, communications and electricity" (GOI, 1973: 9).

Thus, besides food, shelter and clothing, which were initially identified as basic needs, education, health, nutrition, drinking water, communication and electricity were added in the basic needs basket. Needless to emphasise that, these initiatives are necessary interventions. But the question arises whether these can be sustained without sustainable base for livelihood. It goes without saying that overcoming food insecurity and access to nutritious food, housing materials and clothes are by and large dependent on the produce of land and therefore, fulfilment of these basic needs is primarily dependent on access to land resources. Outlining strategies for fulfilment of Basic Need Approach to Fifth Five Year Plan document clearly mentioned:

> "Home-sites are as important as employment opportunities for ensuring to the rural landless a minimum standard of well-being. The problem can be dealt with most economically as part of land reform and consolidation of holdings. Home-sites for the landless may be treated as the first charge on any surplus land that theses measures yield. The surplus land may be transferred to an appropriate location by exchange and allotted as home sites to the landless" (GOI, 1973: 10).

Thus, measures initiated by the government for redistribution of ceiling surplus and gram sabha land for housing, cultivation, fishing, plantation, pottery, etc., are pointers to examine whether these initiatives have been instrumental towards achieving sustainable basic needs for social development through access to land resources. This paper is an exercise towards understanding and exploring the possibility of human development by acquiring sustainable basic needs through access to land resources. This study is primarily intended to examine as to how far access to land has been instrumental in facilitating basic needs for human development on sustainable basis. Primary data for this purpose have been collected from 1126 households through census survey in ten villages—one from each sample block spread over five districts namely, Chandauli, Gorakhpur, Rai Bareli, Muzaffar Nagar and Hamirpur representing different regions and climatic zones of Uttar Pradesh. Households with different size of land holdings and with different operational status have been considered for this examination. Distribution and possessions of ceiling surplus (CS) and gram samaj (GS) land and the impact of land reforms on basic needs and social development in Uttar Pradesh (UP). This study is divided into four parts: Part one deals with agrarian structure, whereas part two discusses agrarian reforms, part three analyses access to land towards fulfilment of basic needs and social development followed by part four as an attempt to consolidate the findings along with policy advocacy forwarded by the rural households.

I. Agrarian Structure

Land has been the basis of productive organisation and rural assets in any agrarian economy. Transformation in productive organisation, assets and structure is an important indicator to comprehend transition process which a rural society experiences. Forms of agrarian structure are reflected in operational holdings of a society and economy. It indicates iniquitous pattern of distribution of land to the tillers. Persisting inequality in distribution of land reflects the existing relations in an agrarian society of Uttar Pradesh (Diwakar, 2000). "Caste – land – occupational relations are inextricably intermeshed and this character of agrarian relations is favourable to those who operate large holdings and belong to the dominant caste." (Mishra, 1982: 79). Studies provide a basis to argue that in fifties distribution of land ownership holdings in Uttar Pradesh was highly inequitous (Singh, et. al. 1964; 28, in which 4340 zamindars spread over 81 villages were studied).[1] Sen Committee Report (RBI, 1984; 76-84, 384-393) categorically underlined skewed distribution of land as one of the major constraints for agrarian transformation of the region of the Permanent Settlement. After the abolition of zamindari system two generations elapsed since then. Although land reforms were decided to be implemented effectively, partly it contributed also in narrowing down inequality in distribution of land, it remained incomplete and neglected in absence of political commitment and will. Meanwhile subdivision and fragmentation of landholdings was witnessed in the process of natural attrition caused by division of family consequent upon growing population. As a result, landholding size in fifty years has decreased and therefore it is also argued that inequality in distribution of landholdings has lost its relevance to some extent. However, percentage distribution of operational holdings shown in Table 1 indicates that about 74 per cent of the households have possessed only 31 per cent of the land area whereas top ten per cent of the households possessed about 44 per cent according to the latest data available so far. This table shows that only 0.2 per cent of the landholders owning above 25 acres of land have about 4 per cent of the total operational area in their possessions. If we add the households above ten acres of land they amount to 2.9 per cent of the total households. But the area of operational holdings that they possess amounts to 21 per cent of the total area of operational holdings. Quantitatively it may appear less iniquitous for many of us but it needs a fresh assessment of the facts. Land holding size in the process of natural attrition has decreased but the question of land controlled by the same privileged class still persists. However transfer of land has widened the land base among middle caste/class and other section of the society also. Moreover family participation irrespective of caste/class has also increased.

Concentration of landholdings measured in terms of Gini Coefficient for macro data of Uttar Pradesh remained almost unchanged irrespective of ownership and operational holdings, although marginal increase was registered in the coefficient in 1982 (Sharma, 1994: A-14 & A-17). Moreover the gap between ownership and operational holdings may be explained through tenancy and fluctuation in it suggests the prevalence of tenancy at will. Quinquennial census data of agriculture suggest that Gini ratio for land concentration of operational holdings has been declining from 0.567 in 1980-81 to 0.505 in 1990-91 and 0.461 in 1995-96. However, individual research studies based on primary data and longitudinal studies show that Gini coefficient with respect to land concentration in Moradabad district of West Uttar Pradesh has rather increased from 0.49 in 1957-58 to 0.52 in 1993. However, value of coefficients remained unchanged when landless households are excluded (Dreze, 1997). Similarly another longitudinal study of Aligarh district of West U.P. suggests that percentage of households owning up to 25 bigha lands has increased from 36.4 in 1970 to 67.6 per cent in 1987.

Table 3.1: Percentage Distribution of Operational Holdings in India and Uttar Pradesh during 1995-96

Percentage

Size of Holdings (Acre)	*India*		*Uttar Pradesh*	
	Number	*Area*	*Number*	*Area*
Less than 2.5	59.4	15.1	75.6	34.1
2.5 - 5.0	18.8	17.4	14.5	23.8
5.0 - 10.0	13.1	23.2	7.3	23.1
10.0 - 25.0	7.1	27.0	2.4	15.8
Above 25.0	1.6	17.3	0.2	3.2
Average size (acre)		0.55		0.90

Source: Statistical Diary, State Planning Institute, Department of Planning, Government of Uttar Pradesh.

However, percentage of land owning households more than 50 bigha lands has declined. Overall Gini coefficient in 1970 was 0.73 for the distribution of owned land on a household basis, and 0.63 on a per capita per household basis whereas corresponding figures for 1987 were 0.74 and 0.65 (Saith and Tankha, 1997; 100). Major concentration of land areas in Allahabad and Muzaffar Nagar lies with Hindu upper castes and Muslims (Srivastava, 1997). The above analysis, thus, suggests that inequality in land distribution has not lost the ground and much is yet to be done to restore the land to the tiller in order to remove the qualitative inequality in distribution of land.

Table 3.2: Operational Land Holding of U.P. and Sample Districts (%)

Sl. No.	*Description of land holding*	*Total U.P.*	*Gorakhpur*	*Chan-dauh**	*Muzaffar-Nagar*	*Hamirpur*	*Rae Bareli*
1	Average holding	0.90	0.58	n.a.	1.09	1.96	0.64
2	Marginal holding (up to 1.0 hec.)	73.82	85.07	85.01	64.56	46.06	80.83
3	Small farms (1-2 hec.)	15.53	9.82	10.07	18.81	23.02	13.18
4	Semi-medium farms (2-4 hec.)	7.69	4.16	n.a.	11.84	17.72	4.86
5	Medium farms (4-10hec.)	2.73	0.90	n.a.	4.59	11.46	1.09
6	Large farms	0.22	0.05	n.a.	0.19	1.73	0.05
7	Total	100.00	100		100	100	100

Source: For Uttar Pradesh See Statistical Diary of Uttar Pradesh year 2000 pp. 98,99 and for sample districts see Statistical Diary of: Gorakhpur 2000, pp. 61, 62, 63; Muzaffarnagar 2000, pp. 46, 47; Rae Bareli 2000 pp. 59, 60, 61; Hamirpur 2000 pg.no.48,49,50.

* Data relate to Varanasi as no land holding data are available for Chandauli, a carved out district from Varanasi

Data from districts level distribution of operational land holdings from select districts given in Table 2 reveal that average size of operational holdings in Gorakhpur and Rae Bareli is lower than the state average (0.90 ha.). Majority of the farmers in state as well as in sample districts is marginal holders followed by small holdings. In Uttar Pradesh marginal and small holdings together constitute about 89.35 per cent. Marginal holders possess only 31.4 per cent of area whereas small holders possess about 24.4 per cent of operational area. Altogether they possess 55.8 per cent of operational area. Semi-medium farms have almost equal proportion of holdings and area in their possession. However, 2.9 per cent medium and large land holders possess 20.8 per cent of operational area. Even if one ignores concealed tenancy, which is pervasive in Uttar Pradesh, there is apparent inequality in distribution of land. Situation of sample districts are not different. This also explains the need for redistribution of land in Uttar Pradesh.

There could be many analytical categories for understanding agrarian structure in terms of distribution of land ownership, operational structure, social caste hierarchy, labour use including family and female participation in agriculture, but this is not the focus of this study therefore it appears prudent to stick to the official category of operational holdings. However, we have used caste-class continuums for this analysis. Data collected from sample villages at the household level suggest (Table 3) that SCC constitutes highest percentage (56.48) followed by OMC (28.6), MSM (6.04), UPC (5.77) and UMC (3.11). Distribution of operational holdings reveals that MRG constitutes highest percentage (51.95 per cent) followed by LL (37.66), SML (5.86), SMED (3.46) and MED+BG (1.07). Marginal holdings along with landless constitute over 89 per cent and caste-wise also OMC and SCC are the major constituents of the social and agrarian structure. In order to understand regional variation in distribution of households by castes and operational holdings we have analyzed the households further by sample districts as shown in Table 4. It is evident that the villages of Muzaffarnagar have the highest percentage of SCC households (70.85) followed by Chandauli (69.96), Hamirpur

(57.08), Rae Bareli (45.75) and Gorakhpur. Except Gorakhpur, where OMC has the highest percentage of households (44.83), in every sample villages SCC has the highest number of the households followed by OMC. In Gorakhpur and Rae Bareli, UPC stands third position so far number of households is concerned. However, percentage in former districts is higher than that of the later one. If one takes distributions of operational land holdings into account, we find that highest percentage of landless households is in Chandauli (64.38) followed by Muzaffarnagar (46.64), Hamirpur (31.42), Gorakhpur (24.14) and lowest in the sample villages of Rae Bareli. However, marginal holdings are highest in Gorakhpur (71.98 per cent), followed by Rae Bareli (67.45), Hamirpur (51.33) and Muzaffarnagar, whereas, the lowest marginal holdings among the sample villages are found in Chandauli district, which have the highest landless households. These two categories constitute major proportion about 90 per cent and above in most of the sample villages.

Table 3.3: Percentage Distribution of Households by Social Groups and Farm Size (Operational Holdings) at the Sample Villages of Uttar Pradesh

Size of Operational Holdings	*UPC*	*UMC*	*OMC*	*SCC*	*MSM**	*Total*
Landless	0.98	1.15	10.21	23.71	1.60	37.66
Marginal	2.49	1.33	15.72	28.69	3.73	51.95
Small	1.24	0.27	1.15	2.58	0.62	5.86
Semi-Medium	0.71	0.27	1.42	0.98	0.09	3.46
Medium-cum-Large	0.36	0.09	0.09	0.53	--	1.07
Total	5.77	3.11	28.60	56.48	6.04	100.00

Source: Mishra & Diwakar, 2005.

Note: UPC =Upper Caste; UMC = Upper Middle Caste; OMC = Other Middle Castes; SCC = Scheduled Castes; MSM = Muslim.

* Muslim is not a caste but a religious classification, which has been used separately indicating entire Muslim Community as other castes are of Hindu community. However, most of them belong to OMC category.

Besides the fact that majority of households in this agrarian

Table 3.4: Percentage Distribution of Households by Social Groups and Farm Size of Net Operational Area and District in Sample Villages of Uttar Pradesh

No.	*Social Groups/Farm Size*	*Gorakhpur*	*Chandauh**	*Muzaffar-Nagar*	*Hamirpur*	*Rae Bareli*	*Total*
I.	Social Group						
	UPC	14.22	3.86	3.59	3.54	3.30	5.77
	UMC	2.59	6.87	--	4.87	0.94	3.11
	OMC	44.83	19.31	25.56	33.63	18.87	28.60
	SCC	38.36	69.96	70.85	57.08	45.75	56.48
	MSM	--	--	--	0.88	31.13	6.04
	TOTAL	100.00	100.00	100.00	100.00	100.00	100.00
II.	Farmers Category						
	Landless	24.14	64.38	46.64	31.42	20.28	37.66
	Marginal	71.98	28.76	41.26	51.33	67.45	51.95
	Small	3.02	3.00	2.69	10.64	10.38	5.86
	Semi-Medium	0.86	3.43	6.73	4.87	1.42	3.46
	Medium-cum-Large	--	0.43	2.69	1.77	0.47	1.07
	TOTAL	100.00	100.00	100.00	100.00	100.00	100.00

Source: Mishra & Diwakar, 2005

structure is of marginal and small farmers, tenancy remains a major source to supplement income of the households. Tenancy market relations are found very strong and despite the fact that intermediary status has lost its legal ground, this class still exists strongly between state and peasants and exploitation of surplus continues through various forms of tenancies such as money rent, fixed produce are pervasive in Uttar Pradesh. Rent in advance has been driving out poor peasants gradually from lease markets, which have been an important source for their livelihood, employment, income and repayment of loan in absence of viable alternative. Thus, tenancy relations are of compulsive nature and mainly share of 50:50 is the modal terms of tenancy. However pre-cultivation advance rent payment system is emerging effectively, which is driving poor out of the tenancy market. Cost sharing mainly in terms of fertilizer seed and occasionally irrigation cost has been found (Diwakar, 2000a).

II. AGRARIAN REFORMS

In agrarian societies, land has been the most important means of production, status of power and prestige and therefore changes in agricultural institutions would have far reaching effects on land based social order. When land reforms emerged as one of the most important development strategies in the post-World War II period, India was not an exception to this phenomenon; rather it added yet another dimension along with peasant struggle, i.e. through peaceful mobilization and persuasion— Bhoodan (Joshi, 1982: 88-89) however, it could not sustain and achieve significance. Needless to mention here that history of land reforms in different parts of the country was not a liberal gift from enlightened government rather it was an outcome of historical process necessitated by protracted peasant struggle (Radhakrishnan, 1989:13). It was an outcome of growing consciousness and realization, irrespective of geographical boundaries and ideological variations, that agrarian reforms would unleash productive forces, enhance productivity, erode feudal struggle, address distributive justice and there by contend resentment towards bringing a peaceful social order.

Land reforms basically aimed at releasing productive forces of agriculture across the globe to spread up growth rate of agriculture on the one hand and enhance the capabilities of poor towards human development on the other. This development Strategy emerged in the post-World War II period. Many colonies achieved their political freedom and the aspirations of major anti-colonial forces mainly peasantry compelled their national government to enact and implement land reforms. Therefore, land reform measures appeared as State initiatives (from above) in consonance with peasants' aspirations. However, Occupational Forces (General MacArthur for example in Japan and Taiwan) were also forced to take active part in agrarian reforms to do away with feudal hurdles of agricultural development (Dorner, 1972:21; Joshi, 1982:36; Radhakrishnan, 1989: 14). Thus, State initiatives were also the outcomes of peasant struggles (from below). Evidences from various countries suggest that France, Netherlands, China, Japan, Russia and many other countries could bring qualitative change in production relations and development process through land redistribution. It is also seen that land reforms provides savings out of conspicuous extravagant consumption and leakages of landlords. Tenants are liberated from illegal exaction and non-market coercion and constraints. This provides surplus to invest in agriculture to increase production and productivity and also works towards diversification of agriculture and non-agricultural activities and thereby changes occupational structure (Bagchi, 2000).

Creating institution for revenue collection was probably the first step towards institutional reform that Indian agriculture witnessed. Imposition of revenue farming as an institutional arrangement dates back to Mughal India, which was not only the root of inequality and poverty but also the seed of the growth of the Zamindar class (Tandon, *et al,* 1936: 2). Land revenue in Mughal India was fixed on the basis of produce and not on size of land area. It was not the rent but taxes, the burnt of which was felt by both lower and upper strata of the peasantry. However, upper strata had to pay less per unit of land than the lower strata. Moreover, intermediaries were authorized to collect excess over the fixed revenue to be paid to the king. Thus, there were inherent regressive tendencies to aggravate inequality between the rich and poor in the countryside (Raychaudhuri and Habib, 1982, Vol. I, Ch. IX, see also Ch. VII). This mechanism of revenue collection was further reinforced by the company government, which entered into agreement with Zamindars (Tandon, *et al*, 1936: 2-3). In this process small peasantries were subjected to exploitation which led to ejection of large section of small peasantry who lost their right of ownership on land and forced to be subordinated as tenants at will to Zamindars. Rampant exploitation of the peasants during colonial rule resulted into a series of peasant movements during national freedom struggle. Champaran, Bardoli, Khera, Malabar, Agra and Avadh unrest of peasants, etc. were to name a few among them. "The efforts of larger landholders to bring rents more into line with prices touched off the wave of agrarian unrest that swept eastern and south-eastern Avadh in 1920-21" (Dharmakumar, 1982: 83). Consequent upon peasant unrests in different parts of country, there was growing realization among national leaders that land reforms were necessary to initiate process of development in India. This was very much reflected in the planning, legislation and enactment regarding abolition of the then land revenue system, abolition of Zamindari and intermediaries, etc. Basic documents that shaped their initiatives were Congress Agrarian Enquiry Committee Report 1936, Congress Economic Programme Committee Report 1948 and the Congress Agrarian Reform Committee, 1949. However, Sampurnanand (1936) had better clarity than other leaders on these issues. He was of the view: "no radical improvement in the condition of peasantry is possible without the abolition of the Zamindari System." He apprehended and warned a note of caution and further emphasised: "we must take care, while eliminating one set of vested interests, not to create another set which might be equally hostile to our ultimate goal, viz. social ownership of the land and its produce" (p.xv).

In independent India, undoubtedly, abolition of Zamindari and intermediaries was a radical step to change agrarian relations. Concern of reducing disparity of ownership of land was very much recorded in Plan documents for structural reforms and agrarian efficiency (Government of India, 1956, pp. 178-179). If enactment would have been the yardstick for commitment and realization it was the largest body of legislation that India could pass after Independence (Thorner, 1976: 18). But "there was apparent unwillingness of the rulers to do anything concrete about changing the production relations in Indian agriculture, which ensured that in most part of India even tenancy reforms and land ceiling laws, enacted in however diluted a form, would never be implemented" (Bagchi, 1988: 2).

Since Lucknow session of the Congress and Congress Agrarian Enquiry Committee Report 1936 Land Reforms was widely debated till 1950, this gave enough time to the Zamindars, Talukdars and other intermediaries to dispose off their land or manipulate through benami transfer. However, Uttar Pradesh got credit of enacting Uttar Pradesh Zamindari Abolition Land Reforms (ZALR) Act, 1950 (Das, 200). Subsequently, Rampur Thekadari and Pattadari Act of 1953, the Kumaon Land Act, 1954, etc. followed and supplemented ZALRA 1950 were enacted. These acts eroded the base of feudal structure and direct relationship between peasants and state was established (Mishra, 1996: 2). However, Zamindars were also confirmed as landholders along with Bhoomidhars, Sirdhars and Asamis (Thorner, 1976: 27). Thus, the term Zamindar was of course eliminated instead of Zamindar as such. As a result, there was hardly any significant change in land distribution pattern (Mishra, 1996P: 2; Singh & Mishra, 1964). Subsequently, Ceiling on Land Holding Act of 1960 was introduced to address the resultant lapses of ZALRA. But this Act was self-defeating in purpose because of provisions of exemptions and other in-built loopholes. This Ceiling Act 1960 was further amended in 1971 and 1973, which provided enough time and opportunities for the landlords in killing the main spirit and objectives of land reform in Uttar Pradesh (Mishra, 1996: p.4).

First Backward Class Commission was set up on 29th January 1953 headed by Kaka Kalelkar. It submitted its report on March 30, 1955. This committee extensively recommended on land reforms and reorganization of rural economy. However, this report could not be placed for discussion before the Parliament. In 1975 Most Backward Classes Commission was set up in U.P. headed by Sri Chedilal Sathi, which submitted its report in 1977. Another Backward Class Commission Report was submitted in 1980 headed by Sri B.N. Mundle. Among many other recommendations this Commission strongly recommended for effective land reforms.

"Until the stranglehold of the existing production relations is broken through radical land reforms, the abject dependence of under privileged on the dominant higher castes will continue indefinitely. In fact there is already a sizeable volume of legislation on the statute book to abolish zamindari, place ceiling on landholdings and distribute land to the landless. But in actual practice its implementation has been halting half hearted and superficial" (GOI, 1980: 13.33, p.60). "It is the Commission's firm conviction that a radical transformation of the existing production relations is the most important single step that can be taken for the welfare and upliftment of all backward classes. Even if this is not possible in the industrial sector for various reasons, in the agricultural sector a change of this nature is both feasible and over due." (GOI, 1980: 13.34, p. 60). "The Commission, therefore strongly recommends that all the State Government should be directed to enact and implement progressive land legislation so as to effect basic structural changes in the existing production relations in the countryside." (GOI, 1980: 13.35, p.60) "Apart from social traditions, the dominance by the top peasantry is exercised through recourse to informal bandage, which arises mainly through money-lending, leasing out small plots of land and providing house sites and dwelling space to poor peasants. As most of the functionaries of government are drawn from the top peasantry, the class and caste linkage between the functionaries of government and the top peasantry remain firm. This also tilts the socio-political balance in favour of the top peasantry and helps it in having its dominance over others." (Prasad, 1980, quoted in GOI, 1980, p. 60).

Besides these, legislative measures regarding abolition of tenancy, distribution of ceiling surplus and Gram Samaj land, consolidation of holdings, etc., were taken to address the problems of land reforms. Distribution of Gram Samaj patta land with implementing emphasis by the government is an added reinforcement. Moreover, in order to remove gender based discrimination in accessibility of land ownership a 'Committee for Gender Equality in Land Devolution in Tenurial Laws' 1998 was set up headed by Bina Agrawal which reviewed the gender inequality in land laws of five northern states (Haryana, Himachal Pradesh, Punjab, Jammu & Kashmir, and Uttar Pradesh). The Committee has submitted its report waiting for consideration.

State came into direct relation with the tenants after abolition of intermediary tenure. However, it proved mere change of nomenclature and there was hardly any substantial change in agrarian structure. To cover up this limitation Land Ceiling Act, 1960 was introduced with further modification in 1973 in order to acquire ceiling surplus land and redistribute among the land poor households. Another significant dimension of the UPZALRA, 1950 was the lease of the government land vested in the Gaon Sabha (GS) for agriculture, fishery, poultry, plantation and residence. It is intended to discuss redistribution of ceiling surplus and Gaon Sabha land—its official status of implementation and micro ground realities going through household survey of the sample village in order to understand the status of implementation and possessions of land to the beneficiaries.

Distribution of Ceiling Surplus Land

Ceiling on Land Holding Act, 1960 was introduced in Uttar Pradesh so that an upper limit of land holdings could be fixed and surplus land would be taken away from surplus farmers for redistribution among land poor peasantry. A limit of 40 acres of land of fair quality was fixed for a family of five members subject to increase in land area up to 24 acres in case of additional family members. However, this Act exempted a few categories of land from ceiling on land holdings used for grove, industrial purposes, cattle shed, compost pits, thrashing floor, residential houses, cremation ground/ graveyard area under plantation of rubber, tea, coffee, land with religious/charitable trusts, poultry and dairy farm, land covered farm roads, etc., (Mishra, 1996: 4). Cut off date for reference was fixed as May 1959. This Act was further amended in 1973 and the cut off date was fixed on 24th July 1971.

Under this amendment upper limit and exemption was reduced. Land areas under grove, used for poultry and dairy farm and farm roads were removed from exemption. Upper limit was brought down to 7.3 hectares in case of irrigated and from 10.95 to 18.25 hectares for un-irrigated land.

Land declared ceiling surplus and process acquire land was initiated by the government. But the process was not smooth. Disputes on settlement of land brought the matter into court of law. Many of them are still subjudiced and to be settled. Details of official records relating to these facts are shown in Table 5. Official data suggest that about 91.6 per cent of land area declared surplus in Uttar Pradesh was under possession of the government. About 70 per cent of the declared ceiling surplus land was redistributed among the landless poor. About 7.9 per cent area are still sub-judiced. Data relating to sample districts display that Rae Bareli is one of the districts where 100 per cent area was acquired. About 78.9 per cent area was distributed to the landless and about 94.3 per cent area of ceiling surplus land was settled till March 2002. In Chandauli only 58.2 per cent area was brought under possession and as high as 41.8 per cent of declared ceiling surplus land was subjudiced followed by Gorakhpur (23.9 per cent) and Hamirpur (20.9 per cent). Thus, data suggest that special effort is needed to expedite the judicial process to benefit the poor peasantry.

In order to comprehend the ground reality regarding distribution of ceiling surplus land findings from field survey, suggest that about 8.9 per cent households in sample villages were the beneficiaries of redistribution of ceiling surplus land. Beneficiary while reporting quality of land in terms of fertility and irrigation shows that all the land areas are not fertile and irrigated. Moreover, all the beneficiary households do not cultivate their land. There is gap between the households of beneficiary and self-cultivator beneficiary.

Distribution of Gram Sabha Land

Normal prescribed procedure of leasing GS land to leaseholders is ideal and democratic. Land Management Committee of the village Panchayat in confidence with Gram Sabha

Table 3.5: Distribution of Ceiling Surplus Land in Sample Districts of Uttar Pradesh 2003

Sample Districts	*Land declared ceiling surplus*	*Declared ceiling surplus land taken possessions by State*	*Subjudiced land stayed by the court order*	*Balance to be taken in possession*	*Allotted land area to the landless*	*Total area of settlement land*	*Area balance for settlement*
1	2	3	4	5	6	7	8
Gorakhpur	6024 (76.08)	4583 (23.92)	1441 (23.92)	1441 (59.94)	3611 (68.99)	4156 (7.09)	427
Chandauli	1311 (58.20)	763 (41.80)	548 (41.80)	548 (43.48)	570 (52.48)	688 (5.72)	75
Rae Bareli	4559	4559 (100.0)	00	00	3723 (78.93)	4298 (94.27)	261 (5.73)
Hamirpur	8749 (79.15)	6927 (20.85)	1822 (20.85)	1822 (71.89)	6297 (72.77)	6374 (6.38)	553
Muzaffar Nagar	6885 (96.14)	6581 (3.86)	304 (3.86)	264 (51.02)	3621 (92.42)	6454 (3.73)	127
Total U.P.	365584 (91.62)	335074 (7.89)	28969 (8.38)	30391 (70.09)	259000 (85.31)	313569 (6.34)	21505

Source: Land Revenue Board, Government of U.P., Nov. 2003.

Note: Figures in parenthesis indicate percentage of land declared ceiling surplus (col.3+col.5=100 per cent) recommends the list of beneficiaries to the SDM through circle officer and the land is allotted to leaseholders. Land vested in Gram Sabha is leased out to the peasants for different purposes by the Sub Divisional Magistrate on the proposal of Land Management Committee. In Uttar Pradesh this scheme was launched in 1975-76 in order to improve economic condition of the SC/ST/ OBC and weaker section of the society. In this scheme under Article 198 of UPZALR Act, 1950 maximum 1.26 hectare area of cultivable land is leased out to the land poor households. The land is leased out on the joint name of wife and husband. Under Article 126 there is also provision to include the name of adult unmarried daughter, divorced, deserted and widow. According to the availability of land annual targets are set. Land is also allotted for fishery, plantation, and pottery. Under Article 122(c), Circle Officer, ADM himself or on the proposal of Land Management Committee, allots land as on recorded order of preference mentioned in sub-article (3). For the people of SC/ST community in rural areas, 100-150 yards square area is given for residence purposes if she/he does not have own residential facility (Citizen Charter, Land Revenue Department, Government of U.P., pp.5-7).

Official details about district-wise distribution of GS land in Uttar Pradesh since 1975-76 to March 2002 is displayed in Table 6. Data suggest that about 54.8 per cent area of Gaon Sabha Land has been distributed among SCs followed by 25.9 per cent to BCs and 19.2 per cent Other Castes. Remaining area has been distributed among STs and Army personnel. District-wise distribution of GS land suggests that Rae Bareli has allotted highest area among the sample districts (3.5 per cent) followed by Muzaffarnagar (1.6), Hamirpur (1.4), whereas Gorakhpur could distribute only 0.5 per cent of total GS land distributed and Chandauli is still worse (0.2 per cent). However, inter-caste distribution of GS land among sample districts suggests that Chandauli has the highest percentage of GS land area distributed to SCs (67.6 per cent) and BCs (30.3 per cent) followed by Hamirpur (60.6 and 28.7 respectively). Sizeable beneficiary of GS land other than SCs and BCs were found in Muzaffarnagar (27.5 per cent) followed by Gorakhpur (22.4 per cent).

Table 3.6: Distribution of Gaon Sabha Land by Caste Category in U.P. Since 1975-76 to 2002

(Acres)

Sample Districts	*Scheduled Castes*	*Backward Castes*	*Other Castes*	*Total Area**
1	2	3	4	5
Gorakhpur	7290 (55.4)	2933 (22.3)	2946 (22.4)	13168 (100.0)
Chandauli	3430 (67.6)	1539 (30.3)	104 (2.1)	5073 (100.0)
Rae Bareli	51510 (54.7)	18835 (20.0)	4112 (4.4)	94228 (100.0)
Hamirpur	22032 (60.6)	10432 (28.7)	3870 (10.7)	36332 (100.0)
Muzaffarnagar	21669 (51.3)	8977 (21.2)	11620 (27.5)	42268 (100.0)
TOTAL	1454619 (54.8)	687213 (25.9)	508217 (19.2)	2652263 (100.0)

* Total includes ST and Army also.

Source: Land Revenue Board, Government of U.P., March 2002.

Note: Figures in parenthesis indicate percentage of the total households.

Findings emerged with regard to ground reality of the households of sample villages suggest that about 41.8 per cent of the households are beneficiary of GS land lease. Out of these households about 11.6 per cent are from Hamirpur followed by Chandauli (9.3 per cent), Rae Bareli (9.0 per cent) and Muzaffarnagar could score 5.7 per cent. Gorakhpur registered lowest spread of beneficiaries (only 0.6 per cent). So far the quality of land redistributed is concerned, 15 per cent of the households reported fertile and 19.4 per cent accepted that the land was irrigated. About 22.6 per cent of the households among 42 per cent were self-cultivating the land redistributed under GS lease. Reported reasons for non-cultivating households mainly two: one, they mainly work as non-agriculture labour; and, two, the households do not have male working member. Mere allotment does not ensure possessions. Even they got papers regarding allotment, possession remains a difficult task. Hence there is always question of under-possession. With regard to gap of allotment and non-possession in case of ceiling surplus and GS land, non-possession in case of ceiling surplus land is about 52 per cent. Implementation status is almost nil in sample villages of Gorakhpur and Chandauli. In Hamirpur non-possession was to the tune of 10.3 per cent and it was nil Muzaffarnagar. So far the lease of GS land is concerned over all non-possession was around 5.7 per cent. However, Chandauli registered about 17.14 per cent. Clubbing these two categories of beneficiary, i.e., ceiling surplus and GS land overall non-possession was around 14 per cent, whereas, Gorakhpur registered a high as 80 per cent of the beneficiary households. Other districts had 2 to 5 per cent non-possession.

One can also take an overall view of possession in terms of caste distribution and farm size category. Major beneficiary of ceiling surplus land was Scheduled Castes as high as 85 per cent. However, possession was with 79.2 per cent of the beneficiary households. In case of farm size category about 65 per cent households were the recipients of ceiling surplus land by marginal farm size, but interestingly there is over-possession by this category of farm size. Over-possession is reported in case of small and semi-medium farm size also. So far area is concerned, under possession is reported on the whole. Although, UPC and UMC have complete possession on allotted land. SCC suffers from under-possession. Under-possession becomes clearer in farm size category. LL could not acquire possession at all, and marginal holding suffers from under-possession. However, other categories have complete possession. Thus, it appears that landless is the worst sufferer and marginal farm holdings and SCC remained under-possession. Distribution of the beneficiary household of the residential land suggests that SCC is the major beneficiary (about 65 per cent) followed by OMC. In terms of farm size category marginal holdings was benefited to the extent of 83 per cent followed by small holdings with 12 per cent of households. Landless households remained at the lowest level, i.e. 1.9 per cent of the beneficiary households.

Possession status of beneficiary of ceiling surplus, GS lease and residential land distribution with respect to allotment in sample villages of Uttar Pradesh brought some gaps.

Dealing further with GS land in terms of allotment and possession for various purposes, such as, cultivation, residence, fishery, pottery and plantation, findings explain gap by caste and farm size in implementation of land reforms. There is hardly any over-possession in case of SCC irrespective of various uses for which land was allotted rather there is under-possession in case of residential allotment. Secondly LL households have no possession on allotted land at all. Over-possessions are found with OMC, MRG and SML category of the households. In case of pottery and plantation there is ideal situation. Picture becomes clearer if one dwells into the gaps of allotment and possession in terms of area of leaseholder. In terms of average area allotted and possession with leaseholder by caste and farm size of the households in sample villages, findings reveal that except plantation, there has been over-possession in case of pottery and under-possession in allotment of residential, cultivable and fishery land area. Looking into caste-wise details it is evident that: there is hardly any under-possession of lease area in case of UPC, MSM and UMC. Rather in case of cultivation and pottery there is indication of over-possession. However, in case of SCC also over-possession is reported for cultivable area and under-possession in case of residential and fishery area. Considering farm size category landless households have been allotted land for cultivation, residence and fishery but they do not have possession. Marginal holdings reported under-possession in case of cultivation, residence and fishery and over-possession in case of pottery. Even medium-cum-big farm holdings could manage land allotment and showing under-possession. This gives clue for the procedural lapses in identifying beneficiaries. Thus, it is clear that under-possession is mainly with OMC and landless and marginal farmers for cultivation and OMC, SCC, landless and marginal farmers for residence and fishery.

This shows that despite having an explicit mechanism of distribution, procedure adopted for distribution of land has many distortions. Findings suggest that the Committee exists in villages but hardly known to everybody. Only 30 per cent of the beneficiary households knew about the committee in existence. Procedure adopted for recommendation and preparation of a list of beneficiary is very flexible. Generally, it is done by the Lekhpal and Village Pradhan in consultation with other a few influential persons of village. However, about 49.5 per cent of the households of beneficiary acknowledged the role of PRI and Land Management Committee in selecting beneficiary of GS land. Findings suggest dominant and decisive role of Lekhpal, Pradhan and a few influential persons. This makes the process complicated and at the will of these persons in the helm of affairs. In this process the beneficiary has to run pillar to post to get the land allotted, at the cost of his wage employment and he is forced to borrow from the moneylender to bribe the Lekhpal and Pradhan. Findings suggest that about 9.1 per cent households of beneficiary admitted that they have lost their man days. About 15 per cent have been trapped in a money-lending usury network. This is not the end of the misery.

Despite all the complications about 13.8 per cent of the beneficiary households reported that they could not get possessions of the allotted land. The land is in the parcels of big farmers and influential persons. The reason behind is explained by the articulated villagers, that at the time of consolidation individual land was consolidated but the land of Gram Sabha and Government remained scattered and fragmented, as patches in the consolidated area of the big landholders. Therefore, even if the land is allotted it has been difficult to take possessions of the land. This is one of the significant disincentives to the potential beneficiary to persuade Lekhpal and Pradhan to allot such land, as it is almost impossible to take possessions on it.

Besides these there are many other reasons as to why deserving potential beneficiary could not get land. It is evident from table that as high as 92.8 per cent of the non-beneficiary households have accepted that deserving beneficiary could not get land because non-deserving beneficiary have been identified and they wrongly got the land allotted. A sizeable households, i.e. 30.8 per cent of non-beneficiary admitted that many of them could not get land as nobody came forward to help them. Secondly, they lacked money to offer bribe to the concerned persons. Those who could afford to bribe they got the land. This raises questions against governance and shows the seriousness of wrong implementations and lapses on the part of concerned agencies and authorities. This is a challenge also as to how this can be overcome to ensure land to the tillers. Is it possible without changing this non-sensitive superstructure in implementing role? To one it appears that there is need of concerted efforts of sensitive officials and agencies and there is need to create awareness among the potential and bona-fide beneficiary to acquire their proper place and positions. Concerted social mobilisation may answer the questions of bad governance and corrupt practices.

III. Land Redistribution towards Sustainable Basic Needs and Human Development

Needless to repeat that basic objectives of the land reforms across the globe was to release productive forces to spread up growth rate of agriculture on the one hand and enhance the capabilities of poor on the other. Evidences from various countries suggest that France, Netherlands, China, Japan, Russia and many other countries could bring qualitative change in production relations and development process through land redistribution. It is also seen that land reforms provides savings out of conspicuous extravagant consumption and leakages of landlords. Tenants are liberated from illegal exaction and non-market coercion and constraints. This provides surplus to invest in agriculture to increase production and productivity. This also works towards diversification of agriculture and non-agricultural activities and changes occupational structure (Bagchi, 2000).

In India, abolition of intermediary tenurial system was one of the major institutional reforms. Although this could not produce desired result, in select pockets where peasant mobilization was effective, land reforms could improve productivity and growth rates in agriculture and liberate tenants from illegal exaction, non-market coercion and bondage. Kerala and West Bengal could witness encouraging results. Kerala could protect civil, political and substantive freedom through egalitarian land reforms (Bagchi, 2001). Operation Barga in West Bengal could improve the status of sharecropper and redistribution of land resulted into higher level of productivity and growth (Sanyal, Biswas and Bardhan, 1998; Gohh, 1998). This led to better participation in education, health and development.

Table 3.7: Impacts of Redistribution of Land for Residential Housing on the Beneficiary Households by Social Groups and Farm Size of the Sample Villages in Uttar Pradesh

Social Group and Farm Size	*Percentage of Beneficiary Households*				
	Residential Land	*Liberated from Bondage*	*Enhanced Social Prestige*	*Const-ructed House*	*Acquired Comfor-table Living*
I. Social Group					
UPC	0.18	0.09	0.09	0.00	0.18
UMC	0.36	0.27	0.27	0.18	0.36
OMC	2.31	0.98	1.24	1.78	2.04
SCC	6.22	3.55	3.82	4.00	4.53
MSM	0.53	0.44	0.44	0.18	0.36
TOTAL BHH	9.59	5.33	5.86	6.13	7.46
TOTAL	100.00	100.00	100.00	100.00	100.00
II. Farm Size					
Landless	0.18	--	0.09	0.18	0.18
Marginal	7.99	4.53	4.88	5.33	6.04
Small	1.15	0.53	0.62	0.62	0.98
Semi-Medium	0.27	0.27	0.27	--	0.27
Medium-cum-Large	--	--	--	--	--
TOTAL BHH	9.59	5.33	5.86	6.13	7.46
TOTAL	100.00	100.00	100.00	100.00	100.00

Source: Mishra & Diwakar, 2005.

In Uttar Pradesh also, land reforms created space for economic security, reduced landlessness, and generated income despite several lapses and shortcomings in implementation. This section is intended to examine relationship between access to land and sustainable basic needs for better quality of life and over all social development. We have considered income, employment, GS land, net operated area, workforce, level of literacy, health status and schooling of girl child for this purpose. We attempted to discuss the role of land redistribution towards fulfilling basic needs and promoting human capital resources taking distribution of ceiling surplus land and GS land into account. Interesting results are visible despite many shortcomings in the implementation of land reforms and redistribution from the study of the beneficiary and non-beneficiary household survey of sample villages.

In case of redistribution of land for residential purposes suggests that there was indication of liberation of poor from bondage as they could acquire their ownership of homestead land (Table 7). About 5.33 per cent of households reported their liberation from bondage as they got ownership of residential land. Majority among them were of SCC social group.

Farm size category in this context suggests that larger beneficiary were of marginal holdings. As they could acquire ownership of homestead land their position in society was elevated. Particularly SCC and marginal holders could construct their houses and to a certain extent they could enjoy comfortable living. Thus, it is evident from table that redistribution of land for residential purpose could liberate the beneficiary from bondage, elevated their social status and they were enjoying comfortable living in a house constructed for their family. Redistribution of land for cultivation is another dimension where tangible benefits were reported. Data suggest that about 28 per cent of the households were the beneficiary of cultivable land in sample villages and majority of them were from SCC followed by OMC (Table 8. In case of farm size category marginal holdings were reported as major beneficiary followed by the landless households. Findings suggest that production of food grains of the beneficiary households has increased which made them comfortable at food front.

Their dependence for borrowing from moneylenders has been reduced. Since, they can afford security before public financial institution getting credit from has become relatively easier than earlier situation. Now they can rear cattle to

Table 3.8: Impacts of Redistribution of Cultivable Land on the Food Security and Income of the Beneficiary Households by Social Groups and Farm Size of the Sample Villages in Uttar Pradesh

Social Groups and Farm Size	*Percentage Distribution of Households Accepted*							
	Beneficiary of Cultivable Land increased	*Production of Food grains*	*Comfortable at food front*	*ML Borrowing Reduced*	*Public Loan Easier*	*Income increased*	*Easy cattle rearing*	*Other Income Generating Initiatoves*
I. Social Group								
UPC	0.44	0.36	0.36	0.09	0.27	0.36	0.18	--
UMC	1.15	0.44	0.36	0.27	0.27	0.27	0.18	0.09
OMC	7.28	5.60	5.60	2.40	1.69	3.82	1.78	0.62
SCC	17.67	15.63	15.81	9.06	6.31	14.03	5.42	2.66
MSM	1.33	1.24	1.24	1.15	1.07	1.51	0.89	0.18
TOTAL BHH	27.89	23.27	23.36	12.97	9.59	19.98	8.44	3.55
TOTAL	100.0	100.0	100.0	100.0	100.0	100.0	100.0	100.0
II. Farm Size								
Landless	6.84	5.15	5.33	2.49	1.69	3.56	0.80	0.44
Marginal	18.47	15.72	15.63	8.97	6.39	14.21	6.93	2.40
Small	1.95	1.78	1.78	0.98	1.15	1.69	0.53	0.53
Semi-Medium	0.53	0.53	0.53	0.44	0.27	0.44	0.09	0.09
Medium-cum-Large	0.09	0.09	0.09	0.09	0.09	0.09	0.09	0.09
TOTAL BHH	27.89	23.27	23.36	12.97	9.59	19.98	8.44	3.55
TOTAL	100.0	100.0	100.0	100.0	100.0	100.0	100.0	100.0

Source: Mishra & Diwakar, 2005.

supplement their income and initiate other income generating activities. Cumulative results of all these stated above placed the households with better income level. However, this can be examined further with detailed study of the economics of cultivation and other income generating activities of the households. Table also suggests that there are gaps in the beneficiary households and the households reporting benefits from redistribution of cultivable land. This also suggests that mere distribution of land is not sufficient condition to pull out the households from the quagmire of poverty. However, it reveals that land ensures access to other benefits necessary for the households.

Table 3.9: Impacts of Land Distribution on Social Development of the Beneficiary Households by Social Groups and Farm Size of the Sample Villages of Uttar Pradesh

Social Group and Farm Size	*Percentage of Beneficiary Households*			
	Improvement in Health Condition of Children	*Proper Clothing for Children*	*Child Schooling*	*Sending Girl Child to School*
I. Social Group				
UPC	0.27	0.27	0.27	3.73
UMC	0.27	0.27	0.18	1.95
OMC	2.40	1.95	3.02	15.10
SCC	9.86	9.33	9.15	29.13
MSM	0.89	0.89	1.24	3.73
TOTAL BHH	13.68	12.70	13.85	56.64
TOTAL	100.00	100.00	100.00	100.00
II. Farm Size				
Landless	2.66	2.49	2.40	19.09
Marginal	9.06	8.35	10.12	27.71
Small	1.51	1.42	0.98	3.29
Semi-Medium	0.36	0.36	0.27	2.49
Medium-cum-Large	0.09	0.09	0.09	1.07
TOTAL BHH	13.68	12.70	13.85	56.64
TOTAL	100.00	100.00	100.00	100.00

Source: Mishra & Diwakar, 2005.

Another dimension of benefits can be examined in this context is from the point of social development. A few indicators have been selected to understand the potential benefits of social development emanating from redistribution of land. Health and schooling are two major areas where responses are very encouraging. Findings as shown in Table 9, about 13.7 per cent of the households accepted that health status of their children has improved as now they can afford proper food to their children. It is consistent that SCC remains larger beneficiary of health followed by OMC. Similarly marginal holdings followed by landless labourers reported major benefits of land redistribution to improve the health status of their children. They could afford proper clothing. Besides health, they could send their children to school as now they could afford initial cost of food, clothes and basic materials required for. Most significant is the impacts on schooling of girl child. Thus, basic indicators of social development such as health and education displayed significant impacts, which beneficiary and non-beneficiary households have acknowledged.

However, findings suggest that impacts of the redistribution of land were marginal. Land is basis in transformation of rural society. As we have seen that land redistribution although with limited results is of instrumental importance to generate employment and income in order to have access to the resources for basic minimum needs and better quality of life. Here we would like to examine certain causal relations for employment, income and quality of life. In case of employment a hypothesis can be constructed that per capita employment (PCEMP) can be increased with increasing per capita net operated area (PCNOA), which enables household to withdraw workforce for capacity building or in other words for human development. Therefore, dependency ratio (DR) may be increased. Precisely it can be said:

PCEMP = f (PCNOA, Dependency Ratio).

Regression result:

PCEMP = 85.528 + 0.11 PCNAO + 0.39 DR

(43.85) (4.283) (14.168)

Adjusted R2 = 0.181, F-Value = 124.447

Findings suggest that PCNOA has significant positive causal relation with PCEMP. It implies that with the increase in per capita employment households can afford higher level of dependency. Although adjusted R2 explains only 18 per cent the model is highly significant revealed in F-Value of this model. Another model we have examined further including policy variables, such as, total workforce in agriculture (TWA) per capita ceiling land (PCCL) per capita GS land (PCGSL) and dependency ratio (DR) for explaining PCEMP. Thus, the model is:

PCEMP = f (TWA, PCCL, PCGSL, DR).

Result:

PCEMP = 101.095—0.467 DR + 0.155 PCGSL—0.005 PCCL—0.24 TWA

t-value = (40.158) (-16.579) (5.857) (-0.210) (-8.666)

Findings suggest that except per capita ceiling land other co-efficients are highly significant. Interestingly DR has negative relation. PCGSL has positive and significant causal relations. Therefore, if PCGSL is increased PCEMP will also increase. PCCL has no significant relation with PCEMP. With a given space of employment TWA has inverse relation with PCEMP. This model explains over 24.3 per cent of variation significantly. Thus, this model explains higher level of variation than earlier. Thus, to increase employment, there is need to increase per capita GS land to rural poor. Employment is important because it provides opportunities to generate income, which gives purchasing power to the households. Therefore, if we have to analyse the quality of life per capita income (PCINC) is one of major constituents. Per capita income can be explained through availability of per worker employment (PWEMP), per worker income (PWINC), Dependency Ratio (DR), PCNOA, per worker land (PWL), PCGSL, PCCL, and PCEMP. Thus, model is:

PCINC = f (PWINC, DR, PCNAO, PWL, PCGSL, PCCL, PCEMP, PWEMP)

Results: PCINC = 1099.568 + 0.884 PWINC — 0.138 DR + 0.552 PCNAO —0.318 PWL

t-value = (7.52) (60.45) (-6.348) (17.747) (-11.745)

0.189 PCGSL—0.141 PCCL + 0.296 PCEMP — 0.215 PWEMP

(-12.908) (-10.231) (12.899) (-9.299)

Findings suggest that the model explains about 84.6 per cent as adjusted R2 is 0.846, which is highly significant as F-ratio is 767.371. Obvious finding is that per worker income has significant positive relation with PCINC. Similarly PCNAO has significant positive relation. This is true with PCEMP also. Since DR has negative relation, here other relations have also turned negative. It is evident that if PCEMP is increased PCINC will increase. Therefore, simply increase per worker employment is not enough to increase the purchasing power of the household. In order to understand implication and impacts of land redistribution on social development, literacy level can be examined with a couple of related variables. Basic assumption is that access to land will widen employment base and level of income which will be instrumental to higher level of access in education. Percentage literacy of household (PCLH) is explained through DR, PCGSL, PCCL and TWA. The function is:

PCLH = f (DR, PCGSL, PCCL, TWA)

Result = PCLH = 17.714 — 0.053 DR + 0.090 PCGSL + 0.030 PCCL + 0.094 TWA

t-value = (1.375) (-1.667) (2.996) (0.995) (3.002)

Findings suggest that constant and PCCL are not different than zero, whereas DR is weakly significant reflecting still inverse relation with literacy. But PCGSL and TWA have significantly positive relation with the level of literacy. Value of adjusted R2 is significant but it explains very little so far the level of literacy is concerned. Excluding PCCL we have tried to estimate another model as follows:

PCLH = 19.506 — 0.057 DR + 0.088 PCGSL + 0.093 TWA

t-value = (1.529) (-1.781) (2.952) (2.962)

Value of adjusted R2 is still very low but significant (i.e. 2.3 per cent). The result suggests that constant is insignificant and not different than zero. DR has weakly significant inverse relation. However, PCGSL and TWA have significant positive relation. It implies that level of literacy can be enhanced through effective GS land distribution to the workforce in agriculture. It also suggests that literacy level for rural poor is not primary concern but it is employment and income for which GS land distribution has important role. It may be recalled that Bahujan Samaj Party (BSP) led government tried to sensitize bureaucracy for effective implementation, but the campaign lost its spirit in the middle itself. In order to comply the pressure, implementation was manipulated through dubious records, as we could encounter in the field. There was apparently general reluctance from the side of bureaucracy and its allies. This is because of over presence of land owning social groups and class in the bureaucracy.

In fact this is not new at all. Even pre-independence slogan of 'land to the tillers' by the political parties could not be sustained for long after independence. Although Zamindari Abolition Act and other Acts related to ceiling surplus land were promulgated but in every stage there was enough time lag to allow the land owning intermediary to misappropriate the ownership status of land. Thus, the hope was ultimately pinned down in the particular ruling class who could identify with the interest of the rural poor at the lower rung of the society. However, this was also not realised even after BSP usurping to power in Uttar Pradesh. Despite apparent willingness to some extent leadership has to compromise with ruling allies against the interest of rural poor. Since the bureaucratic structure is over represented by the anti-poor elements, it has been difficult for BSP government to sideline the anti-poor interest. Rather it has compromised to retain power at the cost of the interest of the poor at least in the case of land reforms and redistribution of land to the poor. Here the very concept of good governance remained helpless to turn right side up. Michael Kalecky has rightly observed "History has shown that lower-middle class and rich peasantry are rather unlikely to perform the role of the ruling class. Whenever social upheavals did enable representative of these classes to rise to power, they invariably served the interest of big business (often allied with the remnants of the feudal system)" (Kalecky, 1976:30). History also suggests that social mobilization has been creating compelling situation for the ruling class in order to contend the resentment of the peasantry and ruling class has been trying its best to convert the effects of mobilization in terms of land reforms from above. And U.P. has not been an exception in this context. Therefore, unless superstructure is radically transformed it is difficult to enforce effective implementation. There is enough evidence that redistribution of land to the tiller has enormous potential to transform the quality of life of rural poor and contribute significantly towards fulfilling basic needs promoting human development, non-compromising political will is the first and foremost essential condition. Unless the class interest is represented substantially in the ruling class this 'Political will' would remain a far-fetched dream. Hopes still lie in consistent social mobilization in the line of class in itself to be transformed gradually into class for themselves.

IV. Findings for Policy Advocacy

Summarising the analysis and discussions in order to arrive at conclusions regarding access to land for sustainable basic needs in Uttar Pradesh we have tried to understand the process of land reforms and various initiatives taken-up by the governments, particularly after independence with special reference to Uttar Pradesh. We found that in order to overcome the shortcomings of UPZALRA, ceiling on land-holdings was imposed and surplus lands were acquired. However this process was also not free from manipulative syndrome. Exemption on various categories of land and sub-judice status on sizable ceiling surplus land provided a significant cover to and in favour of land-owning castes and class. More than 8 per cent of declared ceiling surplus land (i.e. 30,391 acres) is yet to be taken in possession. Moreover, all the land distributed to the peasants is not fertile and irrigated and therefore all the beneficiaries of ceiling surplus land did not cultivate land themselves.

Land vested in Gram Sabha (GS) is leased to poor peasants of different social groups i.e., SC/ST, OBC and army men, since 1975-76 in Uttar Pradesh for residence, cultivation, plantation, fishing and pottery. About 26,52,263 acres land have been distributed among SCs (54.8%), BCs (25.9%), and other castes (19.2%) and remaining land to STs and army personnel. However, mere allotment of land did not serve the purpose. Possession over allotted land remained a difficult task. Non-possession was reported on account of influence and control of big farmers. Landless households were still waiting for possessions. Under possession in terms of area was also found in case of marginal holdings, SCs and Muslims. Over possessions were found with OMC, MRG and SML households. Status of possession became explicit in case of purpose-wise segregated details. Even medium-cum-big farm holdings could manage land allotment reflecting procedural lapses of the scheme. A sizeable non-deserving beneficiary household were selected at the cost of genuine potential households, because of lapses in procedure, bribery, lack of awareness and sensitive implementing agencies.

Even political powers with this given superstructures remain ineffective. Despite ruling of effective implementation with a declared deadline by the state government land reforms remained on the same ground with a marginal difference, as superstructure did not correspond because of their anti-dalit and anti-poor attitude. This suggests that unless superstructure is radically transformed in favour of poor and landless peasants mere usurpation of political power does not empower in real sense to implement the agenda of poor, may be land reforms or basic needs. Vicious nexus of land owning social groups and class embedded with their bureaucratic connivance because of their common interest, all sorts of manipulations of record have been done to foil the efforts of implementation of land reforms. Majority of functionaries from village to secretariats are represented and controlled by the landowning class and its natural allies in politics. Indifferent attitude towards implementation of land reforms and to ensure possession has been quite obvious. Now the land reforms have been pushed to backseat.

Despite the fact that there has been obvious indifference in implementation of redistribution of land and limited implementation, land reforms measures could bring positive and visible results. To the extent of limited implementation, land redistribution could create space for economic security, reduced landlessness, and initiated income generation.

Indications of liberation from bondage on account of ownership of residential land, were found. Poor could erect houses and enjoy relatively comfortable living elevating their social status. In case of the beneficiary households of cultivable land, production of food grain increased which placed them relatively comfortable at food front. Land as collateral security provided access to public institutional network and credit. These could reduce their dependence on exploitative usury network of moneylenders. Allied activities such as cattle rearing to supplement their income became possible. However, due to lack of comprehensive follow-up package much is left to be desired. Findings also suggest that there were considerable differences in terms of indicators of social development, particularly in the areas of health and schooling. It is sad on the part of implementation that land reforms measures, which have enormous potential for fulfilling sustainable basic needs for human development, have become victim of neglect of ruling class and its natural allies. There is an urgent demand of reorienting policies through effective mobilization of poor so that the policy makers and implementing functionary do not have any excuse and option but to work in favour of deprived masses. But unfortunately advocacy and policy for corporate farming has been accepted which prove a drag on accessibility of land for sustainable basic needs for poor.

People's Voice and Advocacy

Based on responses of the rural households, discussion and analysis of this study following suggestion are thrown up for consideration of the implementing agencies and functionaries in order to achieve effective targets of land reforms: (1) There is need of ensuring effective possession of redistributed land through direct accountability of concerned functionaries. A land management committee at village level with proper representation of poor peasants should be formed to verify the implementation status. Undistributed scattered land parcels should be consolidated and redistributed through co-operative ownership. Poor peasants co-operative should be formed and follow up packages, access to credit, etc. should be rooted through co-operative. Pending cases on sub-judiced land should be disposed off on the priority basis and a separate legal committee should be constituted for technical support of the poor peasants. Poor peasant committee should be provided legal support to identify benami transfer of land. The benami land should be declared surplus and those surplus lands should be redistributed among poor households on the recommendation of poor peasant land management committee. Wasteland should be acquired and transferred to landless through their co-operative ownership and follow up assistance should be rooted through co-operative in reference. Assured irrigation co-operatives of landless peasants should be formed to provide irrigation on distributed and other lands. Effective insurance cover on crops should be extended through micro-finance co-operative of land beneficiaries. Ban on individual purchase of redistributed land should be executed effectively. A provision for direct institutional loan on land should be extended to the beneficiary of land directly on producing kisan passbook. Subsidised inputs should be provided to the beneficiaries of land. Indifference and negligence in implementation of land redistribution and possession by functionaries should be treated as cognisable non-bailable offence. Administration and Policy implementing agencies should be made accountable directly for non-possession and should be punished in terms of career of service. Best implementing functionaries should be given incentives. Minimum wages should be implemented effectively. Poor households should be organised and proper support should be extended to safeguard the interest of the beneficiary of land. Participation of poor in co-operatives, PRI and land management committee should be ensured. Illegal possessions of redistributed land by influential persons should be liberated on priority basis. Pro-poor social activists should be involved in organizing poor. Effective flood control measures should be initiated. Rural industrialisation, functional education and women participation should be encouraged. Micro-financial credit groups should be formed and self-help women cooperatives should be promoted. PRI should be empowered to form women co-operatives and Functional Education Groups. Technical support should be ensured to promote women participation. Land Records should be computerized, updated and easy access to the records should be ensured for information. Above all unless poor friendly environment is ensured any amount of attempts or initiatives with pious intention can hardly make substantial dent towards saturating basic needs on sustainable basis.

REFERENCES

Bagchi, A.K. (1988), *Economy Society and Polity,* Oxford University Press.

Das, Sukumar (2000), "A Critical Evaluation of Land Reforms in India", in Sinha B.K. and Pushpendra (eds.), *Land Reforms in India,* Vol. 5, Sage Publications, New Delhi.

De Silva, G.V.S., et al (1988): *Towards Theorisation of Rural Development.*

Dharmakumar (1982), *The Cambridge Economic History of India,* Vol. II, Orient Longmans.

Diwakar, D.M., (2000): "Agrarian Transformation in Uttar Pradesh", *Journal of Social and Economic Development,* Vol. III, No. 1, January-June.

——— (2000a): "Purvi Uttar Pradesh ke Kheti mein Poonji ka Vikas", *Lokyuddha,* November-December.

Dorner, P. (1972), *Land Reforms and Economic Development,* Penguin, Harmondsworth.

Government of India (1980): *Report on the Backward Class Commission,* Vol. I.

Government of India (1973): *Approach to the Fifth Five Year Plan 1974-79,* Planning Commission.

Joshi, P.C. (1982), *Land Reforms in India,* Allied Publishers, New Delhi.

Mishra, G.P. (1996), *Distribution of Surplus Land and Rural Poor,* APH Publishing Corporation, New Delhi.

Mishra, G.P. & D.M. Diwakar, (2005): *Land Reforms and Human Development,* Manak Publications, Pvt. Ltd. New Delhi.

Neale, W.C. (1962), *Economic Change in Rural India: Land Tenure and Reforms in Uttar Pradesh: 1800-1955,* Kennikat Press, London.

Prasad, P.H., (1980): "Rising Middle Peasantry in North India", *Economic and Political Weekly,* Annual Number.

Radhakrishnan, P. (1989), *Peasant Struggles, Land Reforms and Social Change,* Sage Publications, New Delhi.

Raychoudhuri, R.C. and I. Habib (1982), *The Cambridge Economic History of India,* Vol. I, Orient Longmans.

Sampurnanand, B. (1936), *Agrarian Enquiry Committee Report,* Note of Ch.VI, p. XV.

Singh, B. and Shridhar Mishra (1964), *A Study of Land Reforms in Uttar Pradesh,* Oxford Book Company, Calcutta.

Tandon, P.D. et.al., (1936), *Congress Agrarian Enquiry Committee Report, 1936,* Prabhu Publications, Gurgaon (Haryana).

Thorner, D. (1976), *The Agrarian Prospects in India,* Allied Publishers Ltd., New Delhi.

Notes

1. For details see Singh, Baljit, et al (1964): *A Study of Land Reforms in Uttar Pradesh,* Oxford Book Company, New Delhi. In this context Table furnished below can explain inequality in distribution of land.

4

Dalits and Agricultural Landholdings in Andhra Pradesh

Prof. K. Nageswara Rao

The size of landholdings and the productivity of land serve as the engine of economic growth and the ownership of this asset determines the level of social equality and inequality in the society. It is reported that as on 30th September 1996, in India, about 52.13 lakh acres land has been distributed to 51.21 lakh beneficiaries belonging to Scheduled Castes, Scheduled Tribes and other categories including backward classes and weaker sections. 18.08 lakh acres of land accounting for 34.68 percent of the total land was distributed to 18.49 lakh Scheduled Castes beneficiaries at an average of 0.978 acres per household. 7.31 lakh acres of land accounting for 14.02 percent of the total land was distributed to 7.19 lakh Scheduled Tribes beneficiaries at an average of 1.017 acres per household. 26.74 lakh acres of land accounting for 51.29 percent of the total land was distributed to 25.53 lakh other castes beneficiaries at an average of 1.047 acres per household. In all, in India the average distribution of land to all weaker sections in 1996 works out to 1.018 acres per household. It is clear form the data that per household land distribution to Scheduled Castes and Scheduled Tribes is less than the All India average while it exceeded this average for the household groups belonging to other castes. From this analysis it is inferred that the Scheduled Caste and Scheduled Tribe people failed to get their due share in land distribution even after sixty years of independence.

Structure of Land-holdings in Andhra Pradesh

Land reforms introduced in Andhra Pradesh could not result in the identification of surplus land for distribution, but prevented to a larger extent further accumulation of land by the landlords. The details relating to the operational land holdings and the area operated between 1970-71 and 200-01 in Andhra Pradesh are shown in Table 4.1I. Marginal land-holdings (less than 1.00 hectare) accounted for 42.3 percent of the total operational land-holdings with 9.3 percent of the total operational area in 1970-71. With 11.7 percent of the total operational area, small-holdings (1.00 to 2.00 hectares) accounted for was19.4 percent of the total holdings. In 1970-71 small and marginal holdings (less than 2.00 hectares) together constituted 66.00 percent of the total operational holdings with an operational area of 21.00 percent of the total operational area. This reveals the fact that a smaller part of the operational area is controlled by a larger number of land-holders in Andhra Pradesh. In other words, land-holdings are fragments as one fifth of the operational area is controlled by two thirds of the total number of land-holders. On the other hand, large and medium (above 4.00 hectares) land-holdings constituted for 57.0 percent of the operational area owned and controlled by only 14.0 percent of the landholders. This shows a positively skewed distribution of land holdings in favour of large and medium size landholders in Andhra Pradesh state.

In 1976-77 the percentage of marginal holdings and small-holdings to total number of operational holdings were 48.7 and 20.3 percent respectively. Small and marginal holdings together, with 22.0 percent of the total operational area, accounted for 66.1 percent of the total operational holdings. On the other hand, medium and large holdings were 15.6 percent of the total operational holdings controlling 57.7 percent of the total operational area in the state. It is found that the number of small and marginal holdings increased indicating fragmentation of land holdings on one hand and the medium and large holdings and the area controlled by them also increased on the other hand between 1970-71 and 1975-76.

By 1980-81, the share of marginal holdings to total operational holdings increased by 5.00 percent while the area controlled by them increased by 4.00 percent showing the impact of surplus land distribution of land and forest land to Scheduled Tribes. The percentage of small-holdings to total operational holdings increased by 1.00 percent while the operational area increased by 4.00 percent. On the other hand, the size of large holdings to total operational holdings decreased by 1.31 percent and that of the area of large holdings to total operational holdings decreased by 5.00 percent between 1976-81.

Similar trend continued at a slower pace during 1981-87 and the percentage of marginal holdings to total holdings increased by 3.00 percent and that of the area of marginal holdings to total operational holdings increased by 1.00 percent. On the other hand the area under large operational holdings decreased by a smaller rate of 3.00 percent. Compared to 1976-81 the period 1981-87 witnessed a slower rate of land distribution in Andhra Pradesh state.

In 1909-91 more than 56.00 percent of the total holdings were marginal holdings controlling less than one sixth of the total area of operational holdings. On the other hand, 1.27 percent of the total operational holdings were large holdings controlling 12.80 percent of the total area of the operational holdings. A little more than one fifth of the total holdings were smallholdings that were holding a little less than one fifth of the area of the total operational holdings in the state.

In 1995-96 small and marginal holdings (less than 2.00 hectares) together constituted 80.70 percent of the total operational holdings with an operational area of 42.70 percent of the total operational area. This reveals the fact that small-sized operational holdings are controlled by a larger number of landholders in Andhra Pradesh. In other words, land holdings are fragments as less than one half of the operational area is controlled by more than 80.00 percent of the total number of landholders. On the other hand, Large and medium (above 4.00 hectares) land holdings constituted for 31.00 percent of the operational area owned and controlled by only 6.00 percent of the landholders. This shows a positively skewed distribution of land holdings in Andhra Pradesh state

In 2001-02 the number of marginal operational holdings increased to 70.23 lakhs controlling an operational area of 31.04 lakh hectares. In other words, 21.56 percent of the total operational area is held by 60.00 percent of the total operational holdings of marginal size. The number of small holdings and semi-medium holdings grew in their proportion to the total operational holdings along with the area under their control. Another significant feature of land distribution in Andhra Pradesh in 2001-02 is that the share of large and medium operational land holdings and the area under these holdings declined during the period under review. Another important feature is a decline in the share of semi-medium operational holdings with more or less the same percentage of the area operated under them during the decade in the state.

Land-holdings of SCs & STs in Andhra Pradesh

The details relating to the operational land holdings and the area operated by scheduled castes, Scheduled Tribes, other groups during 1995-96 and 2001-02 are presented in Table 4.2. A closer look at the table reveals that 7.38 percent of the operated area of the total land holdings in the state belongs to scheduled castes in 1995-96 and it increased to 7.86 percent in 2001-02. The share of the number of operational land holdings to total land holdings belonging to scheduled castes decreased from 12.12 percent in 1995-96 to 11.86 percent in 2001-02.

The percentage share of the number of operational land holdings to total land holdings belonging to Scheduled Tribes decreased from 7.71 percent in 1995-96 to 4.48 percent in 2001-02. More than 7.50 percent of the operated area of the total land holdings belonging to Scheduled Tribes in the state in 1995-96 increased to 8.27 percent in 2001-02.

The percentage number of land holdings belonging to other social groups to all land holdings in the state remained more or less the same around 80.75 during 1995-96 and 2001-02. During the same period the percentage area of the operational holdings controlled by other social groups to the area of the total land holdings decreased from 85.03 to 83.88.

All this indicates that thee is a marginal shift in the land holding owned by other social groups to scheduled castes and Scheduled Tribes.

The shares of scheduled caste marginal, small and medium size land holders to the total Scheduled Castes land holders and the area controlled by them remained more or less the same during 1995-2002. Infact, marginal land holders owning 37.00 percent of the total area owned by Scheduled Castes accounted for 73.00 percent of the total number of scheduled caste landholders. Small land-holders owning 30.00 percent of the total area owned by Scheduled Castes accounted for 18.00 percent of the total number of Scheduled Castes landholders. Medium land-holders owning 30.00 percent of the total area owned by scheduled castes accounted for 8.00 percent of the total number of Scheduled Castes landholders.

Similarly, the structure of distribution of land holdings among different categories of Scheduled Tribes remained unchanged during 1995-2002. Marginal landholders owning 18.00 percent of the total area owned by Scheduled Tribes accounted for 53.00 percent of the total number of Scheduled Tribes landholders. Small land-holders owning 25.00 percent of the total area owned by Scheduled Tribes accounted for 25.00 percent of the total number of Scheduled Tribes landholders. Medium land-holders owning 52.00 percent of the total area owned by Scheduled Tribes accounted for 22.00 percent of the total number of Scheduled Tribes landholders.

Among the other social group land holdings, the area under the large sized landholders declined by 2.00 percent between 1995-96 and 2991-02. Further, the percentage of medium sized land holdings to total operational land holdings declined by 3.00 percent associated with a decline of 2.00 percent of the area under medium sized land holdings. On the other hand, the area under the marginal landholders increased by 1.00 percent and that of the number of land holdings increased by 2.00 percent between 1995-96 and 2991-02. Further, the percentage of small sized land holdings to total operational land holdings increased by 1.00 percent associated with an increase of 2.00 percent of the area under medium sized land holdings.

Distribution of Land-holdings of SCs & STs in Anantapur District

Table 4.3 gives the details relating to the operational land holdings and the area operated by Scheduled Castes, Scheduled Tribes, other groups in 2001-02. A closer look at the table reveals that 1100 percent of the operated area of the total land holdings in the state belongs to Scheduled Castes as against that of 7.86 percent for the state in 2001-02. The share of the number of operational land holdings to total land holdings belonging to scheduled castes is 7.00 percent as against 11.86 percent for Andhra Pradesh in 2001-02.

The percentage share of the number of operational land holdings to total land holdings belonging to Scheduled Tribes is 4.00 percent as against 4.48 percent for the state as a whole in 2001-02. A little more than 3.00 percent of the operated area of the total land holdings in the state belongs to Scheduled Tribes while it is 8.27 percent in Andhra Pradesh state in 2001-02.

The percentage number of land holdings belonging to other social groups to all land holdings in Anantapur district has been very high in 2001-02. During the same period the percentage area of the operational holdings controlled by other social groups is 90.00. All this indicates that other social groups control larger proportion of land holdings and area operated in Anantapur district.

Infact, marginal land holders owning 20.59 percent of the total area owned by Scheduled Castes accounted for 48.78 percent of the total number of Scheduled Caste landholders. Small land- holders owning 34.91 percent of the total area owned by Scheduled Castes accounted for 30.79 percent of the total number of Scheduled Caste landholders. Medium land-holders owning 42.01 percent of the total area owned by Scheduled Castes accounted for 20.00 percent of the total number of Scheduled Caste landholders.

A look in to the structure of distribution of land holdings among different categories of Scheduled Tribes in 2001-02 reveals that marginal landholders owning 13.1 percent of the total area owned by Scheduled Tribes accounted for 36.90 percent of the total number of Scheduled Tribes landholders.

Small land- holders owning 46.53 percent of the total area owned by Scheduled Tribes accounted for 35.17 percent of the total number of Scheduled Tribes landholders. Medium land-holders owning 49.00 percent of the total area owned by Scheduled Tribes accounted for 26.88 percent of the total number of Scheduled Tribes landholders.

Infact, in Anantapur district 80.00 percent of the marginal holding belong to other groups who control same percent of the area owned by the marginal land-holders and 84.00 percent of the small holdings belong to other groups that control same proportion of the land held by small holders. 90.00 percent of the medium size holders are from other social group and they hold 88.00 percent of the area under medium size holdings. 12.40 percent of the total area owned by other social groups is under large holdings maintained by 1.71 percent of the other social groups land-holders.

Classification of land holdings maintained by males and females in Anantapur district in 2001-02 is shown in Table 4.4. It is found that one fifth of the total land-holders in the district are female and the remaining are males. Similarly, a little more than one fifth of the total land-holders belonging to Scheduled Castes, Scheduled Tribes and other social groups are females. There are no females controlling large holdings among the Scheduled Castes and Scheduled Tribes in Anantapur district, as many belonging to these groups are poor and economically backward. Among the other social groups 12.00 percent of the owners of large- holdings are females.

It is interesting to know that a little more than 22.00 percent of the marginal holdings belonging to Scheduled Castes, Scheduled Tribes and other social groups are controlled by females in the district. 19. 00 percent of the smallholdings belonging to Scheduled Castes, 14.50 percent belonging to Scheduled Tribes and a little more than 20.00 belonging to other social groups are held by females. Females maintain nearly one fifth of the semi-medium holdings belonging to Scheduled Castes, Scheduled Tribes and other social groups. On the other hand, nearly one fifth of the medium land holdings of Scheduled Castes and Scheduled Tribes, are held by females while 13.6 percent of the medium land holdings of other social groups are held by females. This indicates that larger proportion of females belonging to other social groups controls and maintains landholdings compared to females belonging to weaker sections in the district.

Conclusion

From this analysis attempted to study the pattern and distribution of land holdings in Andhra Pradesh the following conclusions may be drawn.

In 19996, in India about 52.13 lakh acres of land has been distributed to 51.21 lakh beneficiaries belonging to Scheduled Caste, Scheduled Tribes and other categories including backward classes and weaker sections at an average of 0.978 acres per Scheduled Castes household, 1.017 acres per Scheduled Tribes household and 1.047 acres per other social groups household. In all, in India the average distribution of land to all weaker sections in 1996 works out to 1.018 acres per household. It is clear from the data that per household land distribution to Scheduled Castes and Scheduled Tribes is less than the All India average while it exceeded this average for the household groups belonging to other castes.

In Andhra Pradesh state 52.40 percent of the geographical is under land-holdings of various sizes belonging to various social groups. The introduction of land reforms changed the distribution of land holdings in Andhra Pradesh state during the last three decades. In 1970-71 one fifth of the operational area is controlled by two thirds of the total number of landholders. On the other hand, large and medium land holdings account for more than one fifth of the operational area owned and controlled by only one sixth of total land holders showing positively skewed distribution of land holdings in favour of large and medium size landholders.

Between 1970-71 and 1975-76 the number of small and marginal holdings increased indicating fragmentation of land holdings on one hand and the medium and large holdings and the area controlled by them also increased on the other hand. By 1980-81 the share of marginal holdings to total operational holdings increased by 5.00 percent while the area controlled by them increased by 4.00 percent showing the impact of surplus land distribution of land and forest land to Scheduled Tribes. Similar trend continued at a slower pace during 1981-87 and the percentage of marginal holdings to total holdings increased by 3.00 percent and that of the area of marginal holdings to total operational holdings increased by 1.00 percent.

In 1909-91 a little more than one fifth of the total holdings were small holdings that were holding a little less than one fifth of the area of the total operational holdings in the state. In 1995-96 small-sized operational holdings are controlled by a larger number of landholders in Andhra Pradesh. In other words, land holdings are fragments as less than one half of the operational area is controlled by more than 80.00 percent of the total number of landholders. In 2001-02 the number of smallholdings and semi-medium holdings grew in their proportion to the total operational holdings along with the area under their control. Further, the share of large and medium operational land holdings and the area under these holdings declined.

In Andhra Pradesh, during 1976-2001 the estimated average area of each landholding for all social groups declined from 2.73 hectares to 1.24 hectares registering a fall of 47.00 percent. During the same period, for the marginal landholders it declined from 0.47 hectares to 0.44 hectares, for the small landholders it declined from 1.47 hectares to 1042 hectares, for the semi-medium landholders it declined from 2.79 hectares to 2.67 hectares, for the medium landholders it declined from 6.17 hectares to 5.70 hectares, for the large landholders it declined from 17.07 hectares to 16.36 hectares. During the same period the number of marginal landholdings increased by percent, small landholdings by percent, semi-medium landholdings by percent, medium landholdings by percent and the large landholdings by percent.

In Andhra Pradesh during 1976-2001 the number of marginal landholdings increased by 145.00 percent, the small landholdings increased by 101.00 percent and the semi-medium landholdings increased by 33.00 percent. On the other hand, the number of medium landholdings declined by 33.00 percent and the large landholdings by 68.00 percent. This indicates the redistribution of landholdings from medium and large landholders to small and marginal landholders.

During 1996-2001 the share of the number of operational land holdings to total land holdings belonging to Scheduled Castes decreased from 12.12 percent. More than 7.50 percent of the operated area of the total land holdings belonging to Scheduled Tribes in 1995-96 and it increased to 8.27 percent in 2001-02. The percentage number of land holdings belonging to other social groups to all land holdings in the state remained more or less the same around 80.75 indicating a marginal shift in the land holding owned by other social groups to Scheduled Castes and Scheduled Tribes. The shares of Scheduled Caste marginal, small and medium size landholders to the total Scheduled Caste land holders and the area controlled by them remained more or less the same.

Similarly, the structure of distribution of land holdings among different categories of Scheduled Tribes remained unchanged during 1995-2002 The percentage of small sized land holdings to total operational land holdings increased by 1.00 percent associated with an increase of 2.00 percent of the area under medium sized land holdings.

In Anantapur district the share of the number of operational land holdings to total land holdings belonging to Scheduled Castes is 7.00 percent as against 11.86 percent for Andhra Pradesh in 2001-02. A little more than 3.00 percent of the operated area of the total land holdings in the state belongs to Scheduled Tribes while it is 8.27 percent. The percentage number of land holdings belonging to other social groups to all land holdings in Anantapur district has been very high.

Marginal landholders owning one fifth of the total area owned by Scheduled Castes accounted for one half of the total number of Scheduled Caste landholders. Marginal landholders owning 13.1 percent of the total area owned by Scheduled Tribes accounted for 36.90 percent of the total number of Scheduled Tribes landholders. 80.00 percent of the marginal holding belong to other groups who control same percent of the area owned by the marginal land-holders. One eighth of the total area owned by other social groups is under large holdings maintained by one sixth of the other social groups land-holders.

One fifth of the total landholders in the district are female and the remaining are males. Similarly, a little more than one fifth of the total land- holders belonging to Scheduled Castes, Scheduled Tribes and other social groups are females. There are no females controlling large holdings among the Scheduled Castes and Scheduled Tribes in Anantapur district. Among the other social groups 12.00 percent of the owners of large holdings are females.

REFERENCES

1. Dharma Kumar, *Land and Caste in South India,* Manohar Publications, New-Delhi, 1992.
2. Radha Krishna, *Agricultural Growth, Employment and Poverty,* 43rd conference of Indian Society of Labour Economics, Bangalore, 2004.
3. Nancharaiah, *Agrarian Reforms and Agrarian Change,* Atlantic Publishers, New Delhi, 2000.
4. Directorate of Economics & Statistics, Govt. of A.P., Statistical Abstract of Andhra Pradesh, 2003, Hyderabad.

Table 4.1: Operational Holdings and Area Operated in Andhra Pradesh

Size group	*Marginal*	*Small*	*Semi-medium*	*Medium*	*Large*	*All Sizes*
1976-77						
No (lakhs)	28.69	12.52	10.72	7.53	2.09	61.55
	(46.6)	(20.3)	(17.4)	(12.2)	(3.4)	(100)
Area (lakh hec)	13.36	18.36	29.93	46.47	35.68	143.8
	(9.3)	(12.8)	(20.8)	(32.3)	(24.8)	(100)
1980-81						
No (lakhs)	38.04	15.91	11.74	6.46	1.55	73.7
	(51.6)	(21.6)	(16.0)	(8.8)	(2.10)	(100)
Area (lakh hec)	18.86	24.12	32.61	39.79	27.95	143.33
	(13.1)	(16.8)	(22.7)	(27.8)	(19.5)	(100)
1986-87						
No (lakhs)	44.6	17.14	12.54	6.57	1.46	82.34
	(54.1)	(20.8)	(15.2)	(7.98)	(1.77)	(100)

Area (lakh hac)	20.54 (14.5)	24.54 (17.3)	33.91 (23.9)	38.65 (27.2)	23.94 (16.9)	141.55 (100)
1990-91						
No (lakhs)	52.11 (56.1)	19.72 (21.2)	13.45 (14.5)	6.44 (6.93)	1.18 (1.27)	92.97 (100)
Area (lakh hac)	23.69 (16.4)	28.26 (19.5)	36.4 (25.2)	37.77 (26.1)	18.48 (12.8)	44.63 (100)
1995-96						
No (lakhs)	63.0 (59.4)	22.62 (21.3)	13.95 (13.1)	5.63 (5.3)	0.83 (0.8)	106.34 (100)
Area (lakh hac)	29.04 (20.2)	32.29 (22.5)	37.36 (26.0)	32.31 (22.5)	12.73 (8.85)	143.72 (100)
2000-2001						
No (lakhs)	70.23 (60.9)	25.18 (21.84)	14.24 (12.3)	5.01 (4.3)	0.66 (0.6)	115.32 (100)
(lakh hac)	31.04 (21.56)	35.65 (24.8)	37.95 (26.4)	28.54 (19.8)	10.80 (7.5)	143.99 (100)

Note: Figures in brackets indicate percentages to All groups

Source: Source: Directorate of Economics & Statistics, Govt. of A.P. Hyderabad, A Report on Census of Land holdings, 2004.

Table 4.2: Category-wise Operational Holdings and Area Operated in Andhra Pradesh 1995-96 to 2000-01

Category	*Marginal*		*Small*		*Medium*		*Large*		*All Sizes*	
	No. lakh	*Area lakh hec*	*No. lakh*	*Area lakh hec*	*No. lakh*	*Area lakh hec*	*No. lakh*	*Area lakh hec*	*No. lakh*	*Area lakh hec*
Scheduled Castes										
1995-96	9.44	3.96	2.27	3.17	1.12	3.33	0.01	0.18	12.85	10.6
	(73)	(37)	(18)	(30)	(9)	(31)	(0)	(2)		
2000-01	10.1	4.13	2.41	3.34	1.14	3.45	0.01	0.37	13.67	11.3
	(74)	(37)	(18)	(30)	(8)	(30)	(0)	(3)		
Scheduled Tribes										
1995-96	3.9	1.9	1.90	2.69	.70	5.73	0.03	0.46	7.54	10.86
	(52)	(17)	(25)	(25)	(23)	(52)	(0)	(4)		
2000-01	4.6	2.23	2.16	3.05	1.99	6.01	0.03	0.55	8.62	11.85
	(53)	(19)	(25)	(26)	(23)	(51)	(0)	(5)		
Other Groups										
1995-96	49.6	23.1	18.4	26.4	16.7	60.4	0.78	12.0	85.6	122.2
	(58)	(19)	(21)	(22)	(20)	(49)	(1)	(10)		
2000-01	55.5	24.6	20.6	29.2	16.2	56.9	0.60	9.86	93.0	120.7
	(60)	(20)	(22)	(24)	(17)	(47)	(1)	(8)		
All Social Groups										
1995-96	62.9	29.0	22.6	32.2	19.5	69.6	0.82	12.7	106.0	143.7
	(59)	(20)	(21)	(22)	(18)	(48)	(1)	(9)		
2000-01	70.2	31.0	25.1	35.6	19.3	66.45	0.66	10.9	115.3	143.9
	(61)	(22)	(22)	(25)	(17)	(46)	(1)	(8)		

Note: Figures in the brackets indicate percentage to All Groups.
Source: Directorate of Economics & Statistics, Govt. of A.P., Hyderabad, A Report on Census of Land holdings, 2004.

Table 4.3: Operational Holdings and Area Operated in Anantapur District 2000-2001

Category	*Marginal*		*Small*		*Medium*		*Large*		*All Sizes*	
	No. 000	*Area 000 hec*	*No. 000*	*Area 000 hec*	*No. 000*	*Area 000 hec*	*No. 000*	*Area 000 hec*	*No. 000*	*Area 000 hec*
Scheduled Castes										
Individual	31.8	17.3	20.1	29.3	13.1	35.2	0.1	1.9	65.2	83.8
Joint	0.2	0.0	0.0	0.1	0.0	0.1	0.0	0.0	0.4	0.6
Total	32.0	17.4	20.2	29.5	13.1	35.5	0.1	2.0	65.6	84.5
	(15)	(15)	(11)	(11)	(7)	(8)	(1)	(1)	(11)	(7)
Scheduled Tribes										
Individual	0.9	5.3	8.9	13.1	6.7	19.7	0.1	2.0	25.2	40.2
Joint	0.0	0.0	0.0	0.0	0.0	0.0	0.0	0.0	0.0	0.1
Total	9.3	5.3	8.9	18.8	6.8	19.8	0.1	2.0	25.3	40.4
	(5)	(5)	(5)	(7)	(3)	(4)	(1)	(1)	(4)	(3)
Other Groups										
Individual	162.9	90.3	155.7	29.0.	176.4	410.0	8.4	126.0	503.5	1058.0
Joint	1.7	0.7	0.7	1.0	0.7	2.9	0.1	3.6	3.4	8.4
Total	164.9	91.1	156.5	230.0	177.4	415.0	8.7	133.0	507.0	1073.0
	(80)	(80)	(84)	(84)	(90)	(88)	(98)	(98)	(85)	(90)
All Social Groups										
Individual	204.	112.0	184.	271	195.8	464.9	8.6	130.0	594.0	1182.0
Joint	2.0	0.8	0.8	1.1	0.8	3.4	0.1	3.8	3.8	9.2
Total	206.3	113.8	185.7	272.9	197.3	473.3	8.9	137.7	598.6	1197.9
	(100)	(100)	(100)	(100)	(100)	(100)	(100	(100)	(100)	(100)

Note: Figures in the brackets indicate percentage to their respective groups.

Source: Directorate of Economics & Statistics, Govt. of A.P., Hyderabad, A Report on Census of Land holdings, 2004.

Table 4.4: Operational Holdings and Area Operated in Anantapur District, 2000-2001

Category	Marginal		Small		Semi Medium		Medium		Large		All Sizes	
	No. 000	*Area hec 000*	*No. 000*	*Area hec 000*	*No. 000*	*Area hec 000*	*No. 000*	*Area hec 000*	*No. 000*	*Area hec 000*	*No. 000*	*Area hec 000*
Scheduled Castes												
Male	24.9	13.4	16.4	24.1	9.5	22.2	1.2	6.7	0.1	1.7	52.2	68.0
Femal	7.2	4.0	3.8	5.5	2.3	5.2	0.3	1.4	0.0	0.3	13.4	16.4
	(22.4)		(18.8)		(19.5)		(19.2)		(00)		(20.4)	
Total	32.1	17.4	20.2	29.6	11.8	27.4	1.56	8.1	0.1	2.0	65.7	84.4
Scheduled Tribes												
Male	7.2	4.1	7.1	10.5	4.7	11.5	0.8	4.8	0.1	1.6	20.0	32.4
Femal	2.1	1.2	1.2	2.7	1.1	2.7	0.2	0.9	0.0	0.5	5.3	8.0
	(22.6)		(14.5)		(19.0)		(20.0)		(00)		(20.9)	
Total	9.3	5.3	8.3	13.2	5.8	14.2	1.0	5.7	0.1	2.1	25.3	40.4
Other Groups												
Male	127.1	70.6	124.7	183.8	105.3	273.4	42.0	245.5	7.6	115.2	406.6	888.6
Female	37.6	20.5	31.7	46.3	23.2	58.6	6.7	38.6	1.0	14.5	100.3	178.5
	(22.8)		(20.3)		(18.0)		(13.6)		(12)		(20.3)	
Total	164.7	91.1	156.4	230.2	128.6	332.4	48.7	285.7	8.6	129.7	507.7	1077.1
All Social Groups												
Male	159.2	88.1	148.3	218.4	119.5	307.0	44.0	257.0	7.8	118.7	478.8	989.1
Female	47.0	25.7	37.3	54.4	26.6	66.5	7.2	40.9	1.1	15.3	119.1	202.9
	(22.8)		(20.1)		(18.2)		(14.1)		(12)		(19.9)	
Total	206.2	113.8	185.6	272.8	146.1	373.5	51.2	297.9	8.9	134.0	597.9	1191.0

Note: Figures in brackets indicate percentage to their respective totals

Source: Directorate of Economics & Statistics, Govt. of A.P., Hyderabad, A Report on Census of Land holdings, 2004.

5

Gender and Food Security at Household Level

Dr. G. Sridevi

Introduction

Macro level analysis of food security masks a large number of issues confronted at household level. Food security at household level indicates the availability as well as access to food over time, and across all the members of the household. At micro level the importance is not only to the national availability but also actual consumption across different social (economic) groups as well as distribution in the intra-household context. Within the household, intra-family consumption behaviour occupies significant space because allocation of food among the members of the household is suspected to be unequal, allegedly discriminating against the female member of the household. Nutrition and food consumption have been among the primary areas of inquiry into the extent of intra-household differences in resource allocation (Sen, 1984). Poor women are most likely to be undernourished than their male counterparts and this has serious implications for the nutrition status of their newborn and yet-to-be-born children. Undernutrition of adult females also constrains the ability of women to earn income, which tends to impair the nutrition status of their existing children. All these could not be analysed with the help of Secondary data as a large number of questions are intricate and are related to the intra household pattern.

Therefore, these issues have to be investigated at household level.

Hypothesis at Micro-level

At the household level, intra-family consumption behaviour occupies significant space because allocation of food among the members of the household is suspected to be unequal allegedly disfavoring the female members. The consequences of getting less Food are more serious in the households within sufficient food entitlements. It can be hypothesized that female-headed households have more food insecurity problem when compared to male-headed households. In such a situation any change in prices of foodgrains and number of days employed will effect the consumption at the household level. If the distribution system is not effective in improving the consumption of food then females in poor households are at the higher risk of food insecurity.

Food insecurity is not faced uniformly by the households belonging to different social groups despite negligible income differential. The uneven access is due to the flaws in the PDS as well as the proverbial acute social discrimination present in the village, despite the best efforts to wipe it out. Therefore, it is hypothesized that the members of a household belonging to deprived castes (Scheduled Caste and Scheduled Tribes) face steeper food insecurity as against the others both in terms of quality as well as quantum of food.

For the purpose of our analysis one village was selected purposively to examine the extent of intra-household food security, working of PDS, and changes in consumption pattern in the recent past. It is well-established fact that an intensive village study helps in identifying the economic and social status of households and problems that poorer classes face in gaining economic access to food (Harriss, 1990).

Keeping in view these points we selected village Kamepalli that comes under Kamepalli panchayat of Khammam District. The village is entirely agricultural with over 90 percent of workers reporting their occupation as cultivators or agricultural labourers. It satisfies all the requirements given above. We are certainly aware of the fact that this is a purposive selection and not a random selection. Our results therefore, should be viewed with this caveat in mind and not a menable to any sweeping generalizations. Our analysis however, throws open quite a few issues and seeks to arrive at some tentative indicators from this rich material.

Issues at Stake

Micro level changes in crop production system (from traditional crops to commercial crops) will have a telling impact on food consumption, through changes in number of mandays employed, wages and availability of food grains. Seasonal variations in the production will effect different sections of the people, the landless labourers, who make a hand-to-mouth existence, may be forced to consume less food during the slack season compared to peak season. Which in turn influence the intra-household distribution of food and non-food consumption, including clothing, housing, and health.

With the introduction of the TPDS a distinction between below poverty line (BPL) and above poverty line (APL) households has become clear, with the two groups treated differently in terms of the quantities of rice distributed and price at which the grain made available to them. Under the new system ration quantity (entitlement) was fixed irrespective of household size, which will lead to reduction in the quantity distributed through the fair price shop (larger families) ,and it will effect individual food consumption at the household level.

Food is the "first necessity," and people whose incomes do not permit them to buy enough food, would spend almost everything on food. Even admitting the existence of other necessities, such as clothing and shelter, it is still the case of poorest households in India who spend more than three-quarters of their budget on food. For such people, the demand for food is elastic with respect to per capita expenditure, so that it might be supposed that the elasticity of nutrient intake would also be high. Not getting enough food impairs productivity to the point where poverty and malnutrition becomes a trap (it is impossible to work because of malnourishment, and impossible to escape from

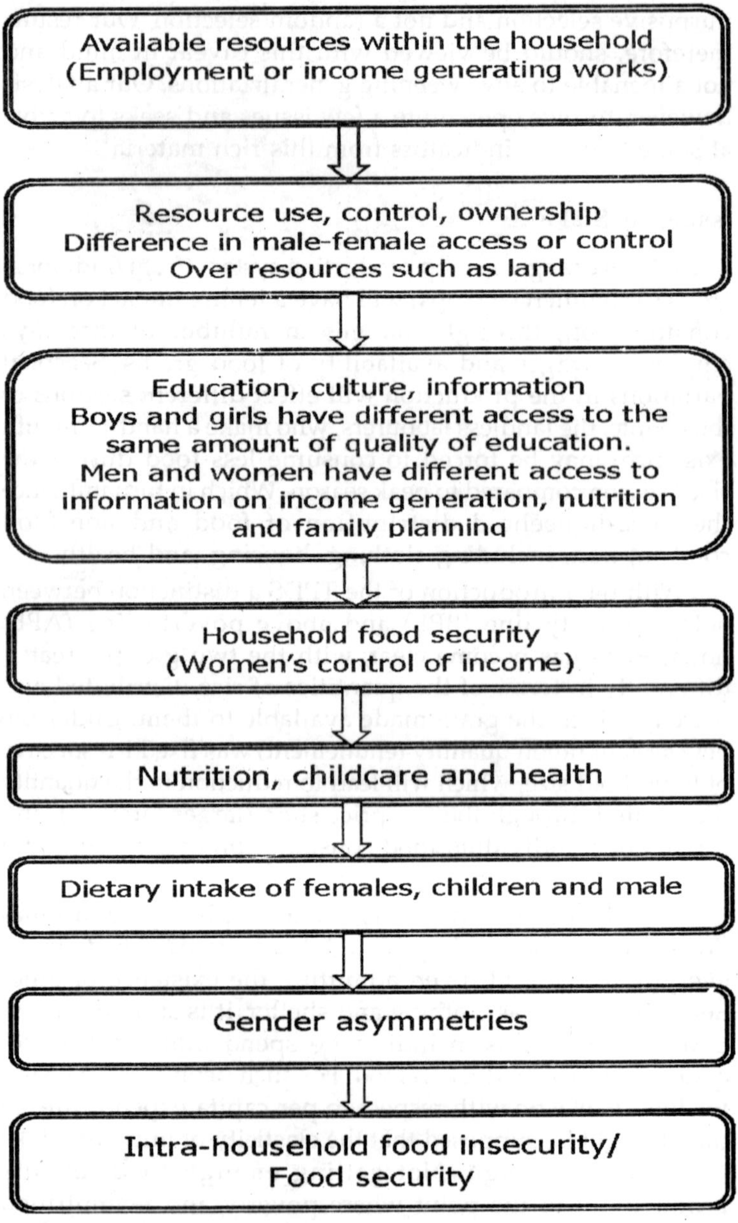

Figure 5.1: Intra-household food security: A conceptual framework

malnourishment without working). In such situations any change in income of the household will lead to unequal distribution of food and other resources in intra-household context. The allocation of the household resources favours males over the females (Dreze and Sen (1989), Harriss (1990), Dasgupta (1993), and Strauss and Thomas (1995).

We have adapted the conceptual framework from FAO/WHO (1992) as is given in figure 5.1 For analysis we have collected information on the cropping pattern, production of foodgrains, quantities purchased from PDS and market wages, seasonal variation in wages, price of food grains, expenditure on food, non-food, daily intake of food, consumption pattern and Anthropometric measures for the members of the household.

The conceptual framework begins with the basic factors underlying nutrition status. This framework is adapted from FAO/WHO (1992).

Characteristics of the Selected Village

Kamepalli village has five hamlets namely Ramakrishnapuram, Gopalapuram, Harichandrapuram, Peddalatchathanda and Kowlyathanda. Peddalatchathanda and Kowlyathanda (see map 5.2).

Total number of households in the village is 1030. We selected randomly 140 households for the purpose of intensive survey. The sample of 140 households was spread in proportion to the density of the each group. Out of 140 households 50 households were agricultural labourers, 70 from the households having less than 5 acres of land and the remaining 20 from the households having more than 5 acres of land and others. These 140 households are selected from heterogeneous communities (SC, ST, BC and upper caste (mostly Khammas). First all the households in the village were grouped by their size of land holding based on a complete census and, with in these groups they were again regrouped based on caste.

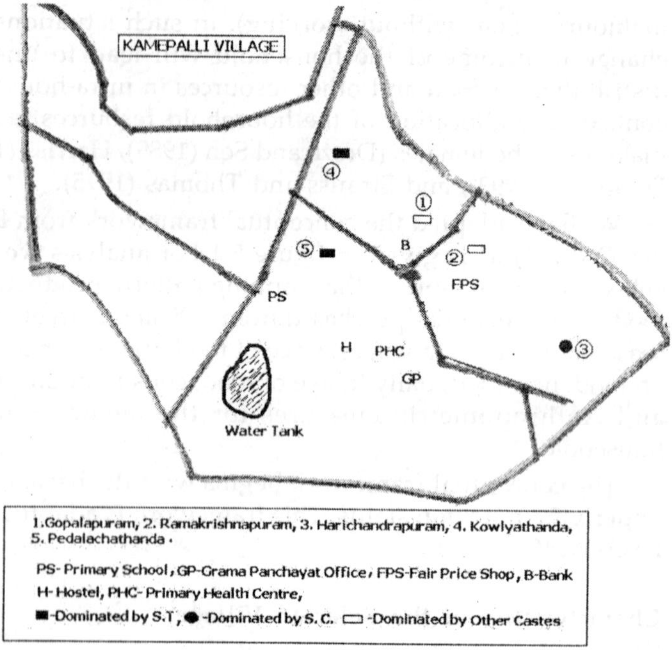

Figure 5.2 Map of the Village

Table 5.1: Some Characteristics of Population of Kamepalli Village, 2000

	Number of Households	*Persons*	*Male*	*Female*
Population	1030	4139	2057	2082
Literacy rate(%)	566	55	65	44
Scheduled Caste population	80	1191	601	510
Scheduled Tribe population	302	1605	817	788
Others	648	1343	639	784

Source: Author's own Field survey.

Then taking the proportion of households from each group and spreading the sample accordingly arrived at umber of households to be selected. The final selection of the sample was done randomly to avoid any election bias. Cultivation occurs on both dry land and land irrigated by ground water or by the tank irrigation. Irrigation facilities in the village are quite meagre but it has most of the amenities like primary health centre, high school and bank. For daily market they depend on a grocery/vegetable shop in the village. Thene are sttown to this village is Khammam, which is 100Kms from this village. A quarter of the households in the village are landless. Households with ownership of land are 712 households (69percent). Table 5.2 shows the distribution of land in the village.

Table 5.2: Distribution of Households by Size Class of Land Owned, Kamepalli Village, 2002

Extent of land owned (acres)	*Number of Households*	*S.C. House-holds*	*S.T. House-holds*	*Other House-holds*
Landless	318(30.8)	38 (3.6)	109(10.5)	171(16.6)
Up to 3	618(60)	42 (4.0)	186(18.0)	390(37.8)
3–5	54 (5.2)	0	7 (0.6)	47 (4.5)
5–10	36 (3.4)	0	0	36 (3.4)
10–20	4 (0.38)	0	0	4 (0.38)

Source: Field survey.

Note: Figures in the brackets indicate the percentage to total.

Households with ownership holding of less than five acres constituted 65.2 percent of all households, only .78 percent of households owned 5 or more acres and no household owned more than 20 acres of land. Basic crops cultivated are paddy, jowar, pulses, cotton and chilli. Till 1980's paddy, jowar and pulses were the most dominating crops but it is now chilli and cotton that dominate the cropping patterns. Out of the total cropped area of 2598 acres, 985 acres enjoy irrigation facility through wells. The farmers told that the returns to paddy crop was not so attractive where as chilli and cotton has more demand in the nearby markets. In addition to this, the water sources are also not sufficient for paddy cultivation. The change in the cropping system affected the agricultural labour households by reducing the employment and the number of working days. The fair price shop serves Kamepalli and hamlets under it. The card holders inspite of the distance do not forego their rice entitlement and purchase rice, whenever, it is distributed at the fair price shop, if they do not have income to buy, they will borrow at exorbitant interest rate from the village money lender keeping some asset as security. Under mid-day meals scheme rice has been distributed to the school-going children through fair price shop, during 2001, 10 Kgs of rice was being distributed to the parents of the school going children (although they got it only once in the year). Most of the ration stock gets exhausted in the ration shops on the day of its arrival in the village, which indicates the extent of scarcity in the village. The village is predominated by poor households, food security is the major concern of the households as there exists least employment opportunities within the village. PDS is supposed to provide food security to the poor through targeting. Given this background we will look into the household food security in terms of gender, caste, income and state interventions (PDS, support as well as schemes).

Support of PDS Towards Food Security

We will be looking into the PDS support through the utilization and income gain. Distribution system was existing in the village since 1980's, it was universal distribution system till 1997. In 1997 the government introduced the Targeted Public Distribution System (TPDS). Provision of basic food to the vulnerable population at reasonable prices is one of the prime objectives of TPDS. But after the increase in the PDS price the context of reasonable issue price for the rural poor households became crucial. In this context the functioning of TPDS at micro-level will have impact on the consumption and distribution of food within the household. Alternative measures are used for finding out the extent of PDS support to food security . The percentage of PDS rice purchases in total rice purchases is only about 22 percent. While the percentage of PDS rice purchases in total cereal consumption is 22.92 percent (Table 5.3). The extent of PDS support declines in general with landholding.

Table 5.3: Percentage of PDS Rice Purchases by Size Class of Holding

Class	*%of PDS rice purchases to total cereals consumption*
Landless labour	40.30
Smallfarmers	30.14
Medium farmers	23.62
Large farmers	15.38
Others	23.95
All classes	22.92

Source: Field survey.

The extent of PDS support declines with expenditure levels of the households (Table 5.4). For the lowest expenditure class the percentage of PDS purchases in total rice purchases in the village is 23.2 percent, which shows PDS support for the lowest expenditure class is low in this village.

Table 5.4: Percentage of PDS Rice Purchases in Total Cereals Consumption by MPCE Class

MPCE class (Rs.)	*% of PDS rice purchases*
< 175	23.20
175–225	22.27
225–275	12.01
275–350	8.14
Above350	1.10
All	22.92

Source: Field survey.

The extent of PDS support improved with the employment level in the village (Table 5.5), even though employment has no direct connection with PDS. However, it is quite expected as employment results in increased purchasing power.

Table 5.5: Percentage of PDS Rice Purchases in total Cereals Consumption by Employment Level

Sl. No.	*Employment category*	*% Of PDS rice purchases*
1.	No employment	8.45
2.	1–10 days employment	20.2
3.	11–20 days employment	28.12
4.	Above 20 days	41.27
5.	All	22.92

Source: Field survey.

Employment is derived in terms of average number of days of paid employment per worker during the reference month. The dependency on PDS by first employment category (unemployed) is low (8.45) due to lack of purchasing power. As among the various castes group's dependence on PDS is low among S.C. & S.T. groups when compared to others (S.C. 18 percent, S.T. 30 percent, others 52). That may be due to lack of white cards and income. PDS is supposed to provide food security to the poor through targeting, but after looking at the PDS support in the village we found most of the poor households are not having access to PDS, in order to look in to this issue we have calculated the targeting errors in the village.

Errors in Targeting

The target group for the PDS comprises households with an expenditure level below the official poverty line. But there are a few conceptual and practical drawbacks in using the official poverty line as an indicator of eligibility of a family for access to food grains through the PDS (Swaminathan, 2000). First, incomes are difficult to measure in an economy, where the majority of the workers do not earn regular monthly salaries. The majority of the workforce is in the unorganized sector, where earnings from casual labourer from self-employment fluctuate overtime. To estimate annual family incomes in such a situation is quite a difficult task. Secondiy a substantial proportion of households above the poverty line are likely to be vulnerable to income poverty and food insecurity.

White cards (BPL cards) were issued to every household having less than 1.5 acres of wet land under assured water resources or 2.5 acres of wet land under other irrigation sources or 3 acres of dry land under commercial crops and 5 acres of land under other crops. These were termed as BPL families. There appear to have been four criteria used locally for exclusion from the BPL category:1. Households having a family member employed in a regular job with assured monthly income. 2. Households having more than 3 acre of land.3. Households owning a pucca house.4. Households owning a television/refrigerator/fan/ motorcycle/scooter (under the guidelines of the State Government). Each of the four criteria were arbitrary criterion on the basis of which to exclude a family from the system of subsidized food scheme. For example the housing criterion, the precise demarcation between pucca and non- pucca is difficult to establish. There fore ,the segregation of groups into BPL and APL has its own construction errors.

The distribution of households by status of cards indicates that the percentage of card-less households in the village was quite high (41 percent), 32 percent are having white cards (BPL) and 27 percent are having pink cards (APL).

Table 5.6: Distribution of White Ration Cards Across Caste Groups in the Village

(Percent to total)

Caste group	*APL (Pink cards)*	*BPL (White cards)*	*NPC*
SC	22.2	29.3	48.5
ST	25.5	35.5	39
Others	26	59.9	14.1

Source: Field survey.

Note: APL–Above Poverty Line, BPL–Below Poverty Line, NPC–Not Possessing Card.

Cornia and Stewart (1993) examined two types of targeting

errors that occur in food and nutrition interventions. Type 1 error refers to the exclusion of genuinely poor or deserving households from a programme termed as errors of 'wrong exclusion'. These were termed 'F' mistakes by Cornia and Stewart (1993) on account of the failure to reach the target population. Type 2 error, refers to the 'inclusion of non-eligible persons or households' in the programme errors of wrong inclusion. These were termed as 'E' mistakes that represent' excessive undeserving coverage'. We categorize the total number of households in the relevant population as follows:

$$A = P^i + P^e + NP^i + NP^e$$

Where A refers to all households, P refers to poor households, NP refers to non-poor households and the subscripts I and e refer to households included and excluded by a targeted programme. With this classification, the error of exclusion can be gauged from the value of P^e, then umber of poor households excluded. Alternatively, P^e/A, the proportion of all households that are both poor and excluded, is used to measure the error of exclusion. In a similar way, the error of wrong inclusion is gauged from NPi, the number of non-poor families included in the programme, or NPi/A, that is, the proportion of all households wrongly included in the coverage of the targeted programme.

Table 5.7: Targeting Errors

	Kamepalli village
Type F error	58.85
Type E error	57.08

Note: F-exclusion of genuinely poor E-inclusion of non-eligible persons.

Type F and E errors are large in the village. Nearly 59 (58.85) percent of the poor households are excluded from the PDS safety nets, and 57.08 percent of the white card holders belong to the non-poor class. A micro level study by Indrakant (1996) in five villages also revealed similar findings that most of the people had access to food from PDS scheme in the developed villages, but a large percentage of beneficiaries were non-poor. He also stated that in the backward villages, a large percentage of poor are excluded while a sizeable percentage of the non-poor were included (Indrakant, 1996).

With high exclusion errors it comes out clearly that PDS is not benefiting all the poor households, the basic purpose of the TPDS is to transfer income to the poor by supplying essential commodities at subsidized price but this seem to by pass a large section due to social engineering process. In efficient targeting will have impact on income gain through the PDS at household level and which intern influences the consumption at individual level. This however, needs to be checked from the sample data. In order to look into the magnitude of the income transfer in rice distribution by the PDS we have calculated the income transfers to the household.

Expected income transfer means the income transfer calculated considering the entitlement of rice to the ration card holders where as, actual income transfer is calculated considering the actual purchases of the household from the ration shop under TPDS.

$$EPY\ e^{TPDS} = \frac{\sum_{i=1}^{n} Qi\ e^{TPDS}(P^M\ P^R)}{TP\ BPL}$$

Where, $EPY\ e^{TPDS}$ expected per capita income transfer through Targeted Public

Distribution Scheme based on entitlement of Rice.

$Qi\ e^{TPDS}$ Quantity of rice entitled through targeted public distribution system

P^M – Price per kilogram of Rice in open market.

P^R – price per kilogram of Rice in TPDS ration shop.

TP_{BPL} – Total population below poverty line.

Based on the above formula we calculated the expected per capita income transfer per month. Only rice is supplied through PDS for BPL and therefore, our analysis pertain to rice only. We found the expected per capita income transfer per person per month is about Rs. 3.40, which will be realized only if the household chooses to take all the entitled of rice. But if there is any differences between the entitlement and the off take of rice, then the actual income transfer will be different from the expected per capita income transfer and it will be lower than the meagre Rs. 3.40 as computed above.

The income gain of villagers from the rice scheme depends upon the coverage of the PDS, quantities supplied through the PDS and the difference between the open market price and the ration price. In order to compute aggregate income gain we utilized the following equation.

$$IG = (P_m - P_f)\, Q_f$$

Where IG is income gain, Pm and Pf are open market and fair price of the commodity and Qf is the quantity purchased in fair price shop. Monthly per capita income gain, which is calculated using the difference between open market price and ration shop price is Rs. 3.50 per person per month. About 23 percent of the white card holders complained about the quality of the commodities supplied. In the village more than 50 percent of the households spend around one to two hours to fetch their PDS allocations. The quantity of rice supplied to poor households (5 Kg of rice per person per month subject to a ceiling of 20Kg. (At Rs. 5.50 per Kg) this is inadequate compared to their consumption requirements.

The PDS support was high during 1980's and early 1990's as there exists a universal PDS system and the price at which rice was distributed was lower than the market price. Most of the poor households depended on PDS for their rice consumption. With the introduction of TPDS it was expected that the targeted group will be served better but we noted that about 50 percent of the poor were actually excluded, and the income gain through PDS has not improved over the years due to increase in the issue price.

It must however, be noted that PDS only helps to substantiate the total consumption and large part of the food grains consumed by the household's depends on open market purchases in order to get the required quantity for consumption. Therefore, any change in the open market price and distribution system also effects the individual consumption at household level In addition to the total consumption the nutrition in take (in terms of calories) helps to understand another angle of food security.

Access to Food and Consumption at Household Level

Although households are often the primary income recipients and are always the units for which we observe consumption, there exists in difference in the allocation to individual members in the household. To examine the question whether and to what extent allocation within the household differ according to the gender and social groups, we looked into the access to food at household level. Two types of measures have been used to quantify the food distribution with in a household:

1. Food intake by individuals converted into nutrients.
2. Heights and weights measures for Anthropometric indices. Much of the literature on gender bias in households in developing countries has been on expenditure data (Dasgupta (1993), Thomas (1995)) and, to a lesser extent, on anthropometric data.

The consumption of rice and other cereals by the households during the reference period (30 days preceding the date of the survey) is considered for the analysis. All the households consume rice, edible oil in all the seasons. Both quality and quantity of rice consumed differed across levels of living of the households. The average monthly per capita expenditure of the sample household is Rs. 200/- that is lower than the official poverty line (expenditure norm) of Rs. 262.94 (1999-00) for rural Andhra Pradesh. More than half of the household budget of the selected household is devoted to food items. The expenditure on cereals varies in the range of 28 to 32 percent of the total per capita expenditure. The share of expenditure on rice varies from 17 percent to 32 percent, it varies across the social groups which shows inter class differences in the expenditure levels. The consumption of cereals in the village varies in the range of 12 to 18 kg per person per month. Cereals intake varied among the caste groups with upper caste groups having higher per capita consumption during both the seasons. Monthly per capita consumption of rice varies in the range of 10 to 12 kgs. Besides this, jowar consumption is quite substantial in the village.

Dietary patterns among the sample varied over seasons and even day-to-day basis. It is erroneous to assume that the food intake will be same across seasons and the type of work (Sukhatme, 1980). We collected across season's data, as the intake, work loads activity levels, and maintenance requirements are known to vary seasonally.

Table 5.8: Average Cereals Intake in the Village by Caste Group

(In grams per person per day)

Caste group	*Slack*	*Peak*
SCs	1695	1790(5.6)*
STs	1605	1605(0.0)*
Others	1785	1975(10.64)*

Source: Field survey. Note: Slack season is from March to August, peak season is from September to February Percent Change Over Slack Season.

From the Table 5.8 we find a clear seasonal variation in the consumption cereals among SCs and other caste groups whereas in case of STs consumption remains to be same during all the seasons.

In order to obtain a clear picture of seasonal variations across different classes we have taken consumption of cereals across different land holding groups for the analysis. Cereals consumption was highest among the non-poor households during both the seasons and lowest across the poor households. The poor households not possessing white cards are the worst affected during the slack seasons. By the land ownership holding, consumption of cereals is lowest among the landless class and highest among the households having more than 10 acres of land (Table 5.9). This clearly shows that any change in income across the board will not change the relative consumption of food by the poor households.

Table 5.9: Per Capita Monthly Consumption of Cereals by Different Types of Landholding Households in Peak and Slack Season

(Kgs)

Land size (acres)	*Peak season*			*Slack season*		
	APL	*BPL*	*NPC*	*APL*	*BPL*	*NPC*
Landless	15.8	15.0	15.4	11.1	11.8	13.3
Up to 1	16.1	15.1	15.9	16.1	13.4	15.7
1 to 2.5	18.1	15.6	16.3	16.2	14.6	11.8
2.5 to 5	20.3	18.6	19.5	16.0	15.8	15.1
5 to 10	20.8	19.3	NA	20.3	17.2	NA
> 10	21.5	NA	NA	20.7	NA	NA
Total	19.2	16.7	15.8	17.8	14.1	12.7

Source: Field survey.

Note: APL– Above Poverty Line, BPL– Below Poverty Line, NPC– Not Possessing Card, NA– Not Applicable

Frequency of meals per day is taken as an indicator of food insecurity at household level. Table 5.10 shows the food availability status for each social group. Only 25 percent of SC and 35 percent of ST groups are getting enough food throughout the year. But 21 percent of the females face chronic food insecurity, as they do not consume required quantity of food on most of the days in the year (Table 5.10).

Table 5.10: Percent of Households Getting Enough Food Everyday

(Percent)

Social group	*Throughout*	*Only some the year the year*	*Infrequently months of*
Total	60	25	15
SCs	25	55	20
STs	35	50	15
Female (total)	41	38	21
Male (total)	60	33	7

Source: Field survey.

The landless women cooked only once a day in the evenings. It was identified among these households that, whatever was left the previous night, was eaten in the morning by those who remained at home without work. Commonly the respondents from poor group said that "when we have wheat, when we don't have we don't eat", a very simple adjustment process indeed.

The calorie intake for a sample household was derived by converting the quantities of food items consumed by the individuals into equivalent amounts of calories by using standard conversion factors (NSSO, 26th Round). We have used the 2,200 calories per consumer unit per day, as a standard against which actual observed calorie intakes are compared. Most of the poverty studies in India are based on nutritional adequacy, but what is an average 'nutritional adequacy' really means has been a debatable issue. Sukhatme (1980) argued that there is a range of dietary intake that may be considered adequate among adults depending on activity levels, climate, etc.

Per capita consumption in female-headed households is generally lower than the male-headed households. Among the ten female-headed households belong to two caste groups (S.C. and B.C.). Income spent on food by these households is lower compared to the others.

Table 5.11: Average Income Spent on Food by Female-Headed Household

(Percent total of the group)

Social groups	*Slack season*	*Peak season*	*Peak percent increase*
SC	22.00	30.0	36.36
BC	25.48	32.52	27.62
All	23.54	30.32	28.08

Source: Field survey.

Low levels of per capita spending on food among the female-headed households suggest a low-level of income. It substantiates our hypothesis that female-headed households have more food insecurity problem compared to male-headed households. From the Table 5.11 it can be seen that the peck percent increase is more than 25 percent in both the caste groups but highest increase is seen in SC household.

Control of food distribution in the household determines the food intake across members. Generally, female members of household do not have control on food budget and therefore, they come at the end of the queue to receive low calorie diets. Here by control we mean decisions about food budget in food distribution. Control can be exercised over material stocks, and over their preparation of food within the household from the raw material stage to that of ready for consumption product. In the selected village, the male heads of household enjoyed sole control of market decisions relating to domestic food in nearly 88 percent of the cases, and jointly with the wife in another 12 percent. There was no significant association between female participation in labour market, their earnings, and the control over food expenditure and purchase decisions. At the same time there was an association between the gender of food controller and their social group. Women were responsible in some of the households for the choice of ingredients, but with respect to quantities of food prepared there is no discernible pattern about heir control (Field survey).

When we looked into the order in which the family avails food consumption, male member or head of the household is given the first priority and the order of food intake differs across the social groups. In all the groups adult male is given the first priority (85 percent), women eat last, by choice, so that male members of the households get sufficient food, but nearly 60 percent of the female members among all the social groups eat the left over food. The position of children is not so determined. Within the households, female members generally go hungry when the available quantity of food is inadequate. This adequately underscores the fact that food insecurity is sharper in the context of gender.

Distribution of Food

To know the differences in consumption among the family members, food consumption of each member food must be compared with the others in the same household. Analysis of the adequacy of food across individuals requires information about their requirements matched with their actual consumption. Requirement is arguably the most controversial concept in human nutrition, but broadly the required consumption is decided by three components viz., physical growth, kind of activity, and maintenance. For the purpose of analysis we considered the norms set by ICMR, for male, female and children nutrition requirements. Head of the household (male) consumption is taken as proxy for the comparison of female and children consumption.

Average nutrient intakes with in the household for individuals in specific age and sex groups has been expressed as a percent of average (actual) nutrient in take of the adult male group. This was termed as Relative Index (RI). There are quite a few sources of bias here are. The variations due to occupation, income, age, and activity introduce first group of bias. Whereas, second group involves the accuracy in measurement. Given these biases and after computing the Relative indices, each RI is then expressed as a proportion of the corresponding Recommended Relative Intake (RRI). Here the RRI is defined as the proportion of the recommended intake for the group under consideration to the recommended intake for adult males 1. Recommended relative intakes are derived from the recommendations for moderate activity levels of the Indian Council of Medical Research. The Index of Relative Intake (IRI) is the ratio of actual Relative Intake (RI) to Recommended Relative Intake (RRI). The index of relative intake indicates the relative deprivation of specific groups compared to adult males in that group. Deprivation is seen in terms of the deficit of intake in relation to the need. Thus, an IRI of 1.0 indicates that the relevant group has the same share as that recommended by ICMR. An IRI greater than unity indicates a favorable consumption of food, and less than unity shows relative deprivation. Deviations of IRI from unity, observed among the households range from 0.2 to 1.

$$RI = \frac{\text{Actual nutrient intake of an individual}}{\text{Actual nutrient intake of the male group}} \times 100$$

$$RRI = \frac{\text{Recommended intake for the group}}{\text{Recommended intake for the males}} \times 100$$

$$IRI = RI/RRI$$

We found the deprivation is higher among the agricultural labour households. From the graphs it is evident that the relative deprivations are different across the social groups as well as landholding groups. Scheduled Castes and Scheduled tribes have lower values when compared with other groups, where as the deprivation is higher among landless and negligible among landed rich.

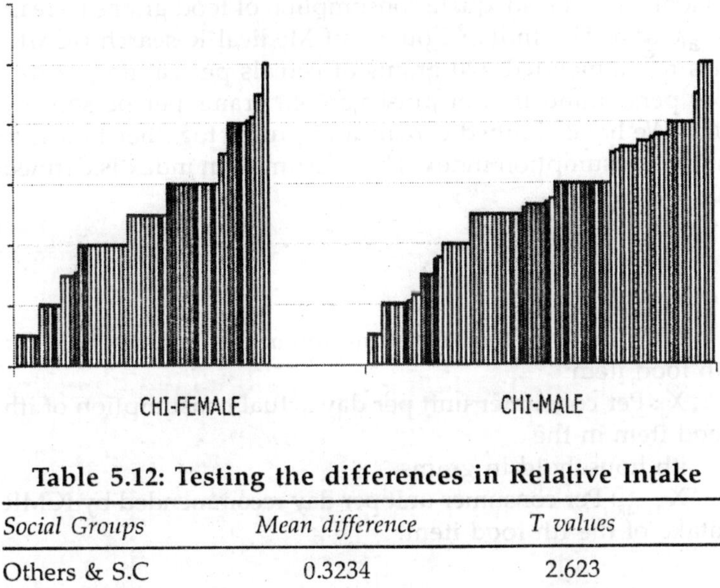

Table 5.12: Testing the differences in Relative Intake

Social Groups	*Mean difference*	*T values*
Others & S.C	0.3234	2.623
Others & S.T	0.00818	0.938
Child-male and Child-female	0.0487	3.597

Source: Field survey.

Note: All the 't' values are statistically significant at 1% level.

We hypothesise that there exists an unequal distribution of food among the individuals within the household and such differences vary across social groups. In order to test this hypothesis we employed Test of difference of means between groups and between individuals with in a household. The results are presented in Table 5.12. The result shows that there exists a difference in the level of deprivation (in terms of consumption of food) among the various groups. Whether of high or low caste, females measure the available food against a set of qualitative and quantitative domestic criteria and match what is available against routine as well as special needs. As they do all this, they also try to balance need against desire and shortages against some form of satisfaction. Obviously, such a balancing feat is most tenuous in poor families.

Consumption index is estimated among the households to look in to the adequate consumption of food grains (cereals & pulses). The Indian Council of Medical Research (ICMR) has recommended 420 grams of cereals per capita per day per person and that of pulses are 40 grams per person per day. We have clubbed cereals and pulses together to arrive at the consumption index. The consumption index is defined as:

$$IFC_{ij} = (X_{ij} / X_{iICMR})$$

Where:

IFC_{ij}: Index of food consumption in the jth household for ith food item

X_{ij}: Per consumer unit per day actual consumption of ith food item in the

jth household in grams

X_{iICMR}: Per consumer unit per day recommended by ICMR intake of the ith food item.

By using this index we found that nearly 55 percent of the households come in the range of 0.1 to 0.53. Which indicates that the consumption of required quantities of food is low among most of the households. This in turn influences the nutritional intake of the individuals.

In addition to these various measures have been used to arrive at the nutritional status of the members of the household such as weight for height and height for age. We have used Body mass Index for the measurement of nutritional status of the individuals.

Anthropometric Indices

Another way of looking at the intra-household differences in consumption of food and across social groups is to analyse food security with the help of Anthropometric measures. Nutritional status of individuals is assessed by means of the body mass Index (BMI). It is computed by using the weight and height of the individual (BMI = weight/height^2). ABMI value less than 16 is an indication of severe malnutrition and a BMI less than 18.5 and more than 16 reflects moderate malnutrition. Table 5.13 shows the incidence of malnutrition among adults and children.

Table 5.13: Incidence of malnutrition among adults and children

Sex	*Proportion of malnourished persons (percent)*	
	Severe	*Severe + moderate*
Male Adult Children (1-15)	24 22	45 69
Female Adult Children (1-15)	36.5 23	57.571.2

Source: Field survey.

Adult female as well as female child are more malnourished compared to men. One explanation for why men are given priority in food consumption compared to female is being a sole earner of the income, to be demanded in the labour market he should be more strong.

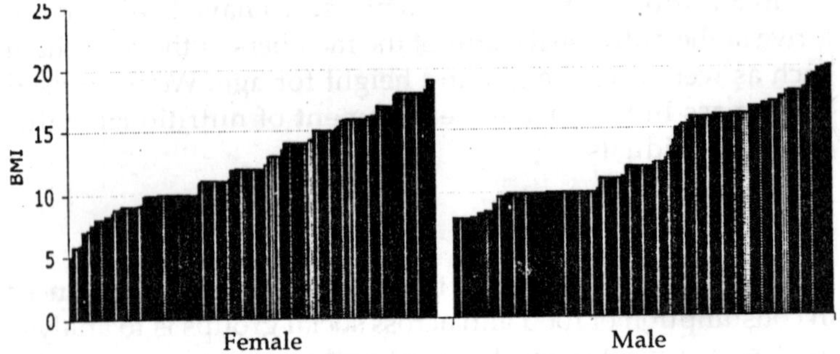

Figure 5.9: Body Mass Index of Adults

We made an attempt to explain variations in the levels of BMI by considering the factors such as total income, size of household, no of days employed and landholding. The estimated equation was

Y = a1 + b1 X1 + b2 X2 + b3 X3 + b4 X4 + e

Where,

Y = BMI

X1=House holdsize

X2=No.of days employed

X3 = Income

X4 = Landholding

E = Stochastic error term

Table 5.14: Regression Results Explaining Variations in BMI

	Dependent Variable-BMI					
Independent variables	*Coefficient*		*t Statistics*		*Significant*	
	Female	*Male*	*Female*	*Male*	*Female*	*Male*
Households size	-.043	-.126	.525	-1.560	.600	.121
No. of days employed	-.091	-.056	-1.065	-.666	.289	.506
Income	.109	.018	2.063	.225	.041	.823
Landholding	.175	-.157	2.63	-.682	.041	.497

Note: R Square = 0.44 for female, and for male, R Square = 0.52

Source: Field survey.

The explanation of variations in the Body Mass Index present interesting results. In the case of females income and size of landholdings have a positive relationship with the dependent variable and that indicates BMI increasing with the higher income an usually expected result. Similar, relation with the size of holding is also visible among females as a group. It is quite unexpected that these variables have emerged with non-significant coefficients in the group of males. There are probably two reasons for such behaviour. First, the variations in BMI for males are not very high for males and most of the males fall in 12-19 range. Second, it is not very easy to find an under nourished adult male as against females. This is quite common among females.

There will be impact of other factors other than food, energy intake on nutritional status. Sukhatme (1980) opined that the conversion efficiency of food in to energy depends on the access to safe drinking water, health care and environmental hygiene.

Food Security as seen Through Non-food Expenditure

The measurement of poverty on nutrition is questioned on the grounds that quantitative formulation of the minimum calorie intake below which there is under nutrition (food insecurity), irrespective of the individual items that contribute to the calories and even more importantly, whether adequacy of nutrition alone can define the status of the poor. Rao (1977) argues that poverty has to be identified with deficiency in the total level of living standard, which means not only energy requirements but also balanced diet needed for health, and the other basic needs essential for human existence at a tolerable level. In the changing context of food security, it is argued that not only access to food but also safe drinking water and health services improve the food security of the poor. In other words the non-food expenditure arguably indicates a proxy for food security. Higher the share of non-food expenditure better is the food security. Food security and non-food expenditure are thus strongly interrelated, though proximate. It is clear that the share of non-food expenditure increases with the increase in food security level of the household.

In this context we will be looking in to the non-food expenditure in the village. Non-food consumption includes clothing, health and other durable consumption expenditure. While empirical evidence tends to suggest a positive association between the calorie intake and nutritional status, the responsiveness is likely to be affected by the factors relating to health and environment. Here is a close link between poverty deprivation and ill health. In the field most of the households responded that they would go for *nattu vaidiyam* instead of going to a doctor, which is more expensive. There is a close linkage between food security, deprivation and ill-health. The linkage between food security and ill-health is directly related. Among the caste groups, ST households spend less on health services compared to others (Rs. 15 per month, S.C. Rs. 20 per month, and Others Rs. 45 per month).

In households where the physical labour of members is the basis of income, work days lost or productivity lowered by illness often constituted the starting point of the food insecurity/poverty. The nature of agricultural work exposed the females to a particular health hazards such as intestinal infections, arthritis, respiratory ailments. When we asked whether health problems interfered with their normal agricultural work, during last month, only 30 percent of the women told that they had been sick and not able to get more wages, which effected their food consumption in the house. There were cultural and gender differences in the subjective perception of illness.

Access to safe drinking water is another important aspect of healthy living. Health also depends on the water in this region as ground water consist of fluorides, for drinking purpose they have to depend on municipal water pipes (Table 5.14).

Tube well installations have compounded the problem of safe drinking water. During summer they will get drinking water twice a week. To fetch the water women have to spend two to three hours and that means a wage loss.

Table 5.14: Households Water Sources for Different Uses

Usage	*Municipal water pipes*	*Pond*	*Well*	*Tank*	*Bore well*
Drinking water	82	0	10	0	8
Bathing	0	20	70	0	10
Utensils	0	0	80	0	20

Source: Field survey.

Wages and Food Security

Men and women play a roughly equal role in the labour inputs to agricultural production, but women are paid less for their work, their daily wage rates are 12-60 percent lower than that men's daily wages. To look in to the impact of their wages on their consumption of food, were grossed real wages on poverty because we generally define the income poverty line to a nutritional norm. Assessing the extent of poverty in the village requires the identification and aggregation, we identified the households based on a cut-off level of income (poverty line based on official estimates), which will facilitate a classification of the population in to its poor and noon poor households. We have used the head count ratio of poverty, which simply measures the proportion of the population in income-deprivation. We found that female wages are not having a major impact on poverty decade back.

Table 5.15: Regression Results—Dependent Variable—Poverty

Statistics	*Real wages of female agricultural labour*		*Real wages of male agricultural labour*	
	1993	*2003*	*1993*	*2003*
Coefficient	-.415**	-4.42*	-448*	-475*
t- value	-1.639	-1.781	-1.807	-1.947
R2	.171	.196	.201	.226

Source: Field survey.

Note: -*Significant at 10 percent level, ** not significant even at 10 percent level.

Increase in wages will improve the purchasing power of the household, hence women in the poor household are compelled to work at low wage, and they do not have bargaining power whereas female workers from food secured households controlled some bargaining power. We looked into the percent contribution to consumption growth by employment and size of household for poor by using decomposition formula. We find more than 83 percent of the increases in per capita consumption of the poor are explained by the employment, rest of the 17 percent is explained by the reduction in the household size. This emphasizes that a positive employment and wage growth will increase the economic access to food.

Economists define poverty on the basis of food consumption and income, which in itself is a mechanical approach as indicated by many social scientists (Rao, 1977), (Sukhatme, 1977). It is argued that poverty goes not only by income but the social deprivation as well as restricted access to income sources. Any type of social deprivation and denial of such access to sources of income makes a person 'feel poor'. And such feeling of being 'poor' is beyond food insecurity/ economic deprivation and do not feature in usual computation. Therefore, we hypothesise that such feeling of deprivation originates from food insecurity but transcends to the other components of livelihood such as shelter, clothing, health and education.

Coping Strategies

The important, food-based coping strategies mentioned by respondents are broadly grouped into two: (i) Intra household adjustments, and (ii) Dependence on the society (which will move the households to ward exploiters).

Intra-household Adjustments

(i) *Eating foods that are less preferred:* Although respondents in all income groups reported long- term trends towards eating foods that were less preferred as a means of adapting to lower real incomes, in a squeeze, there

is all most always an even less preferred and less expensive food to eat.

(ii) *Limiting the quantity of food served to an individual:* Limiting the quantity of food served to an individual was practiced in most of the house holds in the survey, mostly female members of the household reduced their intake (in some cases it was forced). Redistribution of available food favours some household members to the detriment of others.

(iii) *Skipping meals:* eating only one or two meals per day was commonly practiced, Particularly by lower -income groups.

(iv) *Maternal buffering:* Maternal buffering is the practice of a mother deliberately limiting her own intake in order to ensure that children get enough to eat.

(v) *Skipping eating for a complete day:* A severe means of dealing with food insecurity is going whole day without eating anything, it is practiced mainly by the lowest income group and mostly during the slack season.

The changing cropping pattern number of days of available employment has declined over the years for agricultural labour (during early 1990' s it used to be nearly 9 months of employment but now 6-7 months) which intern impacted the purchasing power at the household level. Men and women play roughly an equal role in the labour inputs to agricultural production, but women are paid less for it, as their daily wage rates are lower by 12-60 percent of men's daily wages.

Given the existing patterns of consumption, ensuring adequate food security for the poor is possible by raising their purchasing power. Within the households, female members generally go hungry when available food quantity is low. First priority is given to the adult male and male children of the family. About 60 percent of female households said they do not get sufficient food when they eat. Distribution of food grains plays an important role in providing the food security at household level. Poor households with no ration card are at the higher risk of food insecurity compared to Households with white cards. With the targeting of PDS exclusion errors increased which had a negative effect on consumption at household level. From the analysis it clearly comes out that although there is an improvement in the income levels of the households during 2002, while malnourishment and hunger increased over this period. Based on official poverty line nearly 50 percent of the households are below poverty line but based on BMI 71.2 percent of the female children and 57.5 percent of adult female are under nourished. Our analysis clearly shows that food security did not deteriorated exclusively on the account of non- availability of food but more so due to distributional bottlenecks and administrative lapses resulting into the poor remaining out of the safety nets. The targeting errors are clear indicator of this fact. An adequate quantity of grain needs to be distributed to make a sizeable contribution to household food security. Major improvements are needed in the administration of PDS to ensure a non-corrupt and efficient delivery system. Decentralisation can improve the working of the delivery system.

REFERENCES

Ahmad, A., and J. Morduch, 1993. "Identifying sex bias in the allocation of household resources: Evidence from linked household surveys from Bangladesh". Harvard Institute of Economic Research, Working Paper 1636, Cambridge, Mass., U.S.A.: Harvard University.

Behrman, J. 1988a. "Nutrition, health birth order, and seasonality: Intrahousehold allocation among children in rural India", *Journal of Development Economics,* 28 (1):43-62.

Buvinic, M., and G. Gupta. 1992. Targeting woman-headed households and woman-maintainedfamilies in developing countries: Views on a policy dilemma. International Center for Research on Women, Washington, D.C. Mimeo.

Christian, P., R. Abbi, S. Gujral, and T. Gopaldas. 1989. Socioeconomic determinants of childnutritional status in rural and tribal India. *Ecology of Food and Nutrition* 23(1): 31-38.

Cornia, G., and F. Stewart. 1992. Two errors of targeting. Paper presented at the World BankConference on Public Expenditures and the Poor: Incidence and Targeting, June 17-19, Washington, D.C.

Das Gupta, M. 1987. "Selective discrimination against female children in rural Punjab, India", *Population and Development Review* 13(1): 77-100.

Fauveau,V., A. Briend, J. Chakraborty, and A.M. Sardar, 1990. "The contribution of severe malnutrition to child mortality in rural Bangladesh: Implications for targeting nutritional interventions". *Food and Nutrition Bulletin* 12(3): 215-219.

Haddad, L., and R. Kanbur, 1990. How serious is the neglect of intrahousehold inequality? *Economic Journal* 100 (402): 866-881.

Harbert, L., and P.L. Scandizzo, 1982. Food distribution and nutrition intervention. The case of Chile. World Bank Staff Working Paper 512. Washington, D.C.: World Bank.

Miller, B. 1981. *The Endangered Sex: Neglect of Female Children in Rural North India*, Ithaca, N.Y., U.S.A.: Cornell University Press.

Miller, B.D. 1992. Gender discrimination in intrahousehold food allocation in South Asia: Debates and dilemmas. Paper presented at 1992 Meetings of American Anthropological Association, San Francisco, November 2-6. George Washington University, Washington, D.C.

Pettigrew, J. 1986. "Child neglect in rural Punjabi families", *Journal of Comparative Family Studies* 17(1): 63-85.

Warrier, S. 1992. Patriarchy and daughter disfavor in West Bengal, India. Ph.D. dissertation draft. Syracuse University, Syracuse, N.Y., U.S.A.

6

Depletion and Inequity in Accessibility of Groundwater in Uttar Pradesh

Dr. Sanatan Nayak

I. Introduction

Water is one of the ill-managed resources in India, which is resulting in severe scarcity both for drinking and irrigation as well as environmental problems such as waterlogging, salinity in endowed regions and desertification in fragile regions. Groundwater is considered an important segment of water resources, which covers most of the rainfed regions (covering two third of the total area) of India is more or less neglected. In the absence of any effective policy measures, groundwater regions are plagued with water scarcity, inequitable distribution and environmental degradation. Groundwater is coming under the category of common pool resources (CPRs) and are public goods, which do not represent pure form of open access, communal or state property, as they are mixture of these three idealized types (Singh, 1994). The groundwater basin is a common pool resources in the sense that exclusion of multiple users (pumpers) difficult and costly. Groundwater table go down, as water is extracted beyond optimum yield level and may even lead to drying up of the aquifer in fragile environments. The capital intensity of groundwater extraction makes it easier to exclude rival users especially in fragile resource regions, making the resource privy to a few well-to-do households. This gives rise to free riding externalities, which differ in nature and intensity depending upon biophysical and climatic conditions. These externalities may not be a serious problem in the absence of depletion or unlimited availability of groundwater; however fragile resource regions need external interventions for internalizing these externalities.

In view of above background, the study would like to focus on the following issues in the state. Firstly, to assess the trend of groundwater irrigation across regions in the state. Secondly, the extent of groundwater depletion and the factors held responsible for its consequence across the regions in the state. Thirdly, to estimate the level of inequity in accessing various types of groundwater and minor surface irrigation sources in the state.

II. Trend of Irrigation in the State

It is observed that the share of canal irrigation (both major and medium irrigation) and surface minor irrigation has declined on the one hand and the share of ground water irrigation (private and public) has increased dramatically on the other hand. In a broad sense, the share of public irrigation has declined on the one hand and the share of private irrigation has increased on the other hand. The area under canal irrigation has increased slowly during 70's, remained constant during 80's and slow decline during 90's and early years of the present decade. However, the overall trend looks constancy or decline of the trend during 1970-71 to 2001-02. This has been attributed that high per hectare cost of construction, non-judicious distribution of funds for maintenance of existing canals, decline of real investment, spreading of environmental problems, lack of adequate and timely available of water, inequity in the distribution of water, thin spreading effect, low pricing of water, lack of proper irrigation management causes increase in inefficiency of irrigation sector (Gulati, et al, 2005; Rao, 2005; Raju, 2005; Nayak, 2006).

As a result of the demand for large number of private tubewell and state tubewell, the irrigated area under tubewell has increased from 19.65 lakh hectares (28.70 percent of the net irrigated area) in 1970-71 to 89.42 lakhs hectares (72 percent of the net irrigated area) in the state during 2001-02 (Table 6.1). This is reflected that the CAGR of private pump sets in eighties is 9.20 percent and it has declined to 5.50 percent in nineties and again declined to 4.12 percent in first four years of the present decade. It is reflected that tubewell irrigation is the dominant form of irrigation among all types of irrigation as it has its own advantages. The most important factor contributing the rapid growth of groundwater irrigation is that it is predominantly owned and managed by farmers and water is used timely and adequately (Shah, 1993). The development and availability of electricity at subsidised rate as well as the availability of credit at highly subsidised rate has helped the farmers to increase the area under groundwater irrigation significantly (Shah, 1993; Vaidyanathan, 1994). Moreover, the introduction of free boring schemes also helped the farmers to adopt groundwater irrigation at a rapid rate (Pant, 2004). This has been resulted due to the introduction of free boring scheme, which recommended heavy doses of subsidy for the development of groundwater in the state. Under the programme, free boring facility to the extent of Rs. 3000 was provided to small and marginal farmers. Additionally, subsidies of 33.3 percent and 50 percent were provided to small and marginal SC and ST farmers respectively for the purchase of electric or diesel pumps (Pant, 2004: 2005). As a result, the number of both diesel and electric pumps sets has increased 17.63 lakhs in 1990-91 to 37.76 lakhs in 2004-05. This has been resulted to increase the share of private irrigation from 54 percent in 1970-71 to 75 percent in 2001-02 on the one hand and sharp decline of the share of public irrigation from 45.82 percent in 1970-71 to 24.70 percent in 2001-02. The development of water markets also helped the owner of groundwater schemes, wells and non-wells for further development of the sub-sector (Narayanamoorthy, 1993; Saleth, 1996; Shah, 1993).

Tank irrigation has declined from 3.60 lakh hectares in 1970-71 (5.26 percent of the NIA) to 0.67 lakh hectares (0.54 percent of the NIA) in 2000-01 in the state (Table 6.1). However, it is attributed that encroachment in the tank foreshore, accumulation of silt in the basin or bed, the construction of dams/reservoirs in the upper watershed or catchments area has prevented the water supplies, rapid development of groundwater irrigation in the tank command areas has dried up the tank, breakdown of village institutions because of caste or other conflicts, inadequate attention by the government bodies are the major reason for the decline of tank irrigation in due course of time (Janakiraman, 1993; Narayanamoorthy, 1993; Palanisami et al, 1996; Sivasubramaniyan, 1997; Vaidyanathan, 2001).

There has been constancy in the growth of area under other sources observed during last 30 years in the state. However, irrigation under streams, rivers and surface flow has been accounted under this category. The area under other sources has increased from 2.73 lakh hectares (4 percent of the NIA) in 1970-71 to 3.83 lakh hectares 3.26 percent of the NIA) in 1995-96 and again declined to 2.06 lakh hectares (1.66 percent) at the state level (Figure 6.1).

Table 6.1: Changes in Area Under Irrigation by Sources in Uttar Pradesh (in Lakh Hectares)

Year	*Canal*	*Tube-Well*	*Wells*	*Tanks*	*Others*	*Net Irrigated Area*	*Net Sown*
1970-71	24.98	23.30	18.26	3.60	2.73	68.47	173.05
	(34.60)	(32.28)	(26.67)	(5.26)	(3.99)	(39.57)	
1980-81	28.04	48.28	0.85	1.36	2.96	81.48	169.97
	(34.41)	(59.25)	(1.04)	(1.67)	(3.63)	(47.94)	
1990-91	31.93	65.63	3.70	1.04	3.12	105.42	172.32
	(30.29)	(62.26)	(3.51)	(0.99)	(2.96)	(61.18)	
1995-96	30.90	78.26	3.90	0.58	3.83	117.47	165.03
	(26.30)	(66.62)	(3.32)	(0.49)	(3.26)	(71.18)	
1996-97	30.75	79.92	4.64	0.99	3.70	120.00	166.10
	(25.63)	(66.60)	(3.87)	(0.83)	(3.08)	(72.25)	
1997-98	30.60	79.80	6.03	0.84	2.85	120.12	166.88
	(25.47)	(66.43)	(5.02)	(0.70)	(2.37)	(71.98)	
1998-99	31.08	87.97	4.58	0.95	2.33	126.91	167.32
	(24.47)	(69.32)	(3.61)	(0.75)	(1.84)	(75.85)	
1999-2000	29.88	87.00	4.82	0.82	2.17	124.70	168.01
	(23.96)	(69.77)	(3.87)	(0.66)	(1.74)	(74.22)	
2000-01	27.49	89.42	4.36	0.67	2.06	124.00	168.01
	(22.17)	(72.11)	(3.52)	(0.54)	(1.66)	(73.80)	

Source: Various Volumes of Statistical Dairy, State Planning Institute, Government of Uttar Pradesh

Note: Values in the parenthesis are the percent of respective total.

Figure 1: Changing Pattern of Irrigation Sources in UP (000' hectares)

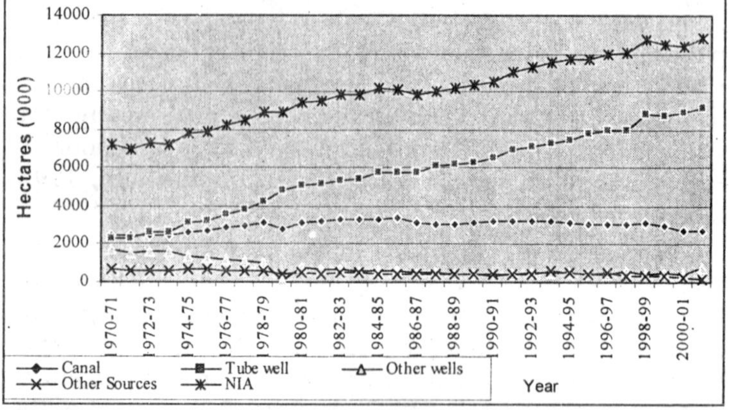

III. Extend of Groundwater Depletion

The depletion of groundwater causes a serious threat on environment, as it affects in different ways. Firstly, declining of water table has major implications for the base flow of the stream. If affects the down stream users' as they loose access to water at critical times. The pollution of both surface and groundwater is likely to increase. It affects many shallow small streams as they become dry after rainy season and even big rivers become dry. This ultimately affects the availability of drinking water. Secondly, as the water content declines in the soil, soil becomes more and more dusty and ultimately become prone to wind erosion. Thirdly, as the water content declines, it affects the trees, grass and other animal for useful needs. Fourthly, over extraction of groundwater affects the water quality directly. Sometimes, pollution poses a serious threat to all groundwater aquifers in the state. With the expansion of irrigated area and increased use of fertilisers and pesticides groundwater gets polluted ultimately causes health hazard.

The level of groundwater depletion can be examined by three sets of data, viz., volumetric data on groundwater, irrigated area statistics, data on water table to analyse the major aspects of groundwater depletion or the decline of water table (Dhawan, 1995). In a volumetric approach, the statistics of groundwater recharge and groundwater utilization are compared with each other. Groundwater depletion is signified by groundwater use for irrigation purpose exceeding groundwater recharge in a long run. The essential of the area approach are similar to those of the volumetric approach, the difference being use of utilization of groundwater irrigation potential instead of groundwater recharge and resources to be created groundwater potential in lieu of groundwater draft. As the information on water table is concerned, depth of water table is measured in selected observation of wells. The most important way of examining the over/under exploitation of groundwater is to measure the water table in a particular period in different areas of the state. However, Ground Water Department, Government of Uttar Pradesh categories, when the water table goes down between 5m to 10m below the ground level, area is considered as safe zone. Moreover, when the water level goes down between 10m to 15m and below, the area is considered as semi-critical and critical zone respectively (Government of UP, 2003).

According to the Third Minor Irrigation Census Report, out of 99, 472 villages surveyed in 2000-01, nearly 32 thousand villages (nearly 32 percent) are under semi critical and critical ground water level zone (Table 6.2). It may be attributed here that rest two third of the villages are under water logging zones or save zone. Under the critical zones, the groundwater level in 7.74 thousand villages is within 15 to 25 meters and 8.18 thousand villages are within 25 to 70 meters, where further extraction of ground water is almost impossible. Among various regions, nearly 40 percent of the villages are under semi-critical and critical level in Western region of the state (Table 6.2).

Some of the districts, viz., Auraiya, Etawah, where all the surveyed villages are under critical level. Some of the other districts, viz., in Agra 69 percent, in Baghpat 50 percent, in Firozabad 67 percent of the villages are under critical level. As Bundlekhand region belongs to naturally disadvantages position, nearly 2371 villages (49 percent) are under critical level. In Banda, Chitrakut, Hamirpur, where more than 70 percent of the villages are under semi-critical and critical level, where as nearly 50 percent of the villages are under semi-critical and critical region in Jalaun. In the Central Region, nearly 5 thousand villages (32 percent) are under semi-critical and critical region. On the one hand, Kanpur rural has 76 percent of the villages under semi-critical and critical level, whereas Sitapur has no villages under such situation. Eastern region of the state is the least affected regions, so far as ground water exploitation is concerned. However, nearly 12 thousand villages (25 percent) are under semi-critical and critical level. However, Azamgarh, Kaushambi, Sant Ravidas Nagar and Varanasi are some of the over exploited ground water regions. It may be attributed here that this region is abundant with the availability of water resources and mostly affected by waterlogging.

Table 6.2: Villages based on the Ground Water Level in the State in 2000-01 (in Nos.)

Regions	*Waterl-ogging and Save Zone <10 mtr*	*Semi-Critical level 10-15 mtr*	*Critical Level 15-25 mtr*	*Over exploitation 25-70 mtr*	*Total*
Western Region	18766	5748	2644	3808	30966
	(60.60)	(18.56)	(8.54)	(12.30)	(100.00)
Central Region	9817	2603	1491	903	14814
	(66.27)	(17.57)	(10.06)	(6.10)	(100.00)
Bundlekhand Region	2516	1279	544	548	488
	(51.48)	(26.17)	(11.13)	(11.21)	(100.00)
Eastern Region	36487	6321	3068	2929	48805
	(74.76)	(12.96)	(6.29)	(6.00)	(100.00)
Uttar Pradesh	67586	15951	7747	8188	99472
	(67.94)	(16.04)	(7.79)	(8.23)	(100.00)

Source: 3rd Census, Minor Irrigation, Government of Uttar Pradesh.
Note: Values in the parenthesis shows the percentages of villages to the total villages under different category.

The comparison between Second Minor Irrigation Census (1990-91) and Third Minor irrigation census shows that the proportion of villages under semi-critical and critical stages has increased during 1990-91 to 2000-01. However, out of 1.23

lakh villages surveyed in 1990-91, nearly 17 thousands (14 percent) and 10 thousands (8.29 percent) are semi-critical and critical stages of groundwater depletion. Similarly, out of 1.07 lakh surveyed villages, 16 thousands (16 percent) and 16 thousand (15 percent) are semi-critical and critical stages of groundwater depletion in the state. It is attributed here due to heavy demand for groundwater irrigation, the area under semi-critical and critical zones are increased over the decade with proper replenishment mechanism.

Heavy uses of water resources for various purposes lead to depletion of ground water table, which makes the existing minor and groundwater schemes defunct. There are mainly four reason for being not use of the existing minor and groundwater schemes, viz., inadequate power supply, mechanical failure, less water recharge or depletion of water table and other reasons (Third Minor Irrigation Census, 2000-01). The Third Minor Irrigation Census estimates that nearly 60 thousand (2 percent) minor surface and groundwater schemes became defunct/under utilised. As a result, 2.63 lakh hectares (2.05 percent of the NIA) are lost as irrigated area in the state. It is attributed here that the lost of irrigated area is mainly caused by less water recharge or over exploitation of groundwater among various other reasons.

IV. Inequity in the Accessibility to Groundwater Sources

Equitable distribution of land and water is an essential pre-requisite for ensuring equitable distribution of income, while alleviating poverty through irrigation led agricultural development strategies. In other words, quantitative assessment of inequality in irrigation water distribution is considered extremely important for strengthening irrigation policy for decision-making to achieve desired development objectives. However, measurement of inequality in irrigation led water distribution implies the distribution of both major and medium surface irrigation as well as minor surface and groundwater irrigation. Here an attempt is made to assess the inequality in accessibility of different types of minor and groundwater irrigation schemes among different size holding in the state, as minor and groundwater irrigation constitute nearly three fourth of the total irrigated area by 2001-02. As distribution of water is very much attached with the manner of distribution of land among different class and ownership, it is here with important to highlight the inequality of ownership and land holding size.

The present study confirms the existence of inequality in the number and distribution of area under various size holdings in different regions of the state. It is attributed here that marginal size class (who holds less than one hectare of land) constitutes nearly 76 percent of the total number of operational holding occupy only 36 percent of the total operational area in the state by 1995-96. However, small farmers constitute nearly 14.50 percent of the total number of operational holdings and they occupy nearly 25 percent of the total area of land cultivated. More importantly, medium (both semi-medium and medium farmers) farmers constitute nearly 10 percent of the total number of operational holdings and they possess lion share of 35 percent of the total area operated at the state level. Finally, large farmers constitute nearly one percent of the total number and they hold nearly 3 percent of the total land. However, similar kind of inequity is spread over the regions of the state. In Eastern region, marginal farmer constitute nearly 83 percent of the total number of operation holding and they occupy nearly 45 percent of the total area under operation in the region. Bundlekhand region is the worst affected, where marginal farmers constitute nearly 50 percent of the total number of operation holding and they majority only 13 percent of total area under operation. In all the regions, medium farmers are the highest beneficiaries, where they occupy highest proportion of area under operation holding.

The Inequality has been measured in two categories. Firstly, GC is measured by taking the number of operational land holding and the number of operation holding under minor surface and groundwater irrigation schemes. Secondly, region wise GC has been estimated in number of surface minor and groundwater irrigation schemes and area under operational holdings in the state. However, the results confirm the existence of wide variations of inequality of number of surface minor and groundwater irrigation schemes and area of operational holding by different size holdings in the state. In the state, marginal farmer constitute nearly 76 percent of the total operation holding and they occupy nearly 49 percent of the total minor and groundwater irrigation schemes. However, small and medium farmers are better off in occupying the minor and groundwater irrigation schemes in the state. Similar situations are observed in different regions of the state. In the Eastern region, the situation is worst, where nearly 82 percent of the operation holders (marginal farmers) occupy only 57 percent of the total minor surface and groundwater irrigation schemes. The result of the GC confirms that the level of inequity is highest in Bundlekhand region of the state (Table 6.3).

Table 6.3: Region-Wise Inequity in Land Distribution Along with Irrigation Schemes

Region	*Number with Area under Land Holding Operation*	*Number of operation holding with Number of Irrigation schemes*	*Area of operation holdings with Number of irrigation schemes*
Western Region	0.42	0.27	0.18
Central Region	0.40	0.24	0.19
Bundelkhand Region	0.51	0.25	0.29
Eastern Region	0.40	0.26	0.17
Uttar Pradesh	0.44	0.27	0.20

Sources: Estimated from Third Minor irrigation Census, 2000-01 and Agricultural Census, 1995-96.

IV. Conclusion and Policy Implication

This may be attributed here that over exploitation and depletion of groundwater resources is progressing in the state. The inequity in the accessibility of groundwater irrigation sources among various farm size operation holdings is significant, in which the farmers of marginal and small holdings are not in a position to access the resource and are the first victims of the externalities arising in the process of resource depletion. As a result of water depletion, majority of farmers of marginal and small holdings lose access to water. In other words, they are denied their genuine share of common pool resources. At present, legislation does not guarantee equity in access to groundwater resources to all section of the community, irrespective of their land ownership. Moreover, there is no legislation that supports the sharing of groundwater equitable. Therefore, there is string case of internalizing these externalities in a systematic fashion. One way of minimizing the externalities is to strengthen the resource base that is replenishing groundwater through rain water harvesting. This calls for policy changes towards prioritization of minor surface irrigation in the fragile regions as well as supporting cheaper access to technology. The following policies need immediate attention. For example, investment on community basis rather than individual basis would be more preferable. Similarly, integration of groundwater development/exploitation with surface water bodies like tanks is a precondition for sustainable water resource management. In addition, economic approaches need to be integrated with institutional arrangements in order to make the policies effective. Community involvement is required to make groundwater a common pool resource in the true sense.

REFERENCES

Dhawan, B.D. (1995), *Groundwater Depletion, Land Degradation and Irrigated Agriculture in India,* Commonwealth Publishers, New Delhi.

Gulati, A.; Ruth Meinzen-Dick; K.V. Raju (2005), *Institutional Reforms in Indian Irrigation,* Sage Publications, New Delhi.

Janakiraman, (1993), "In Search of Hidden Tanks: Some Hidden Facts", *Economic and Political Weekly,* Vol. 28, No. 26.

Nayak, Sanatan (2006), "Land Degradation in Uttar Pradesh: Causes, Extent and Intensity", in Jodha. N.S.; Pushpam Kumar; Sudhakar Reddy (eds.), *Ecology and Human Well-Being,* Oxford Publications, Forthcoming Issue.

Palanisami et al. (1996), Management of Tank Irrigation by Government and Community: An Analysis of Tank Irrigation Performance in Tamil Nadu, A Report on Water Technology Centre of Tamil Nadu Agricultural University, Coimbatore.

Pant, N. (2004), "Trends in Groundwater Irrigation in Eastern and

Western Uttar Pradesh", *Economic and Political Weekly*, Vol. 39, No. 31, July 31.

Pant, N. (2005), "Control of and Access to Groundwater in Uttar Pradesh", *Economic and Political Weekly*, Vol. XL, No. 26, June 25.

Raju, K.V. (2005), "Sustainable Water Use in India: A Way Forward", in Proceedings of Seminar on Statistical Accounting of Water Resources, CSO, Government of India.

Rao, C. H. Hanumatha (2005), *Agriculture, Food Security, Poverty and Environment: Essays on Post-Reform India*, Oxford University Press, New Delhi.

Saleth, M. (1996), *Water Institutions in India, Economics, Law and Policy*, Institute of Economic Growth Studies in Economic Development and Planning, No. 63, Commonwealth Publishers, New Delhi.

Shah, Tusar (1993), *Ground Water Markets and Irrigation Development: Political Economy and Practical Policy*, Oxford University Press, Mumbai.

Singh, Katar (1994), *Managing Common Pool Resources: Principles and Case Studies*, Oxford University Press, Delhi.

Sivasubramaniyan, K. (1997), "Irrigation Institutions under Two Major Tanks in Tamil Nadu", *Review of Development and Change*, Vol. 2, No. 3, July-December.

Vaidyanathan, A. (1994), "Impact of Irrigation on Productivity of Land", *Journal of Indian School of Political Economy*, Vol. 6, No. 4.

Vaidyanathan, A. (2001), "Irrigation Subsidies", Paper Presented in The World Bank Conference On Economic Reforms, New Delhi, 21-22, May.

7

Contribution of B.R. Ambedkar for Annihilation of Social Exclusion and Discrimination

D L. Karunyakara

I. Social Exclusion in European Context

The modern notion of "Social exclusion" is indeed specifically French origin and distinctly European. French Government servant Rene Lenoir is credited with the authorship of the term "Social exclusion". He applied the term in the context of French society, constituting the following as "excluded":

> Mentally and physically handicapped, suicidal people, aged invalids, abused children, substance abusers, delinquents, single parents, multi-problem households, marginal, asocial persons, and other social 'misfits'.[1]

Later on, the scholars tried to locate the definition of the expression—"social exclusion" in contexts other than the French and more generally European. As it has been originally championed by the Europe, the concept of social exclusion is mainly concerned with problems in European countries. Socially excluded thus includes people excluded from multiple forms of social exclusion prevailing in the European society namely from a livelihood; secure, permanent employment; earnings; property, credit, or land; housing; minimal or prevailing consumption levels; education, skills, and cultural capital; the welfare state; citizenship and legal equality; democratic experience, public goods etc.[2]

It is, however, argued that the idea of social exclusion—European in origin, with its cultural specificity—is not a barrier to the use of the concept elsewhere to understand poverty and deprivation, including in Asia and Africa in particular. Amartya Sen (2004) is right some extent to point out that the world in which we live is much more unified today, with shared ideas and concerns, and it would be amazing if socially useful notions developed in Europe would fail to be relevant in Asia just because of their European origin.[3] European understanding on social exclusion indeed, makes a close connection between the ideas of poverty and social exclusion. It treats the idea of poverty as capability deprivation. Based on the European premise Amartya Sen argues that the relational failure with which social exclusion is concerned can be seen to be a constitutively significant deprivation, which is a cause of poverty and inequality of other kinds.[4] In other words, poverty is the cause of social exclusion and capability deprivation.

II. Ambedkarian Perspective of Social Exclusion

In this paper, I shall try to define Ambedkarian perspective of social exclusion, its nature and its relevance to study the idea of social exclusion in India. It provides new insight and contributes to our understanding of the nature of Indian society particularly that of caste and its relation to social exclusion. It helps in identifying causes of social exclusion and discrimination in Indian society. It enriches thinking on policy and social action in alleviating deprived communities.

Ambedkarian perspective studies the social exclusion and discrimination in relation with caste system, which is a peculiar feature of Indian society as it is predominantly Hindu. It makes a close connection between the idea of caste and social exclusion. It treats the idea of caste and not poverty as 'capability deprivation', since poverty is the creation of caste.[5]

In Ambedkarian understanding, social exclusion means a person or a community is being excluded from social relations due to inferior caste. Social exclusion is a state of a person or community not being able to appear in public with pride due to lowborn. It is a ban from taking part in the social life of the nation or community. Thus, caste is the source of exclusion and discrimination. It is a permanent set up of broken social relations.

Ambedkarian approach doesn't recognize the validity of economic interpretation of history to study poverty as the cause of inequalities. It denounces the socialist contention that equalization of property is the only real reform. It privileges social reform over economic reform as it believes that reform of the social order is pre-requisite for economic development.

Ambedkar was not simply a philosopher reinterpreting the Indian society but a leader who tried to reconstruct the society by abolishing discriminative social structures.

Poverty based understanding of social exclusion particularly in Indian context is invalidated by the Ambedkar and locates exclusion entirely in different social realities and provides new theoretical underpinning. The Indian social crisis is unique in its nature due to the presence of caste system. Poverty-oriented approach is not enough to understand Indian variety of social exclusion and discrimination, where even poverty has caste. As Ambedkar asserts that caste is not based on division of labour. It is a division of labourers. In his own words: "Caste system is not merely division of labour. It is also a division of labourers".[6]

III. Ambedkar's Fight against Social Exclusion and Discrimination

Indian context of social exclusion that leads to discrimination is nothing but caste system. Untouchability is the higher degree of social discrimination applied through the ages to discriminate the so-called low castes. It doesn't mean that caste system is only to do with untouchability. The very basis of caste system is social discrimination of all communities except Brahmins, the authors of Hindu social system. The aim of this paper is not to make any polemic bashing of any community or religion particularly the Brahmins or Hinduism. It is to make an objective assessment of Ambedkar's contribution both in terms of his social activities as a leader of the Dalit masses and as a thinker who's thought provoking intellectual stand on various issues particularly pertaining to the downtrodden sections of Indian society that moulded the modern Indian social thought.

The history of Ambedkar's life is full of social protests led against the existing discriminations that aimed to keep the certain sections of Indian society socially deprived forever. Thus, to ensure the larger masses deprived of educational avenues and economic development. Ambedkar fought against this kind of discriminative social system called as caste (Jati or varna) system. He uncovered the bare face of caste by submitting himself for the cause of annihilation of caste. It is difficult to imagine the present India without finding his imprints from the history of Indian social tapestry. Undoubtedly the Independent India would have been trodden with much more inequitable and unjust one without his work.

Ambedkar being an untouchable boy and as a young man had encountered several times the draconian caste discrimination. He adopted a path of conflict to negotiate social cleavages for respectable place and dignified life. Written word is the weapon he employed to fight against the brahminic hegemony. He privileged Buddhism. Ambedkar made a text the battleground where, massing his troops, he launched an attack on the enemy territory, the adversary-text, point by point. The way he handled *Manusmriti, Bhagwad Gita,* Jaimini's *Mimamsa* or Gandhi are apt illustrations of this. Ambedkar thought that winning these battles was crucial for reformulating social relations.[7]

In Indian context the concept of social exclusion covers wide range of social, economic, cultural and political problems. The approach of social exclusion may provide new insight to study the nature of Indian society, culture and history. Social exclusion covers multidimensional nature of deprivation such as exclusion from basic facilities, family, neighbourhood, society, social community, social security, assured holding, labour market, resources—wages, savings, assets—goods and economic services, access to knowledge, legal system, education, health, political rights, justice, public institutions, bureaucracy, migration, accessibility to transport and communications, required information, identity, social visibility, self respect, feeling of oneness and belongingness; and significantly deprivation from common history and culture and above all from human rights. Forms of social exclusion may be the same both in Europe and in India, but the cause differs. Poverty is the cause of deprivation in the former where as Caste in the latter.

Indian understanding on social exclusion, without Ambedkarian approach becomes a borrowed concept from European realities. In European context 'class' is the cause of exclusion and discrimination. The role of class is minimal in India, as poverty stricken class is also divided by caste. Irrespective of class consciousness-rich or poor- human relations in India are predominantly determined by caste. To prove the point one can show many instances such as even in an urbanized educated locality getting a rented house is very difficult for highly paid socially marginalized community. We may argue that European society particularly America has the problem of racial discrimination as equivalent of Caste discrimination. In deed Caste is unique form of discrimination. Caste is a social system where as race is not. Caste is nothing to do with 'Colour'. Racial discrimination based on colour is not supported by sacred scripture of any religion. Caste discrimination is fully supported by all the scriptures of Hindu religion. The religion provides divine justification for committing caste atrocities on outcaste people.

Ambedkar identified caste as the source of social discrimination in Indian society. He also identified Hindu religion as the basis of Caste, as it provides divine sanction to caste discrimination. Thus, Ambedkar wanted Dalits to leave Hindu religion to live life with dignity, freedom and justice. He even asked Hindus to protect India by denouncing Hinduism. He opted Buddhism as an alternative religion that opposed Hindu scriptures like Vedas, Varna (Caste) and stood for equality and social justice. He wanted Hindus to renounce the exclusionary mode of society based on a cleavage framework and to adopt the inclusionary mode of society based on the assimilation framework. For him, Buddhism is the right religion to establish socially inclusive society in India. He preferred Buddhism because in his own words:

> "Buddhism teaches *Prajna* (understanding as against superstition and supernaturalism), *Karuna* (love), *Samata* (equality)."

To sum up, Amedkarian perspective invalidates the idea of poverty as the cause of social discrimination in Indian society and finds Caste as the cause of discrimination. It also finds the divine sanction of social discrimination in India as it is supported by religious scriptures of Hinduism. The remedy is Buddhism as Ambedkar felt Buddhist India means non-existence of social discrimination.

REFERENCES

1. Sen, Amartya. 2004. *Social Exclusion: Concept Application and Scrutiny,* New Delhi, Critical Quest.
2. Silver, Hillary. 1995. "Reconceptualizing Social Disadvantage: Three paradigms of Social Exclusion", in *Social Exclusion: Rhetoric, Reality, Responses,* edited by Gerry Rodgers, et al. Geneva: International Institute for Labour Studies.
3. Lella Karunyakara, *Modernisation of Buddhism: Contributions of Amedkar and Dalai Lama XIV,* Gyan Publishers, New Delhi, 2002.

Notes

1. See Silver (1995), p. 63. See also Sen (2004), p. 3.
2. Silver (1995), p. 63. See also Sen (2004), p. 3.
3. Amartya Sen (2004), p. 21.
4. Amartya Sen (2004), p. 18.
5. As already discussed earlier that Amartya Sen, in European context, treated the idea of poverty as capability deprivation.
6. *Annihilation of Caste, Dr. Babasaheb Ambedkar Writings and Speeches,* Vol. 1, Education Department, Government of Maharashtra, Bombay, 1979, compiled by Vasant Moon, p.47.
7. Valerian Rodrigues, *The Essential Writings of B.R. Ambedkar,* Oxford University Press, New Delhi, 2002, p. 4.
8. " Why I like Buddhism" a talk given on B.B.C. London on 12th May, 1956 by B.R. Ambedkar, reproduced in Lella Karunyakara's *Modernisation of Buddhism: Contributions of Amedkar and Dalai Lama XIV,* Gyan Publishers, New Delhi, 2002, p. Annexure-II.

8

Globalization and Impact on Dalits' Livelihoods

Dr. K.B. Ratna Kumari
Dr. L.C. Mallaiah

The doctrinal basis of today's globalization is provided by the "neo-liberalism" that represented revival of economic liberalism propounded by Adam Smith in 1776 in his famous book titled, *The Wealth of Nations*. Economic liberalism advocated the abolition of the government intervention in economic matters; it considered free trade was the best way for a nation's economy to develop. These ideas were "liberal" in the sense of no controls. Underneath their democratic façade, promotion of individualism and encouragement of free enterprise, they came to mean free hand for the capitalists for exploitation of labour and to make huge profits at any cost. These ideas ruled the world through the 1800s and early 1900s till the Great Depression of the 1930s eclipsed them with the theory of a British economist named John Maynard Keynes. This theory propounded that full employment is necessary for capitalism to grow and it can be achieved only if the governments and central banks intervened to increase employment. It worked well through the post-World War II reconstruction period and thereafter through the mid sixties. The USA which had emerged as the major economy of the world long before the World War II, immensely benefited from the state-coordinated wartime economy so as to assume the reigns of global capitalist order. It zealously guarded the capitalist system against the radical nationalism sprouting at many places, invariably with the use of force under the peculiar terminology of falsehood like "protection against the threat to stability" (a case of overthrow of the first democratic government of Guatemala in 1954 or a blatant military intervention planned in Italy in 1948 in the wake of election results sensing the undesired outcome). With over half of the world's wealth, the USA performed the role of world's banker in the post-World War II system.

However, with the increasing financial crisis of the debt-ridden countries, the Nixon administration decided to dismantle this system, giving rise to huge explosion of unregulated capital flows that totally marginalized the real economy. The composition of the international financial transaction shifted from real economy to speculation. Within just two decades form 1971 to 1990, the percentage of transactions related to real economy came down from 90 % to paltry 10 % and further declined to 5 % over next five years.

A decade into the globalisation-driven economic reforms and the facts indicate a declining livelihood status among Andhra Pradesh Dalits across key socio-economic conditions. Caste discrimination remains a key factor that continues to deny Dalits access to resource and opportunities for socio-economic development, leading to their lower levels of livelihood capitals as compared to other social groups (NFHS 1999). Therefore, bearing in mind that equality in dignity and rights implies an absence of poverty and discrimination, which is the key goal of most livelihood development strategies, it is essential that those involved in livelihood development processes understand the need and begin to analyse globalisation-induced projects and programmes from a Dalit perspective. This applies to the Andhra Pradesh Government through its Vision 2020 and other economic policies, to international development cooperation agencies, international funding agencies, human rights and other organisations working to secure sustainable livelihoods.

A Dalit perspective to livelihoods entails factoring in social exclusion through caste discrimination into assessment of the potential impacts of policies, programmes and projects on particularly Dalits and lower caste-class groups. This factor has been missing from most attempts so far to assess the impact of globalisation driven projects on livelihoods. A more holistic picture of livelihoods in a caste society emerges if one examines caste predication of access to benefits and opportunities, which pinpoints where greater emphasis needs to be laid to bring these communities into the process of development.

Why the need for this emphasis in the broader human rights and development movement? This is because an economic policy that is based on full-cost accounting, which incorporates social and environmental costs and benefits, needs to place special attention on transforming structures that perpetuate inequality, injustice and intolerance, including caste and gender-bias systems. Otherwise, without explicit recognition that Dalit empowerment, that women's empowerment is central to achievement of broad-based socioeconomic goals, these social groups will remain excluded from the process of development. Moreover, without adequate investment in these social groups as well as capital, they are at risk of being further exploited in the new institutions that emerge.

Rooting out caste discrimination and inequality can go a long way towards guaranteeing Dalits freedom to develop secure livelihoods that promote their human dignity and worth in Andhra Pradesh society. In addition, the economic benefits that would potentially flow from securing socio-economic development for Dalits could see Andhra Pradesh finally secure steady equitable economic development for all sections of its citizens. This would boost economic growth for the state as a whole.

Against this background and context, this study seeks to evaluate the phenomenon of globalisation and its impact on the livelihoods of the marginalised, pauperized and hence socio-economically vulnerable Dalits from a human development perspective, one that takes the Dalit well-being and livelihood security as a broad-based central goal over economic imperatives. With the Supreme Court of India deeming the right to livelihood as part of right to life under Article 21 Indian Constitution, this assumes great significance for the Dalits as a community that has the least livelihood security of rural communities in Andhra Pradesh. In the light of these policy changes in the direction of globalization, an attempt is made here to analyse the effects of globalization on dalits livelihoods on the basis of economic theory and available empirical evidence at different level particularly state level.

This study examines the changing status of dalits livelihoods vis-à-vis non dalits livelihoods in the state of Andhra Pradesh since the globalization process was introduced, to assess its impact on the Dalits. This paper will focus mainly on Employment, Education, Land and Health. The information is collected from secondary sources as well as from case studies available on these issues in state and national level.

Globalization in India and Andhra Pradesh

While India commenced liberalization of its market in the 1980s. Economic crisis precipitated the introduction of the New Economic Policy in 1991. This policy was based on an IMF-World Bank macroeconomic stabilization and structural adjustment program. The IMF-World Bank loan conditionalities saw the Indian Government withdraws from the economic sphere through curtailment of government expenditure, particularly in social programs and infrastructure and cuts to state subsidies and price support programs. This was coupled with the rapid expansion of the market- friendly, supply and demand-controlled private sector, reforms to the taxation system and in banking and financial institutions, and increasing import and export liberalization.

A prominent myth promulgated by supporters of unchecked globalization—liberalization and privatization—in India is that globalization processes would be good for growth and the economy, and a growth-driven economy would decrease inequalities, increase incomes, decrease poverty and increase employment. However, over a decade later significant indicators expose the fallacy of this link between economic growth, increased employment opportunities and poverty eradication.

Andhra Pradesh is commonly seen as a testing ground

for globalization processes of trade liberalization and privatization. The State Government commenced reorienting its economic policies in line with current macro-economic policies during the 1990s. A major emphasis was placed during this period on education, roads, ports, fisheries and other industrial sectors, signaling the entry of the private sector into energy, roads and other infrastructure projects. However, during that period the promise of economic reforms to reduce fiscal deficits and promote economic growth proved false, damaging the state's economy. The fiscal deficit more than doubled during the period 1990-91 to 1997-98 from Rs. 967 corers to Rs. 2,428 corers. Meanwhile, total loan repayments, including interest repayments, almost quadrupled from Rs. 807 corers (83 percent of fiscal deficit) in 1990-91 to Rs. 3,153 corers (129 percent of fiscal deficit) by 1997-98. And relatively low revenue creation over the same time period saw the revenue deficit increase from Rs. 158 crore in 1990-91 to Rs.703 crore by 1997-98. This was accompanied by increasing public debt, rising from Rs. 7.017 crore in 1990 to Rs. 17.372 crore by 1997 (State finance 2001).

Vision 2020 of Andhra Pradesh

These trends have culminated in 1999 with the State Government bringing out its 'Vision 2020' policy document, based again upon the World Bank's report, "Andhra Pradesh: Agenda for Economic Reforms". The argument placed before the Andhra Pradesh people was that subsidies and social welfare programmes for the poor are the reason why the state has not grown as it should. This agenda of reducing subsidies to promote economic growth now forms the core of Vision 2020, which needs to raise 80 percent of funds from foreign direct investment in order to meet its targets. While chapter 1 of this policy document emphasizes progress and prosperity through poverty eradication and social welfare, the remaining contents vitiate this development strategy through emphasizing economic growth via further integration into the market economy as the only solution to development in the state.

Salient Features of Vision 2020

- sets an ambitious target for 9 to 10 percent annual economic growth to realize socio-economic development of the state by the ysear 2020. What this would require is a nine-fold increase in the average per capita income.
- Transforms the nature of governance. The government's role in socio-economic development has been till recently as a provider and regulator of development, being the primary Institutional mechanism through which livelihood resources could be re-allocated. Acknowledgement of the socioeconomic inequalities existing in Andhra Pradesh society has seen a series of social welfare programmes specifically targeting Scheduled Castes, including land redistribution schemes and programmes to promote employment diversification among the Dalit community However, this role is now being transformed into the government as a facilitator of market-based development. The idea is to provide an investor-friendly environment in the state wherein private actors are encouraged to take up not only enterprises and infrastructure projects in the state, but also provision of key services including education and healthcare.
- Shifts government's focus towards developing the productive capabilities of people through particularly primary education, job-oriented skills training and primary healthcare. These strategies will allegedly stimulate people's economic efficiency to attract private investment. This in turn will ensure a level of economic growth leading to increasing employment opportunities and, therefore, development in the state.
- Promises to stimulate growth in three major sectors of the economy—agriculture, industry and services to both create employment opportunities as well as generate additional resources for the government to plough into social development measures. Identified `growth engines' for priority investment consist of 19 areas of economic activity in these three sectors.

- Envisages an annual 6 percent agricultural growth rate for the 70 percent of the state's population who depend on agriculture and agriculture-related activities for their livelihoods, double what it has been in the past decades. However at the same time around 20 million people will supposedly shift from agriculture to non agriculture work activities. Stating that the outdated paradigm of small and marginal farmers in agriculture form the new focus for development. However the document makes no mention of how it will provide an alternative agricultural income to those who do not have sufficient natural financial and human capital to compete in the export market.

Therefore, it become necessary to inquiry into how Vision 2020 is being translated into action at the local level, to gauge how a policy promoting economic growth as the solution to poverty in the state, particularly for disadvantage sections can negotiate the myriad of caste to class and gender factors which condition peoples access to resources and means of securing their livelihoods. Already the government has acknowledged that focus upon sustainable livelihoods is supposed to allow the government to link between local issues and wide concerns about policies, institutions and processes to better understand local priorities for development. This is especially so given the modern economic environment.

AP Dalits' Economic Scenario

As of the year 2001, the 10.529 million Dalits in the state, constituting 15.93 percent of the state's population, lag behind the general Andhra Pradesh population on almost every development indicator, their precarious livelihood status is borne out by 50.4 percent being below the poverty line as compared to 32.0 percent for the general population. With around 80 percent of Dalits found in rural Andhra Pradesh, available data up to 1993-94 indicates increasing proportion of Dalit rural household engaged in labour work and particularly agricultural labour work in the 1990s. While there was a decline in the proportion of Dalit rural labour households from 1983-84 to 1987-88, between 1987-88 and 1993-94 there was an increase from 75.90 to 78.46 percent. By contrast, the proportion of non-SC/ST households Involved in rural labour was already around half that of Dalits and their proportionate involvement in rural labour has remained almost the same between 1987-88 and the 1993-94 level of 42.28 percent.

Twice the proportion of rural Dalit households is engaged in agricultural labour as compared to non-Dalit households. Moreover, over the time period 1987-88 to 1993-94 while there has been a 4.26 percent increase in Dalit agricultural labour households to 69.65 percent, non-Dalit households have witnessed a negligible increase of 0.39 percent (RLIR 1994). Minimum wages for agricultural labourers in the state as on January 1999 were as low as 30 to Rs. 36.50. Agricultural labour wage levels have increased by a mere 2.30 on average during the 1990 compared to wage level increases of between 5.17 and 8.73 in all other southern Indian states. Hence, agricultural wages, an important determinant of rural poverty in an agrarian economy, have not risen to meet inflation and rising costs of living in the state. The result can be observed in the vastly different monthly per capita consumption expenditure levels of Dalits as compared to non-Dalits. While the average monthly per capita consumption expenditure in 1999-2000 across Andhra Pradesh was Rs.453.61, the expenditure level for Dalits stood at a mere Rs.381.82 as compared to Rs.564.50 for non-Dalits (NSS 1999).

Further accentuating the gap between Dalits and the rest of the working population, both agricultural and non-agricultural enterprise ownership by Dalits in 1990 accounted for only 6.3 percent of total enterprise ownership, while non-Dalits owned 88.8 percent of enterprises. Moreover, in terms of establishments, this disparity was greater, with Dalits owning only 2.0 percent of establishments as compared to 97.3 percent for non-Dalits (GOAP 1990). Between 1998 and 1994 there was an overall growth rate of around 2 percent in public sector employment for Dalits, while the trend for non-Dalits saw declining public sector involvement (GoAP 1994). The significance of these divergent trends is that with public sector reforms introduced by the State Government in the late 1990s signaling increasing disinvestment and privatisation of public sector enterprises, this alternative avenue of employment for Dalits is slowly being curtailed.

Globalisation and Dalit Livelihoods

The implication, of occupational differentiation between Dalits and the dominant castes, coupled with economic and socio-political marginalisation, is that Dalits cannot access basic entitlements to develop the means and abilities to participate in the market, a political sphere controlled by the dominant castes. Hence, they cannot equally compete with the dominant castes in the shifting economic scenario of privatisation and trade or market liberalisation to secure their livelihoods. This is because competitiveness in the global market produces greater changes and opportunities but also greater economic risks than closed national markets.

The dynamics of these new processes expose Dalits to new forms of vulnerability by further denying or limiting their rights to work, to goods and services and to resources entitlements. Left to rely upon a labour market which is increasingly positioned to favor those with high human capital in the form of education and technical skills as opposed to labour capital, the formal sector is increasingly closing its doors to Dalits. Increasing privatization of public sector enterprises destroys what little work opportunities were guaranteed under reservations to Dalits in the public sector. Possessing little if any physical and natural capitals, this leave, little option for most Dalits but to seek work in the informal and unorganized sector, where lower incomes and lesser employment opportunities due to increasing mechanisation and labour surplus ensure greater chances of under-employment. Particularly where the majority of Dalits are concentrated in low-waged agricultural labour, lessening workdays within the local economy forces them to increase migration to the external economy of waged labour. The result is disruption to social family life and consequent negative implications for Dalit children's development.

Essential goods and services, including education, health services, housing under affirmative action policies, subsidies and the public distribution system, are slowly being dismantled or privatized. The State is withdrawing from direct intervention in these aspects and encouraging private sector participation. However, again, without State intervention to ensure that those possessing the lowest human capital are guaranteed access to these goods and services through reservations and preferential treatment, capital poor Dalits are left to rely upon the market and private actors to provide access.

Access to resource entitlements such as land and common property resources, though traditionally alienated from rural Dalits due to caste discrimination, had slowly been reversed through government programmes for land redistribution. However, with the withdrawal of the State Government from an implementation to a supposed facilitation role, and increasing land allocation to commercial industries and agri-business, Dalits are forced to rely more and more on the open land market. But in a situation with highly skewed landholding patterns, where teasing out depends on landholding size and hence is controlled by dominant castes and leasing in increasingly depends on financial capital, land markets are closed to Dalits due to their lack of financial and socio-political capitals. Moreover, for those Dalits concentrated in small and marginal landholdings, smaller land size, lesser access to agricultural inputs and lesser crop diversity all contribute to lower land productivity than that of the dominant caste large landholders.

Hence their low capital base and prevailing caste discrimination that restricts their possession of socio-political assets ensure that Dalits are excluded from access to the market through denial of access to land, capital, employment and the More-mentioned social services.

As the public sector, which was the next largest source of Dalit employment after agriculture, is being privatised, the majority of Dalits and other 'lower' castes become more and more dependent on the dominant castes for employment. The dependency is not only on the landlords, but also on dominant caste entrepreneurs, industrialists, investors and employers. This leads to increased segmentation and competition between the 'lower' castes and Dalits and hence greater atrocities as the former seek to assert their caste power over the latter and usurp work opportunities from Dalits. In other words, as intensification of pressures on rural livelihoods increase under globalisation, and as Dalits increasingly assert their rights to livelihood and resources to sustain their livelihood, there is a corresponding increase in atrocities against them (DHR, 2000).

Overall, current globalisation processes in a caste-unequal society such as Andhra Pradesh are being seen to merely build upon a 'feudal caste-patriarchal economy', which further institutionalizes inequitable distribution of resource, ownership of the means of production and capital and access to opportunities. This in effect further institutionalises caste subservience of Dalits, by reinforcing denial of the following key freedoms necessary for their development: freedoms from discrimination, from want, from fear, from injustice, to develop and realise their potential, of speech, association and participation in decision-making, free of economic exploitation. Without addressing the social structures that deny Dalits freedom of livelihood choice and opportunity., globalisation-driven macro-economic policies are doomed to further exacerbate systemic deprivation, discrimination and economic disenfranchisement of Dalits.

Importance of Dalit Livelihoods

The majority of Andhra Pradesh Dalits lie outside mainstream socio-economic processes, many subsisting below the official poverty line due to socio-religiously ascribed deprivation under the caste system. The caste system subjects Dalits to widespread caste discrimination on the basis of descent (birth into a particular caste) and work (historically prescribed, immutable degrading occupations), which is reinforced through the social control mechanism of untouchability practices. This limits their socio-economic-political base and mobility, thus marginalising them in the process of development.

In a caste-based hierarchical society, where the fundamental social structure is itself based on social exclusion due to caste discrimination, caste becomes a key factor in understanding how marginalisation from economic, social and political spheres leads to poverty (Rodgers, 1995). Economic marginalisation means that Dalits, as the lowest caste in the social hierarchy, are denied the means and abilities that would allow them to participate in market exchange in land, labour, credit and output markets. The result is their concentration in low income, .unskilled' manual labour occupations and an inability to make investments to increase productivity or own the means of production. This means an inability to protect themselves from risks and thereby increased vulnerability (Figure for 1996).

Therefore, in the context of globalisation processes, there are three key points which mark Dalit livelihoods as separate from non-Dalit livelihoods and which form the basis for assessing globalisation impacts from a Dalit perspective:

1. There is a clear demarcation between the livelihood activities of Dalits and non-Dalits under the caste system, which is legitimized by feudalistic practices of untouchability and caste discrimination. This is being maintained despite alleged socio-economic opportunities thrown open by globalisation processes and despite attempts by Dalits towards economic mobility.
2. Caste-imposed livelihood status disparities between Dalits and non-Dalits in livelihood areas are exacerbated by current globalisation processes with non-Dalits reaping the benefits of globalisation processes.
3. Caste inequality and discrimination in access to livelihood resources, employment opportunities and markets further hinders the ability of Dalits to be equal players in the globalisation process. This is due to creating a level playing field of unequal players and consequently entrenching existing inequalities, discrimination and marginalisation.

The overall result is that caste-ascribed occupations have traditionally dictated and circumscribed the access of different caste groups to the labor market and economic mobility. Access and control over decision-making structures regarding resources allocation and their usage have also been similarly circumscribed. Not only this, the core doctrine being economic inequality, the caste system has legitimized exploitation of `lower' castes for economic gain, sanctioning and legitimizing in effect their poverty. This has pushed particularly Dalits into more subsistence oriented livelihoods, placing in effect a `glass ceiling' over the livelihood choices available to Dalits.

This situation has changed over time, though to varying degrees depending on caste status. The majority of the dominant castes with greater financial resources have been able to shift into new occupations in the process of development, moving from rural to urban employment, and moving into new areas of employment such as information-communications technology or aquaculture, or into the formal, organised sector. And in the rural agriculture and non-agriculture sector most dominant castes have retained ownership of these livelihood activities over the years, aided by their control to a large extent of resources such as land and water and access to credit and land markets.

By contrast, untouchability remains the dividing line between those who can socio-economically progress and those who cannot. As such, for the Dalits economic marginalisation and severely curtailed occupational mobility remain even today. This is due to lack of ownership of production processes, lack of access to and control over resources, lack of skills, lack of socio-political contacts to access opportunities for occupational mobility, due to their `impure' status, untouchability practices and caste discrimination which socially alienate Dalits. These prevent them from forming any social networks that could generate the bridging social capital to tackle the factors that condition their livelihoods.

Effects of Globalisation

According to the Indian government the growth rate of the economy has increased to 6.4 percent in the 1990s and poverty levels have decreased from 38.9 percent in 1987-88 to 26.1 percent in 1999-2000 (Economic Survey 2001) the actual number of those living in poverty has not reduced. The Planning Commission's Special Group on Job Creation estimates that the current unemployment rate is over 7 percent (as opposed to the Governments 1999-2000 estimate of 2.2 percent), with the number of unemployed swelling to at least 45 million by 2007. Job creation in the 1990s, post trade liberalization, is said to be three times less than in the 1980s, refuting the claim that economic growth automatically leads to greater employment opportunities (Outlook 2002). The formal sector employment growth rate has almost stagnated at 0.04 percent in 1999 as compared to 1.44 percent in 1991, with negligible increase in public sector employment and private sector employment growth set at 0.11 percent in 1999 as compared to 1.24 percent in 1991 (Planning Commission, 1999).

Correlating with this declining formal sector growth rate is a higher labor absorption by the unorganized sector, witnessed by increasing casualisation of labour from 29.6 percent in 1987-88 to 32.0 percent in 1993-94. This will be particularly so where employment opportunities generated are human capital-intensive requiring education and technical skills in the formal sector, which excludes the majority of India's poor (NSS, 1994). Privatization and disinvestment have seen the Indian Government slowly reduce budgetary support for welfare measures. Per capita expenditure on health by central and state governments reduced from 1.25 percent of GDP in 1993-94 to 0.90 percent by 1999-2000. Education per capita expenditure reduced from 2.74 percent of GDP in 1993-94 to 2.49 percent by 1997-98 and then rose to 2.75 percent by 1998-99 (CMIE 2000), still well below the prescribed level of 6 percent of GDP recommended by the Kothari Commission. Indian livelihoods have been affected by the lifting of import restrictions on many consumer goods items. The resulting flood of foreign consumer goods entering the Indian market threatens the local consumer market by displacing local products with factory produced mass goods. Moreover, numerous studies are revealing that pressures on particularly livelihoods in rural areas, where 80 percent (and the majority of Dalits) of the Indian population is located and where primary employment opportunities lie in agriculture, are often intensified by patterns of agricultural development that enhance mode of production through economic and technical change, than by lack of development. These patterns, prominent under macro economic policy implementation, are processes of commodification or commercialization of land and labour; formation of markets with social and institutional bias and inequalities, technical change and its environmental effects, such as modern technique of horticulture and sericulture, along with increased mechanization and government policies and practices, that, intentionally or unintentionally, favor those with socio-political assets, namely the dominant rural caste-class groups (Bernstein, 1992).

These processes only result in intensifying social inequalities, particularly on the basis of caste, class and gender, in access to land and natural resources and to opportunities arising out of economic policy shifts. The consequence is further pauperization of already poor and marginalized communities. Poverty and consumption expenditure estimates during the 1990s reveal a marked increase in inequality in terms of increasing disparities in per capita expenditure across states, across the rural-urban divide, and within most urban areas in states.

Access to Land

Greater percentage of Dalit rural labour and agricultural labour households are landless as compared to non-SC/ST households in these categories, higher than the all-India levels. Moreover, by 1993-94 landlessness among Dalit rural labour households and particularly agricultural labour households was higher as compared to two decades ago, indicating a negative shift in land ownership. By comparison there was a huge drop of over 40 percent in landlessness among non-SC/ST rural labour and agricultural labour households. The sharpest disparity appeared in terms of rural agricultural labour households, with 75.3 percent of Dalit households in this category in 1993-94 landless as compared to a mere 15.76 percent of non-SC/ST households (RLIR 1994). Given this widening gap between Dalits and non-SCs/STs in ownership of key land capital, the State Government's land redistribution programme under the Andhra Pradesh Land Reform (Ceiling on Agricultural Holdings) Act 1973, as amended in 1977, has made only a small dent in this trend. Both in 1996 and in 2001 Dalits accounted for around 41 percent of beneficiaries of government land endowment schemes. However, of the total land area declared surplus (795,665 acres) in 1996, the government had failed to distribute around 30 percent of the land. Moreover, the period 1996 to 2001 had witnessed an increase in land cases pending before the courts, around 150,000 acres remaining locked in court cases to the detriment of many Dalit and other beneficiaries (GoAP 1996).

Those Dalits owning land, most fall into the categories of marginal and small landholders. Their smaller plots of land indicate the predominance of subsistence agricultural operations or minor commercial agriculture, the number of marginal Dalit farmers increasing from 67.7 percent in 1981 to 70.7 percent in 1991. This was accompanied by a decrease in all other landholdings categories during the same time period. By comparison, only 56.0 percent of non-Dalits operated marginal landholdings in 1991 (Census 1991).

Dalits owned only around 12.6 percent of the total landholdings and a mere 6.9 percent of the total operated area in 1981. These figures only slightly increased by 1991, with Dalits now owning 12.7 percent of landholdings and 7.5 percent of the total operated area. And with around 60 percent of the gross cropped area in Andhra Pradesh consisting of dry land with non-assured irrigation sources, quality of land in terms of irrigated holdings becomes another point of differentiation between Dalits and non-Dalits. While, 39.7 percent of Dalits in 1981 held irrigated holdings, by 1991 this had reduced down to a mere 17.7 percent, but non-Dalits in 1991 held around twice the number of irrigated holdings.

Education Level

At the start of the 21 century Dalits are still half as literate as the general population in the state, with only 32.35 percent literacy as compared to the general literacy level of 58.10 percent in 2001. Moreover, Dalit literacy in Andhra Pradesh remains less than the national Dalit literacy average. What signals a decline in educational delivery to Dalits is the poor growth rate in literacy levels recorded in the National Census from 1991 to 2001. Whereas from 1981 to 1991 literacy levels among Dalits grew by 13.94 percent, over the decade 1991 to 2001 the literacy growth rate dropped to a poor 0.76 percent. By comparison, general literacy in the state has steadily grown from 1981 to 1991 and 1991 to 2001 at a rate of between 9 to 1 3 percent. Whereas the gross enrolment ratio in primary schooling in 1998-99 was higher for Dalits (106.61) than for the general school children population (85.20), by upper primary school there was a larger drop in the enrolment ratio among Dalit children (48.98). Moreover, while the enrolment ratio in primary and upper primary schooling had increased for Dalit children between 1978-79 and 1988-89, by 1998-99 this ratio had dropped (GoAP 1997).

1999-2000 drop-out rates among Dalit children (67.94) in primary level education continue to be much higher than that of the general school children population (58.29). Notably, dropout ratios increased during the first half of the 1990s when economic reforms were first introduced, while by the second half of the 1990s the rates were again dropping, though at a greater rate for the general child population than for Dalit children. With a still large number of Dalit children dropping out to join primarily the labour force due to such factors as poverty, discrimination or poor quality schooling, they form a large portion of the 34 percent of children aged between 10 and 14 years engaged in child labour in 1993-94 (GoAP 1999). Despite the decreasing enrolment ratio and higher drop-out rates among Dalit children, the Andhra Pradesh Government has steadily decreased educational facilities such as government hostels for Dalit students over the past decade. Whereas in 1991 there were 2,231 hostels with 228,000 Dalit students on government records, by 1997-98 this number had dropped to 2,210 hostels with Dalit student strength of 205,000.

Health and Basic Amenities

While generally rural areas fare worse than urban areas in terms of access to basic amenities of electricity, safe drinking water and toilet facilities, in both rural and urban settings caste disparity is seen in terms of access to particularly electricity and toilet facilities. The 1991 National Census reveals that only 24.17 percent of Dalits as compared to 53.49 percent of non-SCs/STs had electricity in their homes, while only

6.66 percent of Dalits as compared to 22.00 percent of non-SCs/STs had toilet facilities. Only in terms of potable drinking water facilities was greater equity seen, due in part to such schemes as the million wells schemes and other targeted drinking water schemes of the government.

In 1994, a NCAER/ HDI Survey revealed that 66.7 percent of villages with a majority Dalit population in the state lacked access to a health sub-centre or hospital within 5 km of the village, as compared to 52.2 percent for villages in general.

The serious repercussions of lack of access to healthcare facilities for Dalits is seen in the high infant and under-5 mortality rates, the latter rate having increased during the period 1992-93 to 1998-99 from 114.8 to 122.4. By contrast, non-SCs/STs have experienced declining infant and under-5 mortality rates during the same period, the latter rate being 79.0 in 1998-99, indicating better health levels and better access to healthcare (NFHS, 1999).

Dalit women and children have lower health levels than their non-SC/ST counterparts. Whereas in 1992-93 a lesser percentage of non-SC/ST children were underweight than Dalit children, by 1998-99 this percentage had sharply decreased as compared to the slower declining percentage for Dalit children.

The role of state has to be not only economic and also protective to enables dalits to overcome the problems of poverty and social discrimination and access to livelihoods. Their skills are to be improved through expansion of educational facilities. Effective implementation of land reform is essential, given the skewed distribution of land, to reduce the inequalities.

REFERENCES

1. *Economic Survey 2000-2001*, Government of India.
2. See "Labouring under a Misconception", *Outlook Magazine*, 2006.
3. National Planning Commission Reports, 1991 to 1999; National Sample Survey Report, 1993-94.
4. Centre for Monitoring of Indian Economy (CMIE), Public Finance, March 2000.

5. Samuel, I. & Prakasam, G. (1998). "Withering of Welfare State: Liberalised Market and Development Delusion", *Social Watch Country Report*.
6. Bernstein, H., Crow, B. & Johnson, H. (eds). *Rural Livelihoods: Crises and Responses*, 1992, Oxford University Press, United Kingdom, p. 10.
7. Deaton, A. & Dreze, J.: "Poverty & Inequality in India: A Rexamination", *Economic and Political Weekly*, 2002, p. 3731.
8. State Finances: The Factual Position. Finance and Planning Department, June. 1996 & Strategy Paper on Fiscal Problems, Finance Department, 2001, Government of Andhra Pradesh.
9. See <<wvvw.aplivelihoods.org».
10. Chambers, R. & Conway, G.R., Sustainable Rural Livelihoods: Practical Concepts for the 21st Century, IDS Discussion Paper 296. 1991, p. 1.
11. Rodgers, G., "What is so Special About a Social Exclusion Approach", in Rodgers, G., Gore, C. and Figueiredo, J.B. (eds), *Social Exclusion: Rhetoric, Reality, Responses*, 1995, IILS/UNDP, Geneva, at pp. 253-282.
12. Figuerora, A., Altamariano, T. and Sulmont, D., *Social Exclusion and Inequality in Peru*, 1996, IILS/UNDP, Geneva.
13. *Ibid*.
14. Bhalla, A. and Lapeyre, F., "Social Exclusion: Towards an Analytical and Operational Framework", *Development and Change*, Vol. 28 (1997), Institute of Social Studies. 1997, Blackwell Publishers Ltd, Oxford, p. 419.
15. Thorat, S.K., "Inequality and Caste Based Discrimination: Reflection on Theory and Empirical Facts with Respect to Scheduled Caste Wage Labour in India", keynote address. Workshop on Economic Development of the Scheduled Castes with special reference to Agricultural Labourers, Gokhale Institute of Politics and Economics, 2002, Pune and Thorat, S.K. & Deshpande, R., "Caste and Labour Market Discrimination", *ILJE*, Vol. 2, No. 4, Oct.-Nov. 1999.
16. Strategy Paper on Welfare of SCs and STs, Government of Andhra Pradesh.
17. Rural Labour Inquiry, Report of General Characteristics of Rural Labour Households, 1983-84, 1987-88. 1993-94, Labour Bureau, Ministry of Labour, Shimla.
18. National Sample Survey 55th round, July 1999 - June 2000, table no. A-168. 27. Directorate of Economics and Statistics, Government of Andhra Pradesh, 1990.
19. Directorate of Economics and Statistics, Government of Andhra Pradesh, 1999 & 1994.

20. Ellis, F. & Seeley, J., Globalisation and Sustainable Livelihoods: An Initial, Background Briefing Note, 2000, U.K., p. 2.
21. Rassumssen, L. "Economic Inequality, Human Rights and Labor Markets", *Netherlands Quarterly of Human Rights*, Vol. 15/2, 1997.
22. Rural Labour Enquiry Report 1994, Labour Bureau, Government of India.
23. Quarterly Progressive Report on Implementation of Land Ceiling Laws, 1996, Government of India.
24. Census Reports 1981 and 1991 and 2001.
25. Agricultural Census, DES, Government of AP.
26. Educational Statistics, 1998-99, Directorate of School Education, Government of AP.
27. National Family Health Survey, 1999.
28. S. Mahendra Dev, *Baseline Survey Reports* CESS, 2002.

9

Ambedkar's Contribution for the Educational Development of Dalits

Prof. L. Karunyakara

Education is the only route for the empowerment of dalits. Babasaheb Bhim Rao Ambedkar was instrumental in opening the gates of the education to the common people. He was of the firm view that education is not only the birthright of every human being but also a weapon of social change. This essay aims to explore Ambedkar's educational background, his role to establish various important educational institutions and his ideas on the importance of education for the development of dalits.

Ambedkar is known to the World as a social thinker, jurist, economist, historian, constitutionalist and also a great contributor in the field of education. He was a great intellectual of international repute, orator, erudite scholar and prolific writer. The rage of his writings includes economics, sociology, law, constitution, anthropology, political science, religion, history and culture etc. He was a rare specimen of politician armed with high academic qualifications.

Ambedkar, the man of great learning, with humble background, had risen to the great heights, just because of education. He had education from the world reputed universities like Columbia University, USA and London University. It is very interesting to note that Ambedkar was the only Indian political leader of his time who had education from both America and England. He completed an M.A. from Columbia University with a dissertation on 'Administration and Finance of East India Company' and his Ph.D. from the same University on 'National Dividend: A Historical and Analytical Study'. He obtained an M.Sc., degree from the London School of Economics (LSE) and completed D.Sc. with the dissertation on 'The Problem of the Rupee'. He did Bar-at-Law at Grey's Inn, London.

Teaching community should be proud of him because he was not only son of a teacher and also he worked as Professor in the reputed educational institutions of his time. He was a Professor of Political Economy at Sydenham College, Bombay that was then modeled on the pattern of the London School of Economics. From June 1925 to March 1928 he taught mercantile law, part-time, at Batliboi's Accountancy Training Institute, Bombay. He was also Professor of Law in the Government Law College, Bombay from June 1928 to March 1929 and accepted a part-time Professorship in the same college in June 1934, and after a year, was appointed the Principal of this college for the subsequent three years. Indeed, Ambedkar's main intention of constructing 'Rajgruha' his house at Dadar, Bombay, was to make personal library for his books which he purchased in huge quantity.

Ambedkar considered education as the most important means for the nation-building and social well being of the people. He strongly advocated the spread of universal education among Depressed Classes who were denied the same for centuries. Denial of education has thrown the Depressed Classes into the morass of ignorance, a slough of despond, perpetual bondage and eternal deprivation. Ambedkar founded Bahishkrit Hitkarni Sabha in 1924 particularly for the educational development of dalits. On behalf of the Bahishkrit Hitkarni Sabha, on 29 May 1928, he submitted before the Indian Statutory Commission, popularly known as the Simon Commission, on the state of education of Dalits.

It is interesting to study the extraordinary system of colleges started by Ambedkar. He founded colleges, schools to name; the most prestigious Siddharth College of Commerce and Economics and Siddharth College of Law in Mumbai. He worked to promote the spread of education particularly among the dalits and OBCs' by opening hostels, libraries, social centers, study circles and industrial and agricultural schools. He fought for the provision of scholarships for the poor and downtrodden sections of the society and even to send them abroad for higher studies.

Ambedkar was responsible for the establishment of the Depressed Classes Education Society in June 1928 that established hostels in Panvel, Thane, Nasik, Pune and Dharwad for high school students belonging to dalit and backward classes.

On 8th July 1945, Ambedkar founded People's Education Society, Bombay with sole purpose of educational development of dalits. The People's Education Society was instrumental for the establishment of the Siddharth College of Arts and Science, Bombay in 1946. Under the direction of the society, several educational institutions were set up to cater the educational needs of dalit community. They are namely, Siddharth Night School in 1947, Milind Mahavidyalaya in 1950, Siddharth College of Commerce and Economics in 1953, Milind Multipurpose High School in 1955 and Siddharth College of Law in 1956. All these educational institutions testify his significant contribution to the field of education. The products of these institutions have occupied positions of prestige and power in fulfillment of Ambedkar's vision.

Ambedkar was very particular in developing the primary education. He could see that free and compulsory primary education for the children up to the age of fourteen years was included in the Directive Principles of State Policy in the Indian Constitution. According to Ambedkar the object of primary education is to see that every child that enters the portals of a primary school does leave it only at a stage when it becomes literate and continues to be literate throughout the rest of his life.[1]

To achieve this objective he felt there should not be dropouts. The remedy for the problem of dropouts, he suggests to spend sufficient money on primary education to see that every child that enters a school reaches the higher education.[2]

Ambedkar's educational philosophy is not just for dalits and backward classes, indeed it meant for all sections of the society. He wanted to make education to be within the reach of everyone and particularly higher education to be made as cheap to the poorer classes as it can possibly be made. Ambedkar opposed the commercialization of education. He was of the opinion that the Education Department is not a department, which can be treated on the basis of quid pro quo. Education ought to be cheapened in all possible ways and to the greatest possible extent, particularly for the lower classes that were at a stage just to enter into the high schools, middle schools and colleges.[3]

Ambedkar was very much against the education policy that perpetuates disparity in the comparative advancement of education of different classes. He observed that the higher educational growth among the caste Hindus than backward communities due to historical social prejudice that resulted in unequal status and progress within the society. To over come educational disparity among various communities, he emphasized that to give favoured treatment to those who are below the level. He felt that the principle of equality of treatment to people who are unequal is simply another name for indifferentism and neglect. Based on this argument he maintains that to adopt principle of inequality that is to provide special privileges for hitherto educationally neglected communities.[4]

Ambedkar felt education is necessary for females as it is for males. He advised them not to marry at early age and go for higher education.

Ambedkar's educational philosophy is not just for backward classes, indeed it meant for all sections of the society. He wanted to make education to be within the reach of everyone and particularly higher education to be made as cheap to the poorer classes as it can possibly be made. Ambedkar, in his presidential address delivered in Depressed Classes conference held at Mahad on March 19 and 20, 1927, suggested that parents to provide the best possible education to children. He said "there will be no difference between parents and animals if they will not desire to see their children in a better position than their own. The better position is possible only through education."

Ambedkar did not want education for the sake of getting degrees only. For him education is a character builder. In his words, "Education as a sword and being double-edged weapon is dangerous to wield. An educated man without character and humility is more dangerous than a beast. If his education is detrimental to the welfare of the poor, the educated man is a curse to society. Fie upon such an educated man! Character is more important than education".

Ambedkar appealed to the teachers to reorganize University education to meet the requirements of the modern world and to make the University a place for knowledge and not a center for training clerks.

For students, Ambedkar told: "Knowledge is the foundation of a man's life and every effort must be made to maintain the intellectual stamina of a student and arouse his intellect". He also said: "Today everybody is after politics and films, but social service has a greater value because it builds up character. The purpose of education should be social service".

Ambedkar's message particularly to youth and students is: "Everyone must cherish a noble ideal. Whatever might be one's ideal either of national progress or of self-development, one should patiently exert one self to reach it." He further said: "All great things in the World are achieved by patient industry and by undergoing toil and tribulations. One should concentrate one's mind and must on one's goal. Man must eat to live and should live and work for the well-being of society".

Ambedkar wanted that everyone should strive endlessly, sacrifice the present pleasures for a great future and should go through the ordeal of fire and sacrifice till you attain the goal.

Babasaheb Ambedkar visualized particularly the centers of higher learning like Universities need to become places of academic excellence and cater more educational avenues to the people particularly downtrodden sections.

On 18 March, 1956, Babasaheb Ambedkar paid his last visit to the historic city Agra. Addressing a huge public meeting there on that day, he reviewed the past performance and reflected on future prospects of the movement launched by him. Lamenting that the educated people had deceived him, he gave some useful hints to his followers as to how to take the movement forward. As part his speech, Ambedkar urged the Government employees to contribute for the educational development of the fellow dalits. He felt, " there is some progress in education in our society. By acquiring education some people have reached the higher positions. But these educated people have deceived me. I was hoping that after acquiring high education they would serve the society. But what I am seeing is that a crowd of small and big clerks have gathered around, who is busy in filling their bellies."[5]

Ambedkar urged Government employees, "Those who are employed in government services, it is their duty that they should contribute willingly 20th part of their salary to the cause. Then only the society will progress. Otherwise only one family will improve. The boy who is educating in a village, the entire society has expectation from him. One educated social worker can prove a boon for them."[6]

In his same address, Ambedkar appealed to students and youth: "My appeal to the students is that after acquiring education, instead of doing some clerical job, he should serve his village or locality people, by which, exploitation and injustice arising out of ignorance can be stopped. Your emancipation lies in the emancipation of the society."[7]

Ambedkar's perspective of education is to cultivate self-respect among the dalits. He declared, "Self-respect is more important than the material gains. Our struggle is for honour, for self-respect, not only for the economic progress alone."[8]

The purpose of education as Ambedkar perceived is that to develop human mind with pure thoughts and with enthusiasm. He felt that there is a difference between man and animal. Whilst the beast needs nothing save its daily food for existence, the human being who is endowed with the physique and the sentient mind has to develop both. Mind must be developed side by side with the body. Mind should also be filled with pure thoughts.[9]

In his words, "personally, I believe that it would not be in the least advantageous to have anything to do with the countries where people believe that 'eat, drink and merry' should be the motto of life. Keeping in view the masses one should bear in mind that just as we must have a healthy body in order to be free from disease, so in order to keep the body healthy we must also develop the sentient mind, or else it would be futile to say that man is developing and making progress."[10]

For the question that why does the human mind become diseased?, Ambedkar finds the reason that so long as the human body is not free from suffering, mind cannot be happy.[11]

To quote him, "there is a saying by Ramdas, Maharashtrian Saint, that if a man lacks enthusiasm, either his mind or body is in a diseased condition. Now what saps the enthusiasm in man? If there is no enthusiasm, life becomes a drudgery—a mere burden to be dragged."[12]

Ambedkar declares, "Nothing can be achieved if there is no enthusiasm. Why does one lose enthusiasm? Main reason for this lack of enthusiasm on the part of a man is that an individual loses hope to get an opportunity to elevate oneself. Hopelessness leads to lack of enthusiasm. The mind in such cases becomes diseased. One who sees no ray of hope of escaping from the present misery lacks the enthusiasm and is always cheerless. When is enthusiasm created? When one breathes in an atmosphere where one is sure of getting the legitimate reward for one's labours, only then one feels enriched by enthusiasm and inspiration."[13]

Ambedkar felt "if the teachers in school start commenting, 'Oh, this—here is a Mahar (Chamar) boy. How did he secure the first position in his class? What business has he to stand first in the class?.' Only the Brahmins are entitled to secure the first position. Now what enthusiasm, what inspiration, what hope can the Mahar (Chamar) boy have in these circumstances? How will he advance in life and make progress? For inspiration and enthusiasm one must have a healthy and sound mind. Such a man is capable of surmounting all kinds of difficulties. He has confidence, courage and will to rise and that gives him the inspiration and enthusiam."[14]

Ambedkar was opposed to the spread of education based on the ideals of Hinduism as he felt, "unfortunately, Hinduism which is founded on the ideologies of inequality and injustice leaves no room for the development of enthusiasm. So long as the Untouchables continue to slave under the yoke of Hinduism, a diabolical creed—they can have no hope, no inspiration, and no enthusiasm for better life. They might produce no more than a few hundred clerks—poor clerks who will do nothing except filling their bellies. What else can they do? Then we shall need super clerks to protect them from injustices and various kinds of atrocities. Common masses of the untouchables will not gain anything. The Scheduled castes can never feel enthusiastic about and derive inspiration from Hinduism."[15]

Ambedkar is of the opinion that man derives inspiration if his mind is free to develop. He explains, "You know the proprietors of mills. They appoint managers in the mills who extract work from the labour. The proprietors remain so much engrossed in their work that they have little time to develop their minds. While they accumulate wealth and become economic giants they remain mental dwarfs. We have started this movement to develop and educate our minds."[16]

Ambedkar describes his own experience in this context, "I may tell you how I got my education. Owing to the poverty I used to attend school with nothing more than a loincloth on my body. I could not get water to drink in the school. I had to go without water for many days. My mother instructed me to address the strangers with respect. There was a lady peon, Maratha by caste, in our school. Even my satchel was untouchable for her. When thirsty, I was not allowed to touch the tap myself. Untouchability was observed even in Elphinstone College, Bombay. What can be expected in this kind of circumstances?"[17] He utterly disgusted with the prevailing social environment, which had no enthusiasm to provide particularly to dalits.

Narrating another interesting experience about how dalits don't get enthusiasm even if they provided opportunities due to the impact of Hindu social environment, Ambedkar felt that untouchability couldn't be removed by education alone. It is noteworthy that he persuaded Lord Linlithgow, the then Viceroy of British India, to sponsor few Scheduled Caste students for prosecuting their higher studies in foreign Universities. He describes, "During British regime I was a member of the Viceroy's Executive Council. Lord Linlithgow was the Viceroy. A certain amount of money was allocated for expenditure on general education. Out of this a sum of three lacs of rupees was sanctioned for Aligarh Moslem University and an equal amount for the Benares Hindu University. While talking to the Viceroy one day I raised this issue. I told the Viceroy that a sum of Rs. 3,00,000 had been given to Aligarh Moslem university and an equal amount had been made available to Benares Hindu University. The Untouchables are neither Hindus nor Moslems. But they are really more backward than either of these communities. An amount proportionate to their population should also be allotted to the Scheduled Castes people for their education. Lord Linlithgow asked me to give in writing whatever I wanted to say in this regard. I submitted a memorandum. Europeans were generally sympathetic in their outlook. He agreed to my proposal and granted a sum of Rs. 3,00,000 for the Scheduled Castes. Now the question arose as to how to spend that money. Viceroy wanted this amount to be spent on the education of the girls belonging to the Scheduled Castes, and suggested Boarding Houses be built for them.

"If this money is spent in this manner to build Boarding Houses in order to make the illiterate girls belonging to the Scheduled Castes educated, I thought, soon we shall require money for providing them with good, food too. Poor our people are, how shall they get these things for their daughters. From where will our people get money to bear the expenses on food in the Boarding houses? Our girls do not need any training in the art of cooking. What will be the result of this education and then the question of their marriages?

"Meanwhile government spent on other items but withheld the amount earmarked for the education of the Scheduled Castes. I went to Lord Linlithgow once again and had a straightforward talk on this topic. I put this question to the Viceroy, Lord Linlithgow. 'Am I not better than 500 graduates?' 'Yes, of course, you are' replied, Lord Linlithgow. Then I asked him, 'Do you know the reason why I say so?' He did not know. I had to convince the Viceroy that a person who received education in a foreign University was as good as 50 graduates of the Indian universities put together. I am personally equivalent to 50 graduates. My education is so thorough that I am capable of holding any office of the Government with confidence. I need such learned men who should be capable of holding the key position whence they should work in the most effective manner for the betterment of the community. If you really want to do something for the uplift of the untouchables you will have to produce such people as would be able to ameliorate their condition. Merely producing clerks will not do.

"Lord Linlithgow agreed to my suggestion and the result was that 16 boys belonging to the Scheduled Castes were sent abroad for higher education. Out of these sixteen, some took full advantage of this opportunity and others did not. They got only half-baked and returned home. The reason is that there exists no enthusiasm for the Scheduled Castes in Hinduism, though such an atmosphere exists for Brahmins and other castes."[18]

Ambedkar is of the opinion that besides the lack of cheerful atmosphere, congenial for human development there is no equality in Hindu religion.[19] He is of the firm belief that Hindu religion and Hindu social order have ruined dalits. He states, "This religion (Hindu) and this social order has ruined us. But this is not going to stop here. This would ruin the Hindus themselves and ultimately India. I do not accuse the Hindu religion in vain. This religion cannot save anybody. It has no life in it."[20] He feels, "Hinduism cannot save anybody. There is no salvation for anybody in Hinduism. According to the tenets of Hinduism only the so-called higher castes have been benefited. There is no exaggeration in my statement. What have the Shudras (OBCs) or the Untouchables (SCs) gained? As soon as the wife of a brahmin woman conceives, she thinks of the High Court whether any post of a judge has fallen vacant but when our woman becomes pregnant, she cannot think of anything better than a sweeper's post under the municipal Committee. This deplorable situation exists only because Hinduism has inculcated this kind of ambitions to the latter. No change in our status can be expected if we continue to be slaves of Hinduism. If we have any hope it is by renouncing the Hinduism..."[21]

For Ambedkar education is a means of emancipation. He emphasizes on the formal education. He feels that it is seldom possible that a man may earn name and fame in the world without having been imparted formal education and training. So it is very essential that every man, seeking to pursue whatsoever occupation, must receive formal education. If and when such education is imparted to him right from the very beginning, he can later expand his knowledge by means of well-directed studies, but at the root of it all is education and education alone.[22]

With the help of the path found through education, with the help of knowledge attained through studies, Ambedkar felt that Dalits should be able to reorient themselves in whatever circumstances they have been placed. This is to imply that knowledge should be the best companion of Dalits. The first object of human life is to help the humanity with the attainment of true knowledge of useful and mysterious things and to be happy at the realization of God's infinite skills, manifest in the form of visible things and, events, before which the pleasures derived from other carnal sources should seem insignificant. Hence, the need to endow dalits with discipline and virtue. The second object is to become so resourceful that dalits could command means to satisfy their wants and to earn name and fame in the world despite poverty and adversity. Of these two objects, the second one is followed by a larger number than the first.[23] It is a general rule, so to say, that every man is naturally endowed with power of excelling other men in this or that matter. If he receives formal education, he will certainly surpass them in some way or the other.

Ambedkar wanted the education to be useful to ameliorate the conditions of the poor. For him, the system of education should be capable of enhancing the nation's wealth, which is the basis of all human pleasures. It is of little practical value to the occupations of the peasants, the artisans and other people engaged in other useful trades, if education could not enhance the skills of their trades that have been instrumental in multiplying the wealth of the nation.[24] He was of the opinion that due to age-old false educational system only bookish knowledge had accumulated in just one particular class and that should not be seen as the spread of education in our country. Indeed, tradiiional education had not benefited all sections particularly those who toil for the well being of the whole society, from whom the government collected large revenue and particularly the excluded classes.[25]

Babasaheb Ambedkar finds education as the means of social change and urges dalits to give utmost importance to education, since it is a true means of their emancipation.26 It facilitates social mobility and also opens doors for modernization. Ambedkar believed that education would not only enhance the abjuration of traditional values but also inculcate preparation for change. He did not visualize education merely as a means of livelihood but as a powerful weapon to liberate downtrodden masses from ignorance and to strengthen their fight against injustice and humiliation. Education as a prerequisite for any kind of progress is evident from his slogan: *Educate, Agitate and Organize.* For Ambedkar, self-help is the best help for self-elevation.

BIBLIOGRAPHY

1. Dr. Babasaheb Bhimrao Ambedkar: *Writings and Speeches,* Bombay, Government of Maharashtra, Department of Education.
2. Robbin Jeanette, Dr. *Ambedkar and His Movement,* Hyderabad, Dr. Ambedkar Publication Society, 1964.
3. V. Chandra Mowli, *B.R. Ambedkar: Man and His Mission,* New Delhi, Sterling.
4. Madhu Limaye, "B.R. Ambedkar: A Social Revolutionary", in *Prime Movers: Role of Individuals in History,* New Delhi, Radiant, 1985.
5. D.R. Jatava, *The Social Philosophy of B.R. Ambedkar,* Agra, Phoenix Publication, 1965.

Notes

1. *Bombay Legislative Council Debates,* Vol. XIX, pp. 971-76, dated 12th March 1927, produced in *Dr. Babasaheb Ambedkar Writings And Speeches,* Vol.2, Education Department, Government of Maharashtra, Bombay, 1982 p. 40.
2. *Ibid.* p. 40.
3. *Ibid.,* pp. 40-41.
4. *Ibid.,* pp. 41-42.
5. Hindi text with Daya Shanker of Agra. Translated by the Editor, *Dalit Voice,* Bangalore, 1-5 August 1990, reproduced in Lella

Karunyakara's *Modernisation of Buddhism: Contributions of Ambedkar and Dalai Lama XIV*, Gyan Publishing House, New Delhi, Appendix-XI: 'On Past Performance and Future prospects', p. 238.

6. *Ibid.*
7. *Ibid.*, p. 239.
8. This is part of Ambedkar's address delivered on 15th October 1956. On 14th October 1956, he embraced Buddhism, along with half a million of his followers, at a historic conversion ceremony at Nagpur. Next day, on 15th October 1956, in a three hour long speech in Marathi, he traced the history of the suffering of the downtrodden through the ages; his life-long struggle to mitigate their suffering and as to why he had chosen Buddhism. This speech was published in D.C. Ahir's *Dr. Ambedkar on Buddhism*, People's Education Society, Bombay, 1982, pp. 31-43, 47-50, and reproduced in Lella Karunyakara's *Modernisation of Buddhism: Contributions of Ambedkar and Dalai Lama XIV*, Gyan Publishing House, New Delhi, Appendix-XII, p. 244.
9. *Ibid.*, p. 247.
10. *Ibid.*, p. 247.
11. *Ibid.*, p. 247.
12. *Ibid.*, p. 247.
13. *Ibid.*, p. 247.
14. *Ibid.*, p. 247.
15. *Ibid.*, p. 248.
16. *Ibid.*, p. 248.
17. *Ibid.*, p. 248.
18. *Ibid.*, p. 248-250.
19. *Ibid.*, p. 250.
20. *Ibid.*, p. 250.
21. *Ibid.*, p. 251.
22. Taken from "Education: A Means of Emancipation" an editorial published in *Mooknayak*, a Marathi periodical, edited by B.R. Ambedkar, dated October 9, 1920. Translated by Prof. C.D. Naik and produced in *Ambedkar's Vision and Education of Weaker Sections*, edited by D.K. Verma & A. Sohrot, Dr. Babasaheb Ambedkar National Institute of Social Sciences, Dr. Ambedkar Nagar (Mhow) & Manak Publications Pvt. Ltd., New Delhi, p. 21.
23. *Ibid.*, pp. 21-22.
24. *Ibid.*, p. 22.
25. *Ibid.*, p. 22.
26. *Ibid.*, p. 23.

10

Dalits and Elementary Educational in India: Problems and Prospects

Dr. Y. Chinna Rao

Before we go in to the details of the elementary education it would be use to briefly look at the rise and growth of education in India, since Independence. Table 10.1 shows Indian population, areas, density, literacy and public expenditure in comparison to some of our neighboring countries. India is home to 17% of the World's total population accommodated in an area which is 2.4% of the world's total area. As against 2820 languages in the entire world, as many as 325 languages are effectively used in India alone. Local dialects change in India almost after every 8-10 kms. The country has witnessed phenomenal educational development—both in quantitative and qualitative terms, since independence. However, the national goals of universal elementary education and total eradication of illiteracy have still remained elusive. The Government is committed, at least on paper, to achieving these national goals and has been steadily increasing the budgetary allocation for education. India spent 4.02% of its GDP on education during 2001-2002 but about 44% of its adult population still remains to be made literate. Table 10.1 compares the population, area, density, literacy rates and level of public expenditure on education in India and some of its neighbouring countries. Afghanistan with 63.75% adult illiterates is at the top, closely followed by Bangladesh, Nepal and Pakistan.

Table 10.2 shows the public expenditure on education in India during the period 1951-52 to 2001-2002. The expenditure on the education sector was slightly less than 1% of the GDP in 1951-52. The percentage expenditure to GDP shows an irregular rise and fall. It rose to 2.33% in 1972-73 but in 1973-74 declined to 2.15%. It increased to 3.07% in 1979-80 and decreased to 2.83% in 1981-82. Continuing to rise and fall slightly, it has reached a level of 4.02% in 2001-2002. Similarly, the percentage of expenditure on education and training to total expenditure of all sectors during the last five decades indicates that it has increased from 7.92% in 1951-52 to 13.17% in 2001-2002 i.e. by 5.25 percentage points during the last five decades. This translates to an annual average growth of 0.11% during the period 1951-52 to 2001-2002.

There has been a considerable increase in the spread of educational institutions during the period 1950-51 and 2001-2002. This is evident from table-10.3. During this period the number of Primary Schools increased by 3 times, while the Upper Primary Schools and Hr. Secondary Schools increased by 16 and 18 times respectively. The number of Colleges for general education and professional education increased by about 24 and 12 times respectively while the number of Universities increased by 10 times during the period. The state wise details of all the recognized institutions in 2001-2002 are given in Table 10.3.

State wise and management wise number of schools by levels along with percentages during 2001-02 are given in tables 10.4 and 10.5. Table 10.4 speaks about the percentage of primary schools under different managements and table 10.5 speaks about upper primary schools. In 1973-74 Government primary schools were 51% of the total primary schools in India. In 1978-79, 1986-87 and 1993-94 a large percentage of primary schools were under local bodies but the trend again shifted in 1996-97 and 2001-02 in which the percentage of Govt. primary schools was higher than local bodies. Government and local bodies put together continued to own more than 90% of primary schools. The contribution of private agencies, as indicated in the Table 10.4, has been small though increasing over the years and was highest in the year 2001-02 (9.08%). The percentage of primary aided schools has been slowly decreasing over the years while the percentage of unaided schools has been increasing. Government continued to manage a majority of upper primary schools, the percentage of such schools managed by Govt. ranging 40% to 51% from 1973-74 to 2001-02. Government and Local Body schools put together accounted for 75.12% to 79.45% of schools; the private sector (aided and unaided) had a percentage share of 21% to 25% over the years.

Table 10.6 presents the growth of sex-wise school enrolment in different stages of school education from 1950-51 to 2001-2002. The total enrolment at the primary, upper primary, Secondary and Sr. Secondary stages increased by 6, 14 and 20 times respectively since 1950-51. The girls' enrolment increased by 9, 37 and 60 times respectively during the same period in the above institutions. The total Scheduled Castes enrolment at the primary (I-V), upper primary (VI-VIII) and secondary/senior secondary (IX-XII) stages of school education from 1980-81 to 2001-2002 (Ttable 10.7), increased by 1.9, 3.4 and 3.7 times respectively. The Scheduled Caste girl's enrolment increased by 2.5, 4.9 and 6.6 times respectively during the same period in the above stages of school education. State wise and sex wise details of enrolments for the year 2001-2002 are given in Table 10.7.

Government has recently argued that expecting both quality and quantity in elementary education is too much, and the Central government cannot take the burden of such high expectations anymore. Such claims made without any rationale lead to larger issues. How much the government spending on education today? According to Institute of Statistics, UNESCO, India has never spent above 4%, and the average for the past three decades is 3,3% the world average is 4.9% in this respect, even above our highest score, even though there is repeated declaration of spending 6% or more on education. The Tapas Mazumdar Committee, in 1999, calculated this cumulative gap between promise and reality, and estimated that it will require an additional investment of Rs. 13,7000 crores per year for the next ten years to make up the short fall in budgetary commitments, which amounts to about 0.6% of the current GDP i.e., merely 60 paisa of every Rs. 100.

When one looks at the literacy rate of Dalits increased from 10.27 in 1961 to 45.20 in 2001, registering an increase of 34.9. percentage points in the last forty years. It is also seen that the gap between the literacy rates of Dalits and that of non-Dalits/Tribal communities has steadily increased from 17.64% in 1961 to 20.28% in 1991. According to the NSSO Survey of 1993-94, as many as 40.5% of Dalit children in rural areas and 24% in urban areas had discontinued school. This discontinuation has been studied as drop-outs by many social scientists, but it perhaps may be looked as "push-outs" by the caste-Hindu society at large. The performance of literacy rate of Dalits in 2001 in states of Bihar (in 24 districts), Jharkhand (in 4 districts) and Uttar Pradesh (in 4 districts) with less than 30 percent.

Although the enrolment ratios in school has improved considerably in most parts of the country, but some of the states such as Uttar Pradesh, West Bengal, Rajasthan still seem to be inadequate. Significantly the figures reveal interesting insights, when one compares the literacy figures of Dalit with the general populace; perhaps one could then argue that lot of dalits in education even after 50 years of reservations has worsened. Below mentioned table reveal the fact that literacy rate of Dalits (54.7%) is less than the national average (64.8). The share of Dalit non-literate population to total non-literate population is 20.5% whereas in the age group of 15-35 it is 21.3%. It is alarming when we take note of the rural-urban divisions.

Literacy Rate of Dalits Comparison with General Population

Age Group + 7 Years	*Total Literacy*	*Males*	*Females*
Overall	64.8	75.3	53.7
Non-Dalits/General	68.8	78.7	58.2
Dalits	54.7	66.6	41.9
Age Group 15–35			
Overall	71.1	81.1	60.4
Non-Dalits/General	75.1	84.0	65.6
Dalits	60.8	74.1	46.7

There has been large scale external assistance for elementary education since the 1990s, following commitments made by the international community at the Jomitien Conference, Thailand in March 1990. It is widely known fact that in accordance with the Constitutional mandate to ensure free and compulsory education for all children up to the age of 14 years, provision of universal elementary education has been a salient feature of national policy since Independence. Since 1950 the constitution and its legal statements at the national level have consistently upheld the cause of elementary education but also has been a salient feature. Such ideological endeavour has been central to educational policies since the 1950s, for instance:

(i) *Constitutional mandate 1950:* "The State shall endeavour to provide, within a period of ten years from the commencement of this Constitution, for free and compulsory education to all children until they complete the age of 14 years".

(ii) *National Policy of Education—1986:* "It shall be ensured that free and compulsory education of satisfactory quality is provided to all children up to 14 years of age before we enter the twenty first century".

(iii) *Unnikrishnan Judgement—1993:* "Every child/citizen of this country has a right to free education until he completes the age of fourteen years".

(iv) *Education Ministers' Resolve, 1998:* "Universal elementary education should be pursued in the mission mode. It emphasized the need to pursue a holistic and convergent approach towards Universal elementary education (UEE).

Apart from these national level policies, this education Ministers' resolve has been emphatically spelt out in the National Policy of Education (1986) and the Programme of Action (1992). In addition to these national level policies, number of schemes and programmes were launched in pursuance of the emphasis embodied in the NPE and the POA. These include:

(i) *Operation Blackboard (OB):* The scheme of Operation Blackboard was launched in 1987 to provide minimum essential facilities to all primary schools in the country, with three sub-themes: (A)Continuation of ongoing OB to cover all the remaining primary schools especially those in SC/ST areas; (B) Expanding the scope of OB to provide three teachers and three rooms to primary schools wherever enrolment warrants them; and (C) Expanding OB to upper primary schools to provide (a) at least one room for each class/section (b) a Headmaster-cum-office room, (c) separate toilet facilities for girls and boys, (d) essential teaching learning equipment including a library, (e) at least one teacher for each class/section and (f) a contingency grant for replenishment of items, consumable and minor repairs, etc.

(ii) *Non-Formal Education (NFE):* In 1988 when the Centrally Sponsored Scheme of the Non Formal Education was formulated by the MHRD, since 1988 clearly demonstrates that Universal Elementary Education can only be achieved if Non-Formal Education is made available as a viable alternative to formal school education.

(iii) *Teacher Education (TE):* As envisaged in the National Policy on Education, the Centrally Sponsored Scheme of Restructuring and Reorganization of Teacher Education was taken up in 1987 to create a viable institutional infrastructure, academic and technical resource base for orientation, training and continuous upgradation of knowledge, competence and pedagogical skills of elementary school teachers in the country. The scheme has the following five components: (a) Setting up of District Institutes of Education and Training (DIETs) to organize, pre-service and in-service courses for elementary school teachers and for personnel working in non-formal and adult education; (b) Strengthening of Colleges of Teacher Education (CTEs) and development of about 50 of them as Institutes of Advance Study in Education (IASEs); (c) Revitalization of State Councils of Education Research & Training (SCERTs); (d) Mass Orientation of school teachers under a planned programme to be implemented under the supervision of NCERT; (e) Establishment and Strengthening of Departments of Education in the Universities through Universities Grants Commission (UGC).

(iv) *Mahila Samakhya (MS):* The Mahila Samakhya programme was launched in 1988 in pursuance of the goals of the New Education Policy (1986) and the Programme of Action as a concrete programme for the education and empowerment of women in rural areas, particularly of women from socially and economically marginalized groups.

In addition to these national level programmes and schemes, there have been State specific Basic Education Projects like the Andhra Pradesh Primary Education Project (APPEP); Bihar Education Project (BEP); Lok Jumbish (LJP) in Rajasthan; Education For All Project in Uttar Pradesh; Shiksha Karmi Project (SKP); in Rajasthan; National Programme of Nutritional Support of Primary Education (MDM); and the District Primary Education Programme with objectives to provide access to all children to primary education through formal primary schools or its equivalent through alternatives; to reduce overall dropouts at the primary level less than 10 percent; to increase achievement levels by 25 percentage points over and above the measured baseline levels; and to reduce disparities of all types to less than 5 percent.

In all these programmes, policies and schemes, common basic feature is emphasis on elementary education. Why only the elementary education was is stressed upon? It is because; the social justice and equity are by themselves a strong argument for providing basic education for all. It is an established fact that the basic education improves the level of national well-being especially with regard to infant mortality, nutritional status of children, life expectancy and so on. Studies have shown that the basic education significantly contributes to economic growth. Following this a separate Department of Elementary Education and Literacy, headed by an Independent Secretary, was created in November 1999 with the Ministry of HRD to specifically focus on EFA goals and a constitutional amendment has been passed by the Parliament to make elementary education a fundamental right. This new Fundamental Right made it obligatory for the state to provide necessary infrastructure and facilities for provision of elementary education in a given time frame.

Commitment to providing free and compulsory education for all children up to 14 years of age is goal set in the early phase. However, even after fifty years of planned development, providing quality education for all has been illusion. This is not to undermine the significant improvements. Thus, since the earlier programmes and schemes could not realize fully their goals, and once again, after 50 years of Independence, the government has had to tackle the issue with a new scheme eulogizing as Sarva Shiksha Abhiyan. This can be linked partly as response to the on going global concern for education for all, especially following the World Conference on Education for All (EFA) held in Jomtien, Thailand in March, 1990, World Education Forum held at Dakar, Senegal (26-28 April 2000) which adopted a Framework for Action in the process of Education for All programme. The goals adopted in Dakar, came to be popular known as Dakar Framework for Action. This global concern has had crucial influence in the shaping of educational programmes in India. Especially, evident in the policies specified below:

(i) expanding and improving comprehensive early childhood care and education, especially for the most vulnerable and disadvantaged children;

(ii) ensuring that by 2015 all children, particularly girls, children in difficult circumstances and those belonging to ethnic minorities, have access to and complete, free and compulsory primary education of good quality;

(iii) ensuring that the learning needs of all young people and adults are met through equitable access to appropriate learning and life-skills programmes;

(iv) achieving a 50 per cent improvement in levels of adult literacy by 2015, especially for women, and equitable access to basic and continuing education for all adults;

(v) eliminating gender disparities in primary and secondary education by 2005, and achieving gender

equality in education by 2015, with a focus on ensuring girls' full and equal access to and achievement in basic education of good quality;

(vi) improving all aspects of the quality of education and ensuring excellence of all so that recognized and measurable learning outcomes are achieved by all, especially in literacy, numeracy and essential life skills.

Access to education is a basic human right. Elementary education has become a very intensely debated topic in the country in recent years. The intensity of this debate lead the Supreme Court to pass a judgement that Right to Education must be seen in conjunction with the Right to Life. This was followed by Parliament amending the constitution to make the Right to Education a fundamental right for children between the ages of 6 and 14 years. After detailed deliberations, the government of India has launched a new programme, in 2000, known as Sarva Shiksha Abhiyan to achieve the goals of Universalisation of Elementary Education of Satisfactory Quality by 2010. This SSA aim to provide useful and relevant elementary for all children in the 6-14 age group; and to bridge social and gender gaps with the effective participation of the community in the management of schools.

As far as the structure for implementation of this programme is concerned, the Central and State governments together decided to implement the SSA programme in partnership with the local governments and the community. To signify the national priority for elementary education, this programme named after a National Sarva Shiksha Abhiyan Mission is being established with the Prime Minister as the Chairperson and the Union Minister of HRD as the Vice Chairperson. This SSA is expected to work without disturbing existing structures in States and districts but only try to bring the convergence in all these efforts. Its strategies including institutional reforms, sustainable financing, community ownership, community based monitoring etc. Although the 'focus is on targeted groups/communities such as Dalits and Tribals, its positive results are yet to be realized.

Concluding Remarks

There has been large scale funding and assistance for elementary education since the 1990s, following commitments made by the international community at the Jomitien Conference and Dakar framework for Action. Large scale programmes of 'Education for All' emerged in the form of District Primary Education Programmes. These EFA programmes were spread to cover almost half the country along with mass literacy campaigns. Although there has been a substantial increase in the primary and middle schools in India since the fifties, i.e., around three time increase till the nineties itself, the entire population of the country has no adequate access to the facilities for basic schooling, more so in case of Dalits.

A major concern to consider is the level of success achieved in reaching communities such as dalits and tribals, whose children have been traditionally excluded from schools. Although the national statistics show very positive changes, the figures may not represent the field situation accurately. Provision of early childhood care for such groups may be of vital importance due to severe social and economic conditions, and this remains an area that this not adequately addressed by our national policy. For instance, when the SSA adopted the Dakar Framework for Action (which is originally international character), when it got imported to India, they continue to use certain concepts like "vulnerable sections", "disadvantaged children", "ethnic minorities", etc., which are problematic in visualization of the programme in the Indian context. Crucially, no where in its allocation of funding, concentration of a locality where the target communities habitate is given a special thrust in their policy making. Unless and until the policy makes special provisions for targeted groups such as Dalits, and tribals, these groups continued to remain at bay, without any progress. As a result this SSA programme also will remain defunct, at least it will not be of any use to Dalits, as one of many centrally sponsored programmes and schemes that have been winding up. So also the programme, unlike its earlier precedents, needs to recognize the specific needs of the communities and in the process restore their dignity not treating them as objects of

Table 10.1: Population, Area, Density, Literacy & Public Expenditure in India and Some Neighbouring Countries

Particulars	*Population (millons) (2000)*	*Area (Sq.kms)*	*Density*	*Percentage to world*		*Percentage of adult illiterate Population 2000*	*Public expr. on education as % age of GNP (1996)*
World	6055.0*	135604354	45	100	100	20.6	NA
Afghanistan	21.2#	652090	33	0.48	0.35	63.7	N.A.
Bangladesh	129.2	143998	897	0.11	2.13	59.2	2.2
China	1277.6	9596961	133	7.08	21.10	15.0	2.3
India	1027$	3287590	312	2.42	16.96	44.2	3.2
Indonesia	212.1	1904569	111	1.40	3.50	13.0	1.4
Japan	126.9	377801	336	0.28	2.10	NA	3.6
Myanmar	46.4	676578	69	0.50	0.77	15.3	1.2&
Nepal	22.5#	140797	160	0.10	0.37	58.6	3.2@
Pakistan	156.5	796095	197	0.59	2.58	56.7	2.7@
Sri Lanka	18.8#	65610	286	0.05	0.31	8.4	3.4
Thailand	62.0#	513115	121	0.38	1.02	4.4	4.8

Source: Statistical Yearbook, 1999, UNESCO.

reform. This can be possible by ensuring quality education, ensuring access to nutrition, maintenance and motivation of the children belonging to the target communities. However, given the history of state intervention, the SSA is most like to be no different from earlier programmes and will simply be statistical exercise without any change in the lives of various communities who are to be benefited by the SSA.

Table 10.2: Public Expenditure on Education in India (in crore)

Year	*Govt. expenditure on education (Trg. & Rev) by education and other Deptts. (center + state)*	*Total Govt. expenditure on all sector (Rev)*	*GDP at current prices (at factor cost) base year 1993-94*	*% of Expenditure on Education to Expenditure on all sectors*	*% of Education Expenditure to GDP*
1951-52	64.46	814.13	10080	7.92	0.64
1952-53	72.26	857.67	9941	8.43	0.73
1953-54	80.06	908.20	10824	8.82	0.74
1954-55	95.82	973.74	10168	9.84	0.94
1955-56	118.39	1111.26	10332	10.65	1.15
1956-57	132.88	1158.01	12334	11.47	1.08
1957-58	150.26	1416.62	12610	10.61	1.19
1958-59	173.78	1594.36	14106	10.90	1.23
1959-60	207.59	1770.06	14816	11.73	1.40
1960-61	239.56	1997.93	16220	11.99	1.48
1961-62	260.30	2225.40	17116	11.70	1.52
1962-63	278.76	2942.67	18302	9.47	1.52
1963-64	313.93	3488.97	20916	9.00	1.50
1964-65	369.29	3844.91	24436	9.60	1.51
1965-66	432.61	4404.82	25586	9.82	1.69
1966-67	487.83	5100.24	29123	9.56	1.68
1967-68	593.14	5619.77	34225	10.55	1.73
1968-69	649.13	6922.07	36092	9.38	1.80
1969-70	760.23	7908.07	39691	9.61	1.92
1970-71	892.36	8787.12	42222	10.16	2.11
1971-72	1011.07	10610.89	44923	9.53	2.25
1972-73	1150.43	11863.56	49415	9.70	2.33
1973-74	1300.72	12884.48	60560	10.10	2.15
1974-75	1570.67	14625.03	71283	10.74	2.20

1975-76	1849.47	17958.99	75709	10.30	2.44
1976-77	2039.09	20482.83	81381	9.96	2.51
1977-78	2630.60	22666.31	92881	11.61	2.83
1978-79	2994.69	26134.84	99823	11.46	3.00
1979-80	3347.57	30915.39	108927	10.83	3.07
1980-81	3884.20	36398.39	130178	10.67	2.98
1981-82	4435.29	33667.31	152056	13.17	2.92
1982-83	5509.17	43996.18	169525	12.52	3.25
1983-84	6229.53	61889.25	198630	10.07	3.14
1984-85	7455.88	69025.45	222705	10.80	3.35
1985-86	8713.02	67091.41	249547	12.99	3.49
1986-87	9479.13	80454.66	278258	11.78	3.41
1987-88	11798.35	92518.38	315993	12.75	3.73
1988-89	14069.82	107543.75	378491	13.08	3.72
1989-90	17192.50	126045.97	438020	13.64	3.93
1990-91	19615.85	146711.53	510954	13.37	3.84
1991-92	22393.69	170370.38	589086	13.14	3.80
1992-93	25030.30	190327.45	673221	13.15	3.72
1993-94	28279.69	218535.15	781345	12.94	3.62
1994-95	32606.22	251691.92	917058	12.95	3.56
1995-96	38178.09	286194.55	1073271	13.34	3.56
1996-97	43896.48	329389.92	1243546	13.33	3.53
1997-98	48552.14	380728.45	1390148	12.75	3.49
1998-99	61578.91	439768.11	1598127	14.00	3.85
1999-2000	74816.09	512519.33	1761932	14.60	4.25
2000-2001	82486.43	572160.14	1917724P	14.42	4.30
2001-2002	84179.46(R.E)	639048.06	2094013Q	13.17	4.02

Table 10.3: Growth of Recognised Educational Institutions from 1950-51 to 2001-2002

Year	*Primary*	*Upper Primary*	*High/Hr. Sec/Inter/ Pre. Jr. Colleges*	*Colleges for General Education*	*Colleges for Professional Education (Engg., Tech., Arch., Medical & Education colleges)*	*Universities/ Deemed Univ./ Instt. of National Importance*
1950-51	209671	13596	7416	370	208	27
1955-56	278135	21730	10838	466	218	31
1960-61	330399	49663	17329	967	852	45
1965-66	391064	75798	27614	1536	770	64

1970-71	408378	90621	37051	2285	992	82
1975-76	454270	106571	43054	3667	** 3276	101
1980-81	494503	118555	51573	3421	** 3542	110
1985-86	528872	134846	65837	4067	** 1533	126
1990-91	560935	151456	79796	4862	886	184
1991-92	566744	155926	82576	5058	950	196
1992-93	571248	158498	84608	5334	989	207
1993-94	570455	162804	89226	5639	1125	213
1994-95	586810	168772	94946	6089	1230	219
1995-96	593410	174145	99274	6569	1354	226
1996-97	603646	180293	103241	6759	1770	228
1997-98	619222	185961	107140	7199	2075	229
1998-99	626737	190166	112438	7494	2113	237
1999-2000	641695	198004	116820	7782	2124	244
2000-2001	638738	206269	126047	7929	2223	254
2001-2002	664041	219626	133492	8737	2409	272

Table 10.4: Percentage of Primary Schools Under Different Management

Year	*Govt.*	*Local Body(LB)*	*Govt. + LB*	*Private Aided*	*Private Un-aided*
1973-74	50.88	42.47	93.34	5.01	1.64
1978-79	38.96	55.03	93.99	4.42	1.59
1986-87	41.37	51.71	93.08	4.34	2.57
1993-94	44.63	47.47	92.10	3.78	4.12
1996-97	47.78	43.88	91.66	3.34	5.00
2001-02	47.45	43.47	90.92	3.07	6.01

Table 10.5: Percentage of upper primary schools under different managements

Year	*Govt.*	*Local Body(LB)*	*Govt. + LB*	*Private Aided*	*Private Un-aided*
1973-74	50.71	26.86	77.57	17.75	4.67
1978-79	40.31	38.13	78.44	16.90	4.66
1986-87	42.79	32.33	75.12	16.30	8.58
1993-94	45.94	33.51	79.45	9.53	11.02
1996-97	46.41	29.13	75.54	10.25	14.20
2001-02	47.36	29.05	76.41	7.81	15.77

Table 10.6: Enrolment by Stages from 1950-51 to 2001-2002 (In million

Year	*Primary (I–V)*			*Middle/Upper Primary (VI-VIII)*			*High/Hr. Sec./Inter/Pre-Degree (IX-XII)*		
	Boys	*Girls*	*Total*	*Boys*	*Girls*	*Total*	*Boys*	*Girls*	*Total*
1950-51	13.8	5.4	19.2	2.6	0.5	3.1	1.3	0.2	1.5
1955-56	17.1	7.5	24.6	3.8	1.0	4.8	2.2	0.4	2.6
1960-61	23.6	11.4	35.0	5.1	1.6	6.7	2.7	0.7	3.4
1965-66	32.2	18.3	50.5	7.7	2.8	10.5	4.4	1.3	5.7
1970-71	35.7	21.3	57.0	9.4	3.9	13.3	5.7	1.9	7.6
1975-76	40.6	25.0	65.6	11.0	5.0	16.0	6.5	2.4	8.9
1980-81	45.3	28.5	73.8	13.9	6.8	20.7	7.6	3.4	11.0
1985-86	52.2	35.2	87.4	17.7	9.6	27.1	11.5	5.0	16.5
1990-91	57.0	40.4	97.4	21.5	12.5	34.0	12.8	6.3	19.1
1991-92	58.6	42.3	100.9	22.0	13.6	35.6	13.5	6.9	20.4
1992-93	57.9	41.7	99.6	21.2	12.9	34.1	13.6	6.9	20.5
1993-94	55.1	41.9	97.0	20.6	13.5	34.1	13.2	7.5	20.7
1994-95	60.0	45.1	105.1	22.1	14.3	36.4	14.2	7.9	22.1
1995-96	60.9	46.2	107.1	22.7	14.8	37.5	14.6	8.3	22.9
1996-97	61.4	46.8	108.2	22.9	15.2	38.1	15.3	8.7	24.0
1997-98	62.3	48.0	110.3	23.6	15.9	39.5	16.1	9.3	25.4
1998-99	62.7	48.2	110.9	24..0	16.3	40.3	17.3	10.5	27.8
1999-00	64.1	49.5	113.6	25.1	17.0	42.1	17.2	11.0	28.2
2000-01	64.0	49.8	113.8	25.3	17.5	42.8	16.9	10.7	27.6
2001-02	63.6	50.3	113.9	26.1	18.7	44.8	18.4	12.1	30.5

Table 10.7: Enrolment of Scheduled Caste Students in Schools (in 000')

Year	*Primary (I–V)*			*Middle (VI-VIII)*			*High/Hr. Secondary (IX-XII)*		
	Boys	*Girls*	*Total*	*Boys*	*Girls*	*Total*	*Boys*	*Girls*	*Total*
1	2	3	4	5	6	7	8	9	10
1980-81	7213	3768	10981	1621	602	2223	906	246	1152
1981-82	7413	3930	11343	1777	677	2454	973	273	1246
1982-83	7807	4244	12051	1906	741	2647	1091	330	1421
1983-84	8001	4472	12473	2297	999	3296	1395	382	1777
1984-85	8040	4651	12691	2543	1123	3666	1524	429	1953
1985-86	8727	5194	13921	2537	1082	3619	1378	432	1810
1986-87	7871	4655	12526	2315	1099	3414	1090	376	1466
1987-88	9083	5593	14676	2543	1193	3736	1521	507	2028
1988-89	9431	5771	15202	2584	1257	3841	1546	557	2103
1989-90	9523	5877	15400	2623	1298	3921	1701	630	2331
1990-91	9737	6057	15794	2747	1413	4160	1703	635	2338
1991-92	9709	6328	16037	3137	1556	4693	1878	703	2581
1992-93	10317	7034	17351	3478	1933	5411	1822	709	2531
1993-94	10412	7169	17581	3566	2014	5580	1981	827	2808
1994-95	10889	7543	18432	3330	1883	5213	1788	803	2591
1995-96	11284	7892	19176	3453	1992	5445	1854	887	2741
1996-97	11754	8368	20122	3621	2176	5797	1952	975	2927
1997-98	11898	8659	20557	3786	2283	6069	2026	1048	3074
1998-99	11123	8377	19500	3748	2388	6136	2068	1149	3217
1999-2000	11810	8625	20435	3881	2420	6301	2385	1399	3784
2000-01	12059	9136	21195	4066	2628	6694	2418	1394	3812
2001-02	12251	9253	21504	4551	2945	7496	2693	1622	4314

NOTES

1. Satlaj Dighe, "Education: Disadvantaged Communities, Girls and Budget Analysis &Tracking", Document downloaded from the website of Asian South Pacific Bureau of Adult Education, p. 4.
2. Report of the Planning Commission, Government of India, 2005.
3. A. Mushtaque R. Chowdhury et.al (eds.) *Hope not Complacency: State of Primary Education in Bangladesh 1999*, (Campaign for Popular Education, The University Press Limited, 1999), p. 1.
4. For details see the Report of the Committee of State Education Ministers on implementation of the proposal to make elementary education a Fundamental Right, Government of India, Ministry of HRD, Department of Education, New Delhi, 15 January 1997.
5. Education For All, National Plan of Action India, Department of Elementary Education and Literacy, Ministry of HRD, Government of India, New Delhi, 2006, (first published in 2003), p. 3.
6. Gopal Guru, "Understanding Dalit Concept of Education", paper presented at 'South Asian Conference on Education', (November 14-18, 1999), Department of Education, University of Delhi, pp. 15-16.
7. As many as 130 centrally sponsored schemes getting winding up, including Scheme for Hostels for Scheduled Tribe boys and girls; Rehabilitation of Bonded Labour; Integrated Forest Management Scheme; National Welfare of Fisherman and Training, which are major concern of these marginalized vulnerable categories. For details see Chetan Chauhan, "130 Central Schemes face Phase-Out", *The Hindustan Times*, (13 November, 2006), p.11

REFERENCES

Aggarwal, Yash, *Education and Human Resource Development*, (New Delhi: Commonwealth, 1988).

APEID, Towards equality of Educational Opportunities, (Bangkok: UNESCO, 1985).

Haq, Mahbub-ul and Khadija Haq, *Human Development in South Asia*, (Islamabad: HDC, 1998).

MHRD, Selected Educational Statistics, 1997-98, (New Delhi: MHRD, 1998).

National Plan of Action, India, Education for All, (New Delhi: Department of Elementary Education and Literacy, MHRD,2006), (first published in 2003).

Oakes, J., "What Educational Indicators? The Case for Assessing the School Context", *Educational Evaluation and Policy Analysis*, Vol. 11, (1989).

Tyagi, P.N., *Education For All: A Graphic Presentation*, (New Delhi: NIEPA, 1993).

11

Education and Social Mobility Among the Middle Class Dalits

Dr. G. Srinivas

Introduction

Education is a very important indicator of social and economic mobility, mainly in the case of the Dalits who had been kept away from access to education earlier for centuries together. Both Nationalist movement and the socio-religious reform movements strongly advocated education among the Dalits, to empower them, to overcome their social, economical and political disadvantages. Similarly, the post-independence Indian State too laid emphasis on the development of the Dalits through education. Hence, the reservations in employment and political representation were considered more important rather than economic development.

It is evident from such efforts by the Government that, there is a steady progress in literacy among the Dalits, though such progress is sluggish and slight compared to other communities. Notwithstanding this effort, noticeable growth in educational rate among the Dalits had began only recently due to several factors. It was random in nature and confined to very few regions, communities and often to individual families. At a general level, efforts towards education began only recently and it is still a comparatively recent phenomenon. Consequently, the educated among the Dalits in general are predominantly first generation educated.

Education is the major source of social and economic mobility among the Dalits as proved by the emergence of a middle class among them in recent times. Education is the means for achieving social and economic mobility and middle class status in general. It is the same for the Dalits as well. It is evident from the sample that in certain occupations, technical educational credentials are a prerequisite to obtain/ achieve it. In the case of the current constitution of Dalit middle class, education is a deciding factor for membership. The education profile of the respondents of the present study also reflects these claims.

This paper attempts to analyze the role of education in the social and economic mobility among Dalits with a special focus on Dalit Middle Class. By way of substantiation, it heavily draws up on the empirical evidence collected from Hyderabad city during 2002-04.

Higher the educational qualification of an individual, higher is his/her social status among the Dalits. Highly educated Dalits are greatly admired within the community. Even among the respondents, the display of admiration for highly educated Dalits was evident in their constant reiteration that education had been the sole factor contributing to their social and economic mobility.

Until very recently, in spite of having the facility of reservations in education and employment, very few Dalits could make an entry into the modern occupations and professions. Owing to which, the average age of middle class Dalits in these occupations and professions is less compared to other communities among these categories in the middle class.

Educational Profile of Middle Class Dalits

The data presented below pertains to a study conducted by the author during 2002-04 in Hyderabad city as part of his Ph.D. thesis.

Since the respondents belonged to diverse occupational categories ranging from clerks to university faculty, accordingly, their education profile too reflects these variations. It ranges from matriculation to PhD. As part of reservations in employment in government sector, the Dalits are provided

Table 11.1: Educational Profile of Respondents

Respondents' occupation	*Educational profile*					*Total*
	Below Graduation	*Graduation*	*Post Graduation*	*Technical degree*	*PhD*	
Officer cadre	-	2 (1.9)	10 (9.5)	1 (1.0)	2 (1.9)	15 (14.3)
Clerk cadre	1 (1.0)	6 (5.7)	7 (6.7)	1 (1.0)	-	15 (14.3)
University faculty	-	-	3 (2.9)	-	12 (11.4)	15 (14.3)
Bank employee	-	3 (2.9)	12 (11.4)	-	-	15 (14.3)
NGO	-	3 (2.9)	8 (7.6)	4 (3.8)	-	15 (14.3)
Advocate	-	-	-	15 (14.3)	-	15 (14.3)
Doctor	-	-	-	8 (7.6)	2 (1.9)	10 (9.5)
Journalist	-	1 (1.0)	3 (2.9)	1 (1.0)	-	5 (4.8)
Total	1 (1.0)	15 (14.3)	43 (41.0)	30 (28.6)	16 (15.2)	105 (100.0)

with concessions pertaining to minimum qualification for eligibility to these posts. However, the respondents of the present study possessed minimum and in some cases additional educational qualifications. None of the respondents seem to have utilized such concessions.

As seen in Table 11.1, more than half (56.2%) of the respondents have post graduation or more educational qualifications. While 30 (28.6%) have technical qualification, one is an undergraduate and 15 (14.3%) are graduates. Interestingly, there are 16 (15.2%) PhDs spread across university faculty in the sample, (11.4%), officer cadre (1.9%) and 2 doctors (1.9%). Ideally, PhD is a desirable qualification for university faculty alone. However, the fact that there are 2 (1.9%) officer cadre employees and 2 (1.9%) doctors with a doctorate degree indicates their individual interest and motivation in pursuing higher studies and their learning aptitude, which high profile professions demand.

The educational profile of the respondents' parents and grandparents suggests that majority of the respondents were first generation educated. In few instances, wherein either the parents and/or the grandparents were educated, the respondents' had benefited in terms of resources and guidance with respect to their education and career. Second or third generation educated respondents were highly educated in comparison to the first generation educated respondents.

Table 11.2: Educational Profiles of Respondents, their Parents and Grandparents

Education level	*Respondent*	*Father*	*Mother*	*Grandp-arents**
Illiterate	-	55 (52.4)	73 (69.5)	98 (93.3)
Literate	-	10 (9.5)	4 (3.8)	2 (1.9)
School level	-	28 (26.7)	27 (25.7)	1 (1.0)
Below Graduation	1 (1.0)	-	-	-
Graduation	15 (14.3)	7 (6.7)	1 (1.0)	-
Post Graduation	43 (41.0)	-	-	-
Technical Education	30 (28.6)	5 (4.8)	-	-
PhD	16 (15.2)	-	-	-

No Response	-	-	-	4 (3.8)
Total	105 (100.0)	105 (100.0)	105 (100.0)	105 (100.0)

* In cases of variation in educational qualification among grandparents, only the highest education of one or more grandparents has been counted.

While the respondents' educational profile ranges from under graduation to PhD, among parents and grandparents, education levels ranged mostly from graduation to school level respectively. Among them, fathers were comparatively highly educated. This indicated that Dalits had access to education only in recent times. Apart from that, Dalit men had the privilege of being highly educated in comparison to Dalit women. The educational profile of the respondents' fathers, mothers and grandparents shows that the majority among all the three categories are predominantly illiterate. Few of the respondents' fathers, mothers and grandparents had been educated up to the school level; they were 26.7%, 25.7% and 1.0% respectively. There were 6.7%, graduates among fathers and mothers. One percent of the mothers had completed graduation and 4.8% of the fathers had had technical education as well.

The pattern of occupation too corresponds with that of education, placing fathers over mothers and grandparents. Similarly, Dalit men were better placed in modern occupations compared to Dalit women.

Education in Paternal Family

In the case of the respondents of the present study, more than half were second generation educated. However, the previous generation's level of education was very less. In few instances, such a background helped the respondents to set high goals for themselves education-wise. In few other instances, the respondents' siblings, largely elder brothers, had been educated, thereby motivating and encouraging them to set higher goals educationally for themselves.

Table 11.3 Education in Respondents' Paternal Family Started with

Respondents' occupation	*Education in the respondents' family started with*					*Total*
	Respo-ndent	*Father*	*Brother*	*Sister*	*Paternal grand father*	
Officer cadre	6(5.7)	6(5.7)	-	-	3(2.9)	15(14.3)
Clerk cadre	5(4.8)	5(4.8)	3(2.9)	1(1.0)	1(1.0)	15(14.3)
University faculty	4(3.8)	7(6.7)	2(1.9)	-	2(1.9)	15(14.3)
Bank employee	3(2.9)	5(4.8)	3(2.9)	-	4(3.8)	15(14.3)
NGO	4(3.8)	6(5.7)	2(1.9)	-	3(2.9)	15(14.3)
Advocate	7(6.7)	5(4.8)	3(2.9)	-	-	15(14.3)
Doctor	3(2.9)	5(4.8)	2(1.9)	-	-	10(9.5)
Journalist	2(1.9)	2(1.9)	-	-	1(1.0)	5(4.8)
Total	34(32.4)	41(39.0)	15(14.3)	1(1.0)	14(13.3)	105(100.0)

Overall, education in the respondents' families began with other family members. While in 34 (32.4%) instances, the respondents were the first to be educated, in cases where the other members of the family were the first to be educated, the figures were: father: 41 (39.0%) instances, brother: 15 (14.3%) instances, sister: 1 (1.0%) instance and paternal grandfather: 14 (13.3%) instances. A comparison between male and female respondents shows that, the female respondents were mostly second generation educated, the proportion of educated women in the families of the respondents had risen by almost three times the original figure and in the case of male respondents, the proportion of educated men had doubled. Thus, significant changes seem to have occurred for women in comparison to men, in terms of access to education and motivation and encouragement from family members, which was absent earlier. Another important factor is that access to education becomes possible for Dalit women only when a relative in the previous generation had availed of education. This becomes significant when we find that 28 male respondents and 5 female respondents were first generation educated.

An occupation-wise comparison shows that, respondents

employed as officer cadre, university faculty, bank employees, NGO professionals and journalists were second generation educated, while in the case of clerical cadre and advocates, majority were first generation educated. Only in the case of doctors, equal numbers of first and second generation educated were found. The present generation of the respondents had entered into a diverse range of occupations, partly facilitated by the attempts by the earlier generation to acquire some level of education.

Table 11.4 Respondents' Education, Occupation and Monthly Income in Comparison with their Siblings

Gradation	*Respondents' education, occupation and monthly income in comparison with their brothers & sisters*		
	Education	*Occupation*	*Monthly income*
Similar	3(2.9)	6(5.7)	9(8.6)
Lower	60(57.1)	54(51.4)	64(61.0)
Higher	2(1.9)	-	-
Some higher & some lower	29(27.6)	34(32.4)	21(20.0)
Not Applicable*	11(10.5)	11(10.5)	11(10.5)
Total	105(100.0)	105 (100.0)	105 (100.0)

* No siblings.

A comparison of the respondents' and their siblings' education, occupation and monthly income showed that in majority of the cases, the siblings had lower levels of education (57.1%), occupation (51.4%) and monthly income (61.0%) compared to the respondents. In the case of other respondents, where some siblings had higher and lower levels of education (27.6%), occupation (32.4%) and monthly income (20.0%), the figures shown were significant due to their implications for the social and economic mobility of the respondents. In two cases, the respondents' siblings had higher levels of education than the respondents; however, this difference is absent in the occupation and monthly income categories.

The social background of middle class Dalits, particularly

Table 11.5: Respondents' Education, Occupation and Monthly Income with that of their Spouses

Spouse's	*Grading*								*Total*
	Lower		*Equal*		*Higher*		*NA*		
	*SMR**	*SFR***	*SMR*	*SFR*	*SMR*	*SFR*	*SMR*	*SFR*	
Education	64	-	11	17	-	4	5	4	105
	(61.0)		(10.5)	(16.2)		(3.8)	(4.8)	(3.8)	(100.0)
Occupation	65	17	6	1	4	3	5	4	105
	(61.9)	(16.2)	(5.7)	(1.0)	(3.8)	(2.9)	(4.8)	(3.8)	(100.0)
Monthly Income	64	18	7	-	4	3	5	4	105
	(61.0)	(17.1)	(6.7)		(3.8)	(2.9)	(4.8)	(3.8)	(100.0)

*SMR= Spouse of male respondent

**SFR= Spouse of female respondent

the respondents suggests that, in general, compared to their present socio-economic status, their paternal family's socio-economic background is low. The education, occupation and income levels of the respondents are higher compared to their paternal families. There is a visible upward mobility in the case of respondents. At the same time, their paternal family's low socio-economic status has a bearing on their upward mobility.

In Table 11.5, education, occupation and monthly income of respondents' spouse were analysed. In the case of occupation and monthly income, spouses of respondents who were employed in lower occupational categories and those who are not employed were classified under lower occupation and monthly income category.

The educational profile of the male respondents were either equal to or higher than their spouse , while in the case of female respondents, not only their spouse's education, but occupation and monthly income were also equal or higher compared to their own. In the case of male respondents, education of their spouse was less than theirs (68.6%), while in the case of female respondents, it was equal (14.3%) or more (8.6%) compared to their spouse. Similarly, occupation and monthly income of male respondents were more than their spouse in comparison to female respondents.

The figures reveal that in the case of occupation and monthly income of spouse, female respondents were better off compared to male respondents since it had implications for social and economic status in terms of a higher standard of living.

A comparison between the age and education of respondents' children showed that, of the 90 cases in which respondents had children, there was similarity in terms of age group distribution and education among respondents' children. While 77 (73.3%) of them were below 25 years of age and pursuing their studies, children of 1 respondent (1.0%) in 26 and above age groups had completed their studies, and 1 (1.0%) respondent had children in both age groups, with some pursuing their studies and some who had completed their studies.

Table 11.6: Age and Education of Respondents' Children

Age	*Education of respondents' children*				
	Studying	*Studies completed*	*Few studing & few completed studies*	*Not Applicable*	*Total*
Between 0-25 years	77 (73.3)	-	-	11 (10.5)	88 (83.8%)
26 years and above	-	1 (1.0)	-	-	1 (1.0)
Both age groups	-	-	1 (1.0)	-	1 (1.0)
Not Applicable	-	-	-	15 (14.3)	15 (14.3)
Total	77 (73.3)	1 (1.0)	1 (1.0)	26 (24.8)	105 (100.0)

In this regard, the problems faced in terms of children's education at school, college and university levels were analyzed in order to understand the nature of such problems and the coping mechanisms adopted. Table 7 presents various such problems faced with regard to education of children.

Table 11.7: Experiences of Problems Regarding Children's Education

Problems faced by respondents' children are related to	*Experiences of problems regarding children's education*					
	At School level		*At College level*		*At University level*	
	Yes	*No*	*Yes*	*No*	*Yes*	*No*
Fees	1 (1.0)	-	-	-	-	-
Standard of institute	1 (1.0)	-	-	-	-	-
Related to learning	12 (11.4)	-	-	-	-	-
Fees & Standard	2 (1.9)	-	-	-	-	-
Not Applicable	-	89 (84.8)	-	105 (100.0)	-	105 (100.0)
Total	16 (15.2)	89 (84.8)	-	105 (100.0)	-	105 (100.0)

As can be seen in the table, only those respondents' children who were pursuing school-level education had problems. Majority of these problems were related to learning and a few were related to fees and standard of the school. These implied their economic inability to afford fees and thereby access to good schools, though it could not be ascertained whether this was due to multiple demands on their limited income. However, in some cases respondents' children were pursuing studies at college and university levels, but no problems were reported in these cases, indicating general affordability among these respondents to provide their children with a good education.

Aspirations Regarding Children's Future

Aspirations regarding children's future are reflective of the Dalits' own achievements and their aspirations for future generations. Higher the occupational status and income, higher are the aspirations for their children. Along with stability, high income and social prestige, there are other expectations

Table 11.8: Respondents' Aspirations for Children's Future

Respondents' occupation	*Respondents' aspirations for children's future*						*Total*
	Government job	*Settling abroud*	*Independent professional*	*Entrepreneurship*	*Children's own choice*	*No response*	
Officer cadre	9 (8.6)	-	1 (1.0)	-	-	5 (4.8)	15 (14.3)
Clerk cadre	4 (3.8)	-	2 (1.9)	-	6 (5.7)	3 (2.9)	15 (14.3)
University faculty	4 (3.8)	-	3 (2.9)	1 (1.0)	4 (3.8)	3 (2.9)	15 (14.3)
Bank employee	4 (3.8)	1 (1.0)	3 (2.9)	-	1 (1.0)	6 (5.7)	15 (14.3)
NGO	4 (3.8)	-	1 (1.0)	-	4 (2.9)	6 (5.7)	15 (14.3)
Advocate	5 (4.8)	-	4 (3.8)	-	2 (1.9)	4 (3.8)	15 (14.3)
Doctor	2 (1.9)	-	3 (2.9)	-	3 (2.9)	2 (1.9)	10 (9.5)
Journalist	2 (1.9)	-	-	-	2 (1.9)	1 (1.0)	5 (4.8)
Total	34 (32.4)	1 (1.0)	17 (16.2)	1 (1.0)	22 (21.0)	30 (28.6)	105 (100.0)

from the children's career. In the case of those social groups among the Dalits, which have achieved a certain level of social and economic mobility, their children are expected to either achieve more or keep up with their own level. Thus, employment in a similar or higher occupational category is a normal expectation of children's future.

Significantly, the respondents who wanted their children to take up occupations similar to theirs were located in government or public sector jobs. Irrespective of occupation and profession, majority wanted their children to be settled in secure occupations like Government service. Among all occupational categories, the major tilt was towards Government job or an independent profession that was secure and remunerative. Other options like business or settling abroad are still a distant dream for the Dalit middle class given their relatively lower level of achievement with respect to economic and social mobility. However, 22 (21.0%) respondents wanted their children to exercise their own choice with regard to career options. Among the 30 (28.6%) respondents who did not respond in this regard, half of them were unmarried and the remaining did not have any children.

Conclusion

The educational profile of the respondents' parents and grandparents suggested that majority of the respondents were first generation educated. In few instances, wherein either the parents and/or the grandparents were educated, the respondents' had benefited in terms of resources and guidance with respect to their education and career. Second or third generation educated respondents were highly educated in comparison to the first generation educated respondents. This indicated that Dalits had access to education only in recent times. Apart from that, Dalit men had the privilege of being highly educated in comparison to Dalit women. The educational profile of the respondents' fathers, mothers and grandparents showed that the majority among all the three categories were predominantly illiterate. The pattern of occupation too corresponded with that of education, placing fathers over mothers and grandparents. Similarly, Dalit men were better placed in modern occupations compared to Dalit women.

REFERENCES

Ram, Nandu, 1988, *The Mobile Scheduled Castes: Rise of a New Middle Class*, Hindustan Publishing Corporation, New Delhi.

Srinivas, G., 2004, Ideology and Identity: A Study of the Dalit Middle Class in Hyderabad, (Ph.D. Dissertation, Mimeo, University of Hyderabad).

Vishwanathan, G. and K. Narasimha Reddy, 1985, *Scheduled Castes: A Study in Educational Achievement*, Scientific Services, Hyderabad.

12

Dalits and Forestry: An Analysis of Participatory Forest Management in Andhra Pradesh

Dr. V.M. Ravi Kumar
G. Ravi

Forest policies in India have undergone perceptible transformation after the 1990s. Concepts like equity, sustainability and partnership with communities were incorporated into new policy initiatives. This process was aimed at crafting a decentralized institutional mechanism to create a platform for peoples' participation in forest management. This resulted in promulgation of Joint Forest Management (JFM) in the early 1990s and subsequent adoption by most of the states in India as a strategy for forest management. Andhra Pradesh (AP) represents one of the progressive forest departments in India, credited to have gone 'beyond' JFM to 'Community Forest Management' (CFM) with the support of the World Bank funding. This process has initiated a wide range of micro and macro level changes in forest management in terms of governance and livelihoods of people. However, after a decade of implementation, PFM found to have not only underperformed than expected level but also initiated widespread exclusion of forest dependent communities. This paper examines the implementation process of Participatory Forest Management (PFM) and assesses its performance in terms of governance and livelihoods.

To analyze the impact of PFM on Dalits' livelihoods in

Andhra Pradesh, the present study organized into four sections: introduction followed by analytical frame work and methodology were mentioned in the first section; section two analyses how the SC/STs were excluded in the decision making process related to forest governance; section three shows how the SC/STs livelihoods were effected after implementation of PFM and final section documents some broad summary and conclusions.

I. Conceptualization of Exclusion

Economic liberalization process of 1990s, had initiated changes in peoples' livelihood systems in India. This change could be tracked in two changing livelihood trajectories. One, due to inherent and structural advantages, certain communities experienced upward trajectory of livelihood change. Second, certain communities, mainly majority of SC/ST and to some extent BCs lack of voice and bargaining powers experienced downward trajectory of livelihoods systems (Farrington et. al., 2006). It is the downward trajectory that majority of the Dalits, and the rural marginalized poor experienced in the context of globalization in India. The word dalit is used in this paper to refer to SC&ST and BC communities who subjected to deprivation due to socio-economic, political, cultural and historical reasons.

Economic liberalization paved the way for globalization process, which significantly alter the demographic composition of India. Rural areas began to experience high level unemployment and weaker sections were excluded from development process. In this context, globalization driven projects, which aimed at elevation of rural poverty human rights and sustainable livelihoods approach to development gained prominence in development discourse. It is argued that "the right to development is an inalienable human right by virtue of which every human person and all people are entitled to participate in, contribute to and enjoy economic, social, cultural and political development, in which all human rights and fundamental freedom can be fully realized'.

In the context of globalization process, which is mainly driven by the market forces certain countries and communities were further marginalized. It is this situation that given rise to human development approach to development process driven by globalization. It is defined as 'the process of enlarging people's choices—not just choices among different detergents, television channels or car models but the choices that are created by expanding human capabilities and functionings—what people do and can do in their lives' (UNDP 1999). It has been also defined as 'need to put people—their needs, their aspirations and their capabilities—at the center of the development effort. And the need to assert the unacceptability of any biases or discrimination, whether by class, gender, race, nationality, religion, community or generation. Human development had arrived (UNDP 1999).

The advocacy of decentralized forest management put forwarded in the context of three-macro level processes: one, structural adjustment reform introduced in the name of liberalization, where scaling down of state functions in several sectors was advocated (Burden, 1996, Hoblley, 1996, Harries, 2000, Manor, 1999, Sharma, 2006, Bauman et. al., 2003); second, application of livelihood centered approach to forest management (Casten, 2005, Sunderline, 2005, Solesburey, 2003, Menzine, 2004, Baumann, 2000, Hoblley and Shelids, 2000) and third process weakening of single party domination and emergence of regional parties, which were compelled to address the voices of marginalized sections (Desai, 2000, Chatterjee, 1999, Kaviraj, 1999, Farrington et. al., 2006).

Implementation process of decentralized institutions in forest management was critiqued by several works. Some studies argued that the objective of equitable distribution of benefits has fallen short in participatory development resulting in poor performance in poverty eradication (Blair, 1996, Adhikari, 2005, Agwral and Gupta, 2005). A study, on performance of decentralized governance in natural resource management in AP and Karnataka, (Bammuan et. al., 2003) proposed that decentralized forest resource management has not significantly increased access of the rural poor and tribals to forest resources. Some of the works demonstrated that envisaged economic benefits have not been achieved in PFM in India (Agrawal and Gupta, 2005, Kumar, 2002, Samata, 2005). The main reason for this underperformance has been the ineffectiveness of institutional structure created by forest management. Recently, some studies have demonstrated constraints for efficient institutional functioning in India. For instance, Madhu Sareen argued that the attitudinal change in forest department, essential for successful PFM has not been achieved in India (Sareen et. al., 2003, Sareen, 2005).

Some of the studies have advocated that globalization driven development projects should take the cognizance of unequal social structures crafted and sustained by caste system in Indian context (Kumaran 2000). The effective implementation of participatory forest policies and their success critically depends on the socio-political dynamics at the ground level. That is, how the existing social or political structures receive or absorb the programme determines the success and sustainability of the programme (Reddy et al, 2005). There has not much work been done on how the unequal social opportunities in the targeted communities have affected the implementation process of participatory forest management? The present paper shows how the SC and STs were excluded from the decision-making process on the one hand and how their livelihoods are getting negatively affected in the context of participatory forest management in Andhra Pradesh.

I. 1. Methodology

Three districts were selected purposively to reflect the three agro-climatic regions of the state. Forest density and concentration of VSS were used as criteria while selecting the districts from each region. Accordingly, Visakhapatnam from coastal Andhra, Kadappa from Rayalaseema and Adilabad from Telangana were selected. The target 'population' for village-level study was the range of forest dependent communities, in particular those, affected by the implementation of PFM, both directly and indirectly. Three VSS village from each district, totally nine VSS were selected by using a stratified random sampling on the basis of the VSS ranking by FD in terms of performance (Table 1). Qualitative methods such as focused group discussions with different stakeholders, semi-structured discussions, personal interviews, case studies, transect walks and village public meetings were mainly used in the present study.

Table 12.1: Details of the Sample Villages

District	*VSS Villages*
Adilabad	Pandhirlodhhi
	Sainagar Thanda
	Heerapur
Kadapa	Ramachandrapuram
	S.R. Palem
	Mudireddypalle
Visakhapatnam	Sobhakota
	Gudlamveedi
	Nandivalasa

II. Participatory Forest Management and Governance Process, Exclusion of Inclusion?

CFM in AP was introduced in 2002 by incorporating several flexible rules to facilitate peoples' participation in forest management. Under CFM, 5000 villages, spread over 14 districts and covering 13,79,862 hectares of forest area were extended funding. It is funded by the World Bank with the total outlay of Rs. 652 crores for the period of five years. The CFM targeted to benefit 55,000 families living in below poverty line (GoAP, 2002). The main object of the CFM scheme is "to reduce rural poverty through improved forest management with community participation" (Go AP, 2002).

Information and awareness about CFM among beneficiaries is an important factor for successful implementation of the programme. This would facilitate active peoples' involvement in the implementation process. In AP, Forest Department (FD) and NGOs played an important role in information dissemination and awareness building on PFM This was aimed at to gain peoples' acceptance to the programme. FD officials projected PFM as a wage employment scheme than a management system. As a result, people perceived PFM mainly as a wage employment scheme than a forest management programme (table 2). In village meetings, forest officials projected CFM as wage employment programme and the entire process of institutionalization, which involved creation of MC, GB and preparation of MC was done hurriedly

Table 12.2: Peoples' perceptions about PFM

Name of the District	*Landless*	*Small and marginal farmers*	*Women*
Adilabad			
Wage Employment	100	100	100
Forest protection	60	75	70
Livelihood improvement	40	65	60
Village development	40	60	50
Kadapa			
Wage Employment	100	100	100
Forest protection	50	60	50
Livelihood improvement	35	50	40
Village development	40	50	40
Visakapatnam			
Wage Employment	100	100	100
Forest protection	40	55	30
Livelihood improvement	50	65	50
Village development	40	60	40

Cutting across all sections, people perceived CFM mainly as wage employment shame (Table 2). While imparting details on CFM, FD officials made several false promises like granting pattas, and loans to muster support from people. This resulted in different perceptions among people on forest management. While majority of landless and women were unaware of the livelihood importance of PFM, small and marginal farmers were aware of benefits. On the role of PFM in forest protection and village development, awareness among landless and women was low. While landless and women were mainly interested in wage employment and the small and marginal farmers are interested in forest protection as they intend to use the grass and wood for agricultural implements that grow in VSS area. As landless could not utilize the forest products like grass, they do not show interest in forest protection, rather look for wage as a main benefit.

II.1. Institutionalization of VSS (Vana Samrakshana Samathi)

The process of institutionalization of CFM starts with creation of VSS with a General Body (GB), with households of the village as members. The Section Officer convenes the meeting with all the households of the village. Presence of 50% households was fixed as quorum for the meeting. After explaining the concept of CFM, VSS was constituted (GOAP, 1992). In the sample villages, forest officials approached the village leaders to convince the people on implementation of CFM. While in Adilabad and Visakhapatnam no NGO was associated in the formation of VSS, in Kadappa, NGOs were involved in formation of GB.

II. 2. Preparation of Micro Plan

Traditionally forests are being managed by the working plans prepared by FD. These plans are prepared with the objective of revenue generation through silviculture treatment and neglected the needs of communities. The concept of Micro Plan (MP) in PFM aimed at incorporating the local priorities and management practices, which benefit communities. It registers the agenda to be followed in VSS works by incorporating local needs in forest management. In CFM policy, emphasis was given to involvement of various actors like Panchayat, NGOs, FD, and communities in conducting the Participatory Rural Appraisal. But as (Profemberger, 1998) argues, since FD field staff needs to create thousands of VSS, they do not have time and training to prepare in-depth plans with community members. This resulted in little responsiveness and relevance to local priorities.

MP drafting has received lot of criticism from civil society in CFM. As per guidelines MPs were supposed to be prepared with the involvement of communities and NGOs. But in practice, the FD played an authoritative role. While preparing MP, PRA was conducted superficially. In case of species selection, design of various works, and other decisions, FD officials played a dominant role. For instance, in Adilabad, FD officials played a dominant role in preparation of MP and in Visakhapatnam and Kadappa MPs were prepared by NGOs under the instruction of FD. While preparing MPs, NGOs have followed FD instructions as they receive financial assistance from FD. NGOs were pressurized to prepare MP in a short period of time. For instance, NGO members in Kadappa informed that NGOs were given two to three days time to prepare MP. This process could not allow preparing a MP that incorporates the needs and choices of communities in forest management.

II.3. Decision Making Process in VSS Management

Decision-making process is an important aspect in institutionalization of forest management process. GB/MC are representative bodies to carry out the management of VSS works with the help of FD. They are expected to take decisions in VSS management with the consent of all BG members. Thus, the success of PFM depended on how better the interests of all groups in communities are addressed (Sarin, 1998). New forms of cooperation have developed, but FD retains the power to author the programme implementation (Sunder *et al,* 2000). This led to prioritisation of FD choices in decision-making process in VSS management. Thus, decision-making process in GB/MC appeared to have caught up in several constraints, which undermined the interests of the poor who depended on forests for livelihood support.

As per CFM guidelines, GB meeting should be conducted at least once in six months and MC meeting should be organized in every month. In the sample villages, frequency of meetings and attendance of members observed to have come down. For instance, in Mudiriddey Pelly VSS in Kadappa, MC meetings were not conducted for more than one year due to conflicts in the village. In other villages, MC meetings were conducted only at the time of fund arrival, and most of the MC members were not aware of the nature of the works to be undertaken in VSS.

Table 12.3: Nature of the Decision taken for VSS Management

Functional Aspects	*VSS*	*FD*	*Other NGO*
1. Organisation of meetings, GB/MC	√	√	√
2. Selection of Forest areas for VSS		√	
3. Micro Plan preparation	√	√	√
4. Identification of works		√	
5. Species selection		√	
6. Carrying out of works		√	
7. Supervision of works		√	
8. Estimating the costs		√	
9. Funds allocation		√	
10. Distribution of harvesting income		√	
11. Distribution of forest products	√		
12. Entry point activities	√	√	√
13. Minute writings	√	√	√
14.NTFP value editions		√	
15. Distribution of livelihood enhancement activities		√	
16. Marketing of forest products		√	
17. Selection of training programme		√	

Source: Data from Field Survey.

The nature of the role played by different actors in decision-making process related to VSS management indicates that all important decisions of VSS management like the forest area to be given to VSS for management, identification of works, species selection, supervision of works, management and conservation models to be adopt by VSS and other important decision are taken by FD (Table 7). Thus, envisaged devolution of powers and autonomy in decision-making, were not delegated to communities. It also shows that as FD plays a dominant role in VSS management ranging from allocation of fund to identification of works, MC became more accountable to FD than people. For instance, RC Puram and SR Palm in Kadappa district, chairpersons behaved like spokespersons of FD. Similar attitude was observed in the tribal areas of Visakhapatnam and Adilabad districts. Elite domination in nexus with FD officials had narrowed down the scope and benefits that were envisaged in the CFM policy. Thus, scope for wider accommodation of peoples' interests in forest management is jeopardized by FD dominance in decision-making process.

Table 12.4: Governance Indicators across Social Categories (in Percentage of response)

Parameters		*Less Hetero-geneous*	*Moderately Heterogen-eous*	*More Heter-ogeneous SC&ST&BC &OCs*
Frequency of att-endance in VSS meetings	Regularly	36	26	8
	Occasionally	60	72	88
	Never	4	2	4
Ability to influence the decisions in the meetings	Always	60	59	74
	Occasionally	24	34	19
	Never	16	7	7
Knowledge about VSS assets includi-ng Common funds	Yes	56	59	83
	No	24	21	10
	No Idea	20	20	7
Accession to meeting minutes	Yes	84	82	87
	No	16	18	13
Does VSS repres-ent majority me-mbers' view?	Yes	88	84	98
	No	12	16	2
How has JFM af-fected Social Coh-esion in the village	No Change	28	11	43
	Increased	33	76	50
	Reduced	39	13	7
How has JFM hel-ped in overall Aw-areness in the village	No Change	60	30	32
	Increased	36	67	67
	Reduced	4	3	1

II. 4. Women Empowerment

Discourse on eco-femininism proposes for the involvement of women in PFM because of their closeness to nature (Shiva, 1989, Kameswari, 2002). Women participation in participatory development schemes has been perceived as an important factor. CFM policy proposed 50 % membership for women in GB/MC. Besides either VSS chairperson or vice-chairperson post is reserved for women (table 10).

Table: 12.5. Women representation in MC

DISTRICT /VSS	*NO. OF MC MEMBERS*	*CP*	*V. C P*
Kadapa			
MR Pelly	8	Male	Woman
SR Palme	8	Woman	Male
RC Puram	8	Woman	Man
Adilabad			
Sai Nagar Tanda	8	Male	Woman
Pandurllludi	8	Male	Woman
Heerapur	8	Male	Woman
Visakhapatnam			
Sobhakota	8	Male	Woman
Gudalemvedi	8	Male	Woman
Nandivalasa	8	Male	Woman

MC= Management Committee, CP= Chairperson, VCP= Vice-Chairperson.

Though the CFM rules ensure the membership for women in GB/MC, women participation in VSS activities was undermined by three factors: one, women chairpersons, belonging to dominant social group were not accessible to poor women. For instance, in Kadapa district, Chairperson of SR Palem is a wife of a government teacher and not accessible to village women. In RC Puram, women chairperson does not even inform the decisions taken in MC meetings. Thus, elite capture of CFM scheme prevents wider women participation in CFM programme. Second factor is, FD staff exclusively consist of men tend to dominate women chairpersons and on the other, women members could not interact with FD staff due to social inhibitions. Third factor is lack of information on GB/MC meetings and VSS works.

Most of the time women remain as passive wage workers than decision makers in VSS management. For instance, a women member from R.C. Puram felt that "we hardly know when the management committee meetings take place. In fact, many members of the management committee do not know what decisions were taken in meetings. Forest officials and NGO members come to village and talk to Chairperson and launch the works. Villagers are informed about VSS works only after the decision was taken". Another factor is that husbands or sons of women chairpersons take lead in management of VSS. For instance, in RC Puram of Kadappa district, Chairperson's take all decisions on behalf of his mother.

In the tribal areas of Adilabad and Visakhapatnam districts, women participation was very low in VSS management activities. Practically, men decide VSS works and all decisions relating to VSS works. A woman from Adilabad district informed that: "All decisions related to VSS works are being taken by men and after the decisions are taken they inform us, we do not have any role in VSS functioning". Increase in women membership in GB/MC does not seem to have ensured their involvement in forest management.

The poor participation of women in MC meetings, especially in tribal areas, is due to lack of information (Table 12). Generally, women participation in MC found to be low, though they attended they could not speak due to taboos and inhibitions. Some of the important constraints for women participation are, many women felt that in GB and MC men dominate and their views were not taken into consideration. They were not informed about MC meetings and decisions taken for VSS management. Thus, male dominated social system was reinforced in PFM operational process resulting in exclusion of women in each and every stage of operational process of PFM in AP. Consequently women choices in forest management are excluded from decision-making process. This resulted in ineffective planning and protection of VSS areas.

Table: 12.6. Status of Financial Transparency in CFM

Name of VSS	*Name of the District*	*Is financial Transparency exist*	*Reasons for existence and non/existence to Transparency*	*DO VSS*
Pandhirlodhhi	Adilabad	Yes	Chairperson is dynamic and accounts of fund and works are published in community hall	NO
Heerapur	"	No	Chairperson and FD officials has close nexus and misuse VSS money	NO
Sainagar Thanda	"	Yes	GB members are informed of expenditure and fund details promptly	NO
Ramachandra-puram	Kadappa	No	Majority people felt, VSS chairperson and FD misuse money and no accounts of VSS funds and expenditure are maintained	NO
Sri Rangaraju Palem	"	No	Funds are not adequately spent by MC, and shows fake accounts of works	NO
Mudireddy Palle	"	No	Fraction of sanctioned money was spent on VSS works and money is misused by chairperson with the support of FD.	NO
Sobhakota	Visakhapatnam	No	MC committee don't shows accounts of VSS works	
Gudlamveedi	"	Yes	Chairperson is honest and put up works of CFM in community hall	NO
Nandivalasa	"	No	MC led by chairperson misuse money for their personal gains.	NO

Though in some VSS like Pandruluddi and Gudlemvedi are in better position in terms of financial transparency, due to the personal initiatives of chairpersons, in the remaining VSS people informed that funds are being misused by MCs in nexus with FD officials (Table 14). Chairperson of Mudireddypallay SC colony informed that FD officials

Table: 12.7: Percentage share of different livelihood activities in study cities

District/. VSS	*Own cultivation*	*Podu.*	*Farm activities, labour*	*Non farm activities*	*Forests/ NTFP/ podu*	*VSS Works*	*Migration*	*Total*
Kadappa								
MR Pelly	10		45	30	5	5	5	100
SR Palem			60	10	15	10	5	100
RC Puram			20	25	45	5	5	100
Adilabad								
H. Pur	10		20	30	10	5	25	100
S N Tanda	50		20	10	10	5	5	100
P. Luddi	60							
	20	-	15	5	-	100		
Visakapatnam								
S. Kota	10	35	25	-	25	10	-	100
G. Veedi	15	40	15	-	20	10	-	100
N. Valasa								
	20	25	20	5	20	5	5	100

Source: Field study.

demand bribes to sanction money for VSS works. At the same time, no VSS has passbooks, muster role registers, estimate copies, and other documents as they are report with FD officials. Chairperson of Ramachandra Puram informed that FD officials took their documents and for the past six months they did not give them in spite of several requests.

III. Livelihood Impact of PFM

In AP, as per latest estimates, about 14 % of population, predominantly belong to tribes; have been critically deepened on forest products as an important source of livelihood. The CFM programme, aimed meeting the livelihood needs with multidimensional strategies. The following table shows the livelihood dependency of people on forests in our study sites.

The above-mentioned table shows that forests provide an important source of livelihoods, particularly in agricultural slak season. In tribal villages, forest dependency is significantly high, together with VSS works. In Visakhapatnam, it constitutes above 50%. Having completed most of the treatment practices in JFM, CFM focused on income generating activities with diversified practices. Due to this, wage based works have significantly declined. The following table shows the wage works undertaken in CFM.

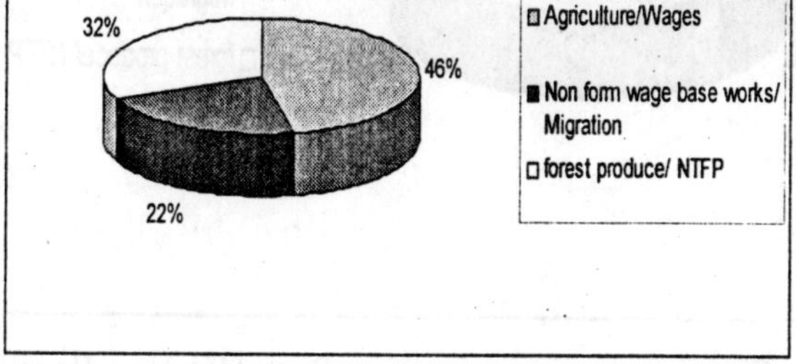

Fig 1: Change in income for Poor HH Poor HH Before JFM in Adilabad District (RS)

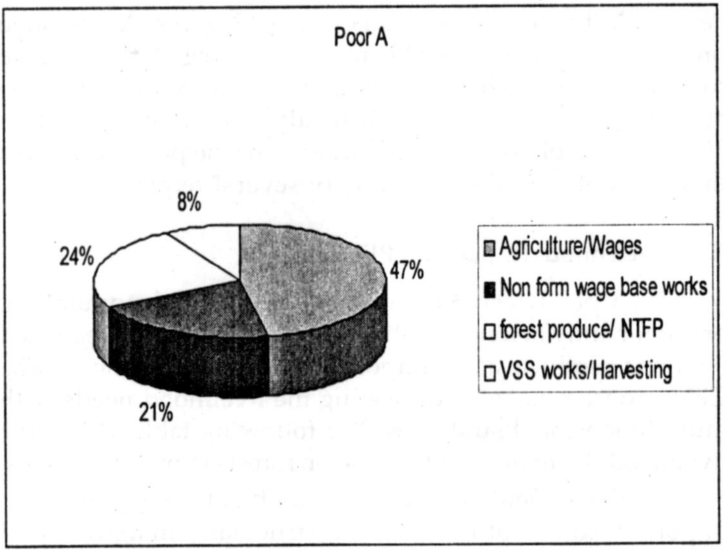

Fig 2: Change in income for After JFM in Adilabad District

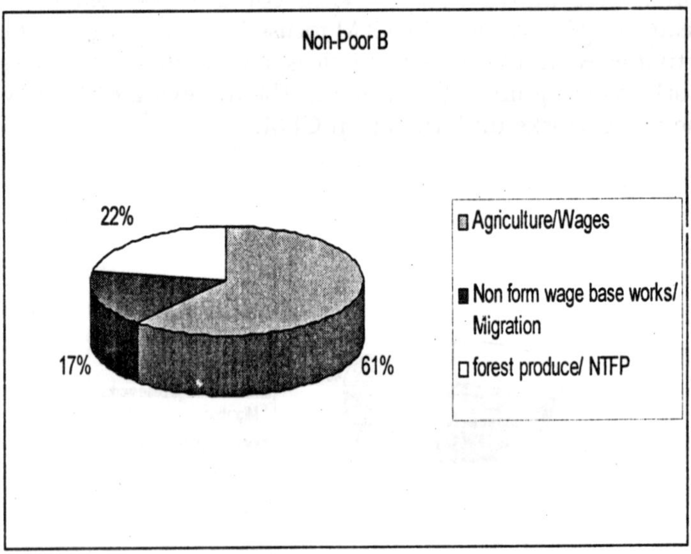

Fig 3: Change in income for Non-Poor HH Non-Poor HH Before JFM in Adilabad District

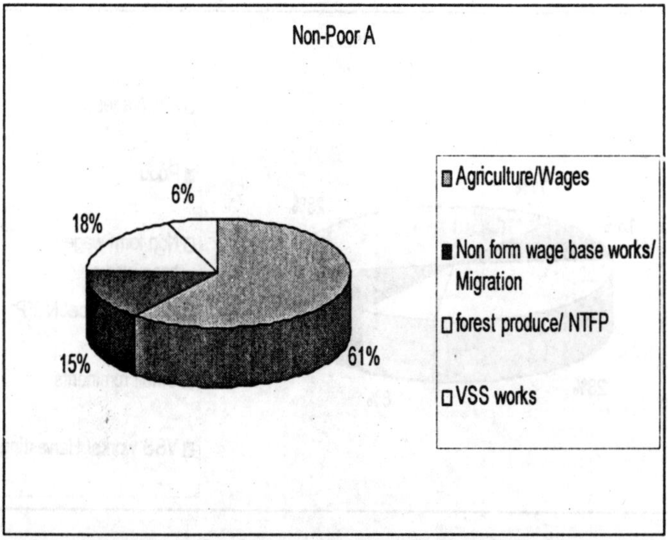

Fig 4: Change in income for After JFM in Adilabad district

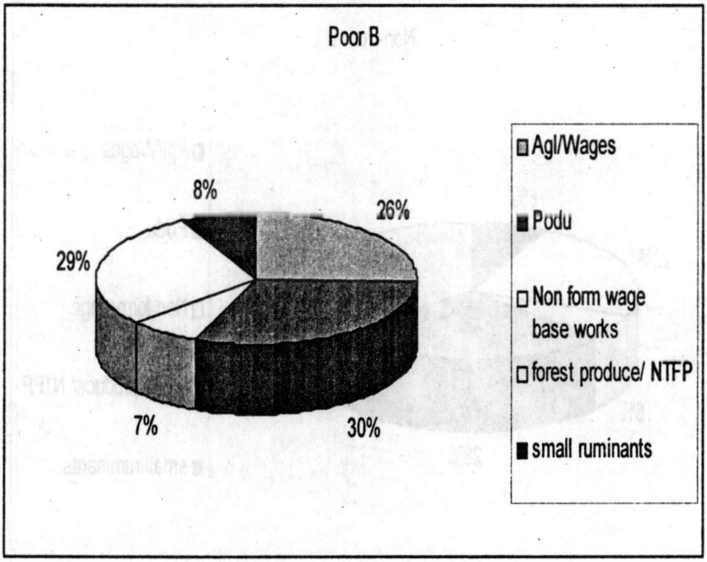

Fig 5: Change in income for Poor HHH
Before JFM in Visakhapatnam District

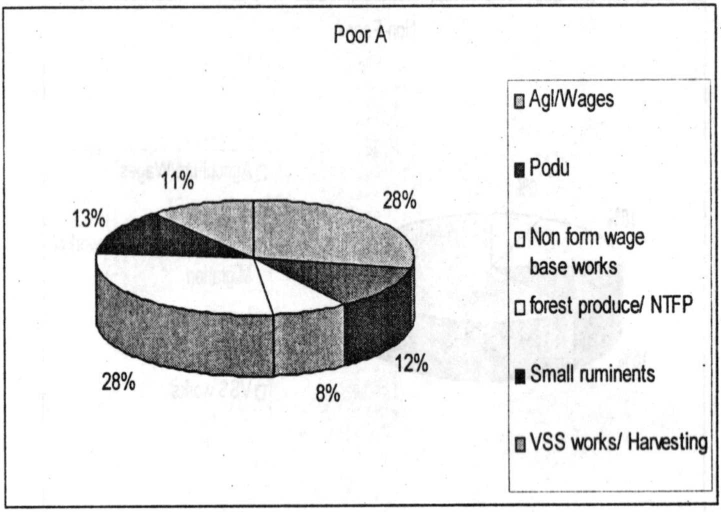

Fig 6: Change in income for Poor
After JFM in Visakhapatnam

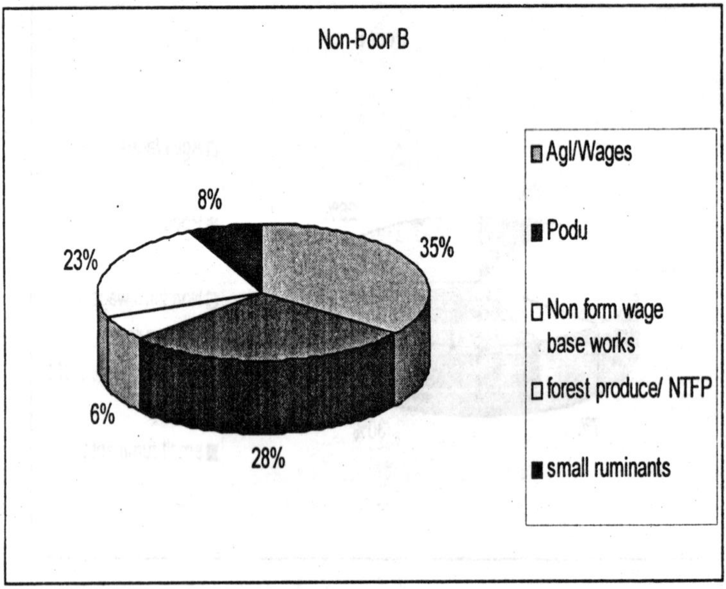

Fig 7: Change in income for Non-Poor HH Non-Poor HH
Before JFM in Visakhapatnam district

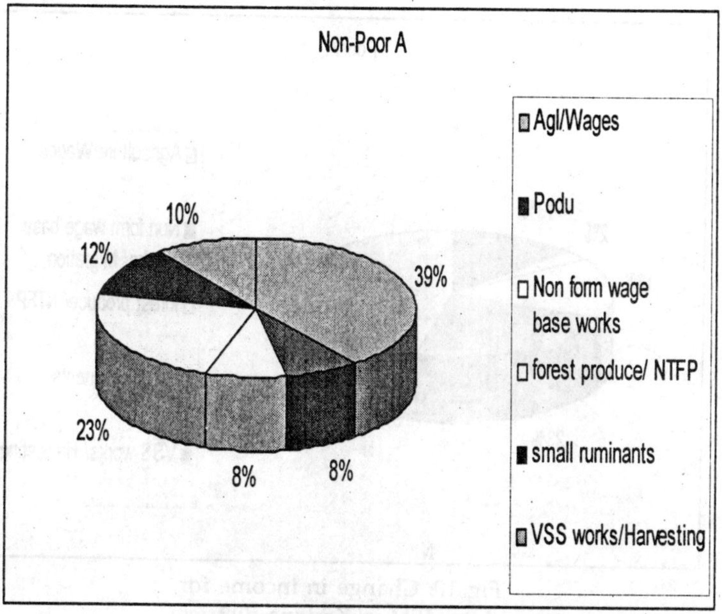

Fig 8: Change in income for
Before JFM in Visakhapatnam

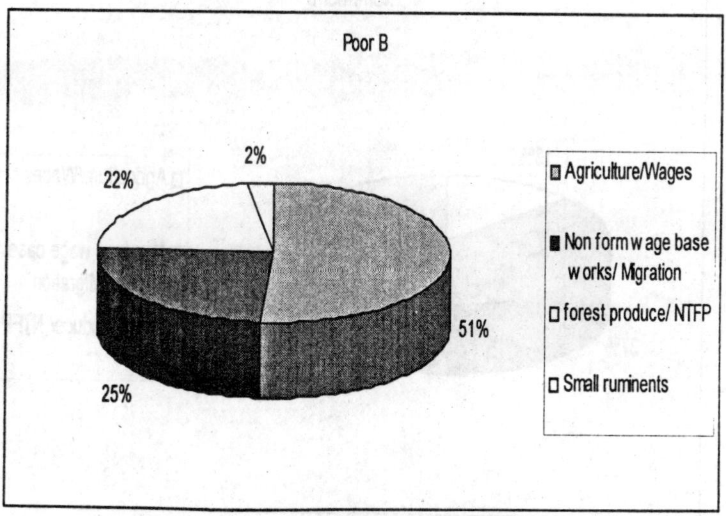

Fig 9: Change in income for Poor HH Poor HH
Before JFM in Kadapa district

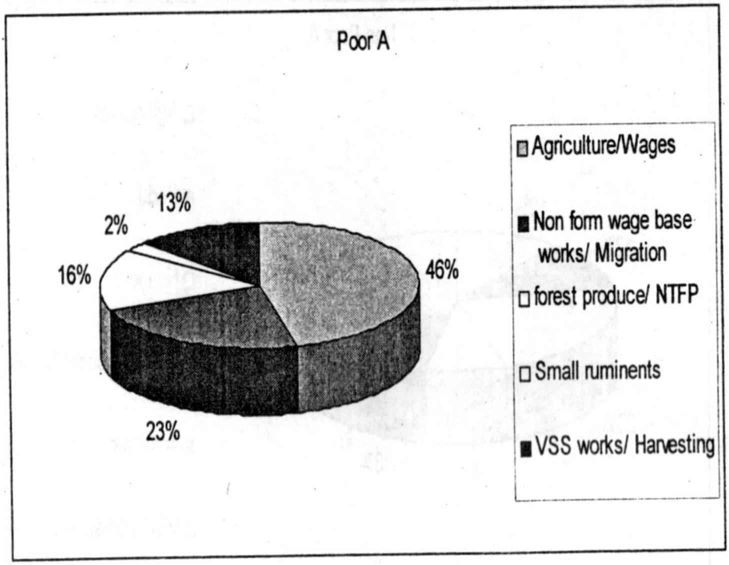

Fig 10: Change in income for
After JFM in Kadapa district

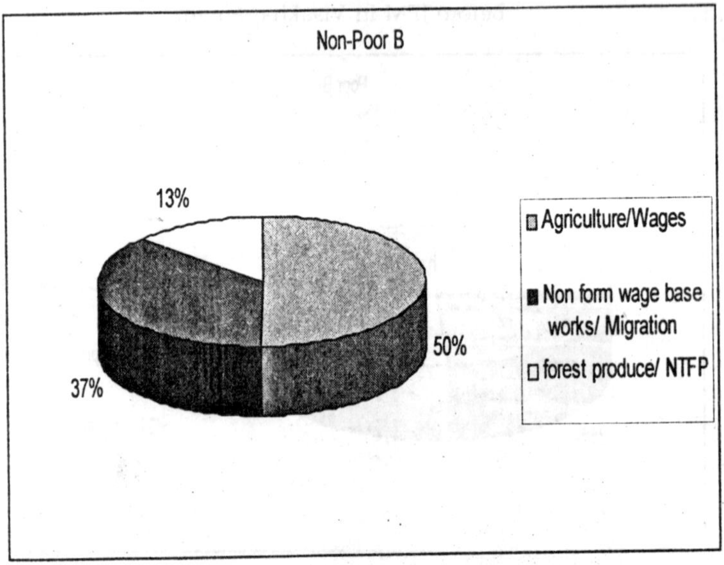

Fig 11: Change in income for Non-Poor HHHH
Before JFM in Kadapa district

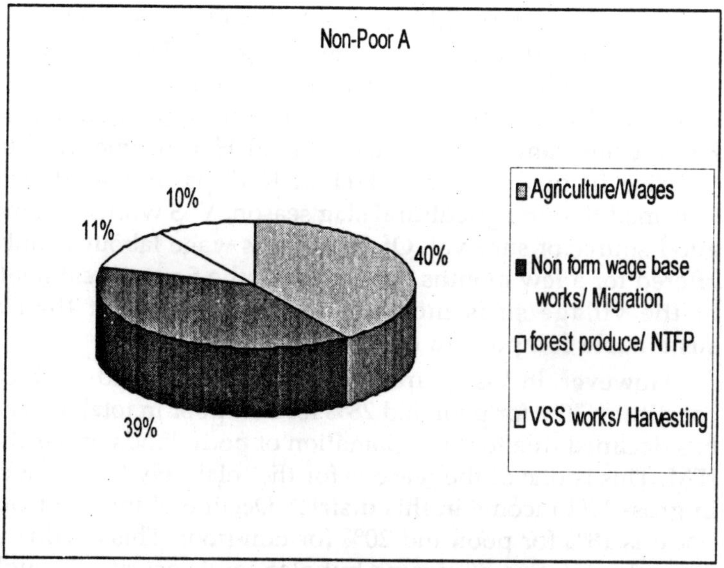

Fig 12: Change in income for Non-Poor After JFM in Kadapa district

In most of the cases the contribution of NTFP is greater among the poor HH. Though the contribution of forest is more for the poor farmers (landless, marginal and small), the share of forestry is about Rs 2,000 per year per household in the case of non-poor HH and it is between Rs. 1500-2500 in the case of poor HH. Kadappa has low contribution from NTFP to the HH income in two of the sample VSS. The contribution of VSS related wage labour is more among poor HH.

The comparison of before and after scenarios clearly indicates that there is an increase in HH gross income across all VSS for poor and non-poor HH. Part of this is due to the normal price rise (inflation). The rise in gross income is more in Adilabad followed by Kadappa and Visakhapatnam (Appendix Table A3). The Contribution of VSS wage income to HH by JFM constitutes 10% of total income for non poor and 13% for poor in Visakhapatnam, in Kadappa and for non poor 10% and poor 13% and in Adilabad for non poor 8% and poor 10%. Thus, non-poor HH have increased their incomes more than poor HH. The percentage of NTFPs in

HH income has declined in all field sites. Of course both poor and non-poor HH experienced the decline in NTFPs. However, it is observed that income has increased from all sources. VSS wage works have become a new and important source of HH income range from 8-10% of total HH income. Due to the rise in income levels HH in Kadapa and Adilabad informed that in agricultural slag season, VSS works became good source of survival. Of course this wage labour is only offered for a few months per year over the 5 year 'treatment' of the village so is more of a welfare payment than a sustainable compoinent of livelihoods.

However, In Visakhapatnam, income from podu, which constitutes 30% for poor and 28% for non-poor in total income has declined due to the reclamation of podu lands under the JFM. This is one of the reasons for the relatively low growth in gross HH income in this district. Decline of income from podu is 18% for poor and 20% for non-poor. This decline is not only in terms of income but also food security. Though the decline of Podu income is compensated to some extent by the VSS wage works, which constitutes only 11% for poor and 10 for non-poor, tribal lost income and food security due to JFM.

The source wise HH income brings out two interesting observations. One is dependence on forest per se is less than the income from agriculture even in the high value forest regions like Adilabad and Visakhapatnam. Due to the advent of VSS the share of NTFP has declined or remained stable for poor as well as non-poor HH in all the VSS. (Fig. 8b). Agriculture is the main contributor to HH income as in the plains. This explains the demand for land, which is reflected in the incidence of encroachment in these regions. Forest adjacent populations follow diversified livelihood strategies, and although, the major livelihood strategy for the forest dwellers or the people residing near the forests is to achieve or increase private land assets, collection of forest produce, forms a major livelihood component, of particular importance to complement inadequate income from agriculture or labouring, especially in the hot season.

Conclusion

The envisaged objective of peoples' centric orientation to participatory forest management has not been achieved due to multiple social and political inequalities on the one hand and unequal power relations between forest department and communities on the other. The institutional and structural changes introduced for inclusive development of forest dependent communities were jeopardized by the indifferent attitude of government to implement reform hurtfully. Unless Participatory Forest Management in Andhra Pradesh go beyond temporary arrangements to comprehensive structural changes focusing on long term and short terms strategies emancipation of the marginalized communities would continued to be remained as distinct dream.

REFERENCES

Farrington J, Priya Deshinkar, Crig Johnson and Daniel Start (2006), *Policy Windows and Livelihood Futures: Prospects for Poverty Reduction in Rural India,* OUP, New Delhi.

UNDP, (1999), Human Development Report, prepared by United Nations Development Programmee.

Bardhan, Pranab, (1996), "Decentralized Development", *Indian Economic Review,* Vol. XXXI, No. 2, pp. 139-156.

Hobbley, Mary (1996), "Institutional Change within the Forestry Sector: Centralized Decentralization", Working Paper 92, ODI.

Harries, J., (2000), *De-politicizing development: The World Bank and Social Capital,* Left Word, New Delhi.

Manor, James (1999), *The Political Economy of Democratic Decentralization,* Washington, DC, The World Bank.

Sharma, C.H. (2006). "Decentralization Dilemma: Measuring the Degree and Evaluating the Outcomes", *The Indian Journal of Political Science,* Vol. LXVII, NO. 1, Jan.-Mar., 2006, 49-64.

Baumann, Pari, Rajesh Ramakrishnan, Manish Dubey, Rajiv K. Raman, and John Farrington, (2003), Institutional Alternatives and Options for Decentralized Natural Resource Management in India, ODI, Working Paper 230

Castern, Tukka, (2005), "Ownership and Incentives in Joint Forest Management: A Survey", *Development Policy Review,* Vol. 23, pp. 78-104.

Sunderline, W., Angelsen, A. Brian and others (2005), "Livelihoods,

Forests and Conservation in Developing Countries: An Overview", *World Development*, special issues, Vol. 33, No. 9, pp. 1383-14302.

Solesbury, Willam, (2003), "Sustainable Livelihoods: A Case Study of the Evolution of DFID Policy", Working Paper 217, Overseas Development Institute.

Desai, M., (2000), *Development and Nationhood: Essays in the Political Economy of South Asia*, OUP, New Delhi.

Kaviraj, S., (ed), (1998), *Politics in India*, OUP.

Chatterjee, P., (1999), *State and Politics in India*, Oxford University Press (OUP), New Delhi.

Blair W. Mary, (1996), "Democracy, Equity and Common Property Resources Management in the Indian Subcontinent", *Development and Change*, Vol. 27, pp. 475-499.

Adhikari, Bhim, (2005), "Poverty, Property rights and collective action: Understating the distributive aspects of common property resource management", *Environment and Development Economics*, Vol. 10, pp. 7-31.

Agrawal, Arun and Gupta, Krishna (2005), "Decentralization and Participation: The Governance of Common Pool Resources in Nepal's Terai", *World Development*, Vol. 33, pp. 1101-1114.

Baumann, Pari, Rajesh Ramakrishnan, Manish Dubey, Rajiv K. Raman, and John Farrington, (2003), *Institutional Alternatives and Options for Decentralized Natural Resource Management in India*, ODI, Working Paper 230.

Samatha (2005), Andhra Pradesh Community Forest Management Project: A Preliminary independent evaluation of a World Bank Forestry Project, Hyderabad.

Kumaran, K.P., (ed), (2000), 'Impact of Economic Reforms on SCs&STs', National Institute of Rural Development, Hyderabad.

Government of Andhra Pradesh, (2002), *Community Forest Management Report*, Vol. I, prepared by Project Monitoring Unit.

13

B.R. Ambedkar and the Indian Christians

Dr. Nina David

Milton Massey, the name familiar to me since childhood, is evocative of Bhim Rao Ambedkar's choice for his Personal Assistant in his Delhi office. Inspite of Christianity wanting in many respects as it did not remove 'paganism out of the converts, caste, superstition, rituals of Hinduism...'[1] Ambedkar, to the exclusion of all its inherent problems (association with British Imperialism, a foreign religion, personally unsuitable to him) accepted it for its services to Indians, the majority of whom were Hindus. In fact, he went on to say that since it failed in winning a sizeable number of converts 'the term Indian Christian is just a statistical phrase. There is no community feeling behind this phrase ....' Indian Christians today do not count for more than 2.5 Percent of the total population of India lends substantial credence to his observation made more than half a century earlier. Hence 'Christianity a religion and Indian Christians cannot be separated in evaluating Ambedkar's thought.'[2]

On the other hand, for all of Dr. Ambedkar's arguments favoring Christianity, he continued to dislike its proponents and propagators (Christian Missionaries). On 24th May 1956, he converted to Buddhism as 'self-respect is more important than material gains'. He continued to add, 'nor have we imported it (Buddhism) from outside'. Hence for him conversion to Christianity was tantamount to 'denationalisation'. Eleanor Zelliot, a well-known authority on Ambedkar believes that its foreign importation was the reason for his antipathy to Christianity. Indian Christians Raj Kumari Amrit Kaur, a prominent Nationalist from the State of Kapurthala, Mahatma Gandhi's aide and Independent India's first Health Minister expressed her ideas on the subject slightly differently. She wrote that she preferred the use of the term 'Christian Indians'. The British had de-nationalized them by giving them European names. Not impervious to verbal attack, she launched a scathing criticism of the nomenclature.

But Ambedkar always denied that his demands for a separate electorate would create anti-national spirits. This was a very different issue. Its was worth fighting for along with the Sikhs and Muslims, the Indian Christians were 'also loyal to the National cause'.[3] He had also felt that Christianity was dangerous to Nationalism Influenced by The Sermon on the Mount.[4] as 'unsurpassable as a directory for human conduct', Ambedkar's chose from the Old Testament (A part of the Bible)to validate his arguments on kinship. He quoted the case of Ruth,[5] daughter-in-law of Naomi who accepted Naomi's Jewish community by accepting her religion. Naomi had asked Ruth to leave her after the death of her son if she wished but Ruth had replied 'Thy people shall be my people and thy God my God.' In this manner 'common religion becomes the basis of kinship'. (James Massey). But, quick to discern Ambedkar also remarked that Chapter 1 of Genesis in the Old Testament only explains the creation of man; there is no mention of the social classes which were existent in Jewish society. For Ambedkar the Christian doctrine 'preaches brotherhood of man and when applied leads to equality of man'.[6]

He liked Gibbon's interpretation of Christianity as a 'Religion of the poor.......' a means to bring social Justice. Christianity defined classless as such was never accepted by the so-called higher classes because it meant surrender of power and prestige which was drawn from system of Chaturvarna. The 'Purusha Sukta' refers to the origin of the social classes. The Idea of class division was specially repugnant to him even when it was non-existent (as stated in the Holy Scriptures). So, Ambedkar acknowledged class in all its manifestations saying 'I am deeply interested in Indian

Christians because a large majority of them are drawn from the Untouchable Classes'.[7]

Now while acknowledging that Christianity in India cannot be separated from the Indian Christians Ambedkar's writings reveal his own interpretations of why Christianity had no appeal for the Brahmans. He blames the lack of Philosophy in it for them. In this respect, I say that Ambedkar chose not to look for it in Christianity. He merely blames the Brahmans as he as a Hindu himself failed to discover it.

Mahatma Gandhi had objected to the spread of the Christian gospel among the Untouchables Ambedkar had replied 'service by Missionaries to suffering humanity is for Christians an essential requirement of their religion'. Christ himself had said 'faith without works is dead'. 'What so ever you do to the least of your brothers you do unto me'. There are innumerable examples of social duties in Christianity. Viewing the community dispassionately Ambedkar knew the elements to be accepted and rejected in the Indian context of Christianty. In fact, the neglected class was rescued by the Missionaries, elevated to a recognizable status finally winning the approbation of Ambedkar. Here it is noteworthy that he accepted the deprived status of the Indian Christians while overlooking their Imperialist connection. Social Justice was necessary for them too, like the rest.

Having made a study of the denominations within Christianity, he was aware of the dissensions within which prevented it from being a unifying force. (Almost despairing of not being able to weld them together, he also observed that they only turned to Christian Missions). If they had being dependent on government help, they would have to 'mobilize, to agitate, to organize........for effective political action.'[8] He also conceded that Dalits became Christians hence his favourites.

Ambedkar went on to give explanations for the failure of Dalit Christians to found a movement. He blamed educated Christians for not taking up cudgels on their behalf, because of class divisions. Dalit Christians were hence leaderless (today Udit Raj takes the lead). Then, their mental make-up does not let them break away from the past. Lastly, he blames the teachings of the Christian church which promises forgiveness of sins on conversion. (This is not understandable as this was redemption and 'Mukti').

Taking off from this point again, Ambedkar clarifies his personal distancing from Christianity. It was founded on 'Divine Omnipotency'. God-based religion was unacceptable to him, as God was 'an embodiment of hatred and injustice'.[9] (He has drawn upon references from the Old Testament more revered by the Jews).

Struck by 'service to humanity', (essentially a Christian duty) Ambedkar gave the Untouchables another faith. It was not based on theism or non-theism. 'The conduct and character of Christ influenced the poor people of India.'[10] But as he has time and again questioned how Christianity has solved the problem of the Depressed Classes, he expressed his disillusionment with the religion by finally saying that it has not served mankind.

In the same context he speaks out against not calling the Schedule Castes a minority by the 'High and Mighty Hindu Majority'.[11] Anticipating a similar agitation by the Muslims today, against a recent High Court Judgment supposedly treating them at par, Ambedkar always spoke in favour of the deprived classes irrespective of the religion they belonged to.

Expanding on the theme of Christianity.[12] Ambedkars cites three main reasons which impeded its growth out of which he singled out the bad morals of the early European settlers, 'struggle between Catholic and Non-Catholic Missions for supremacy in the field of proselytization and the wrong approach of Christian Missionaries in charge of Christian propaganda.' Predicting that 'Christianity has come to stay in India will live and grow in numbers and influence for good' he proved right.

He despaired that the Indian Christians were either too poor or too devoid of ambition to pursue higher education. Their hospitals and Institutions of learning were for Caste Hindus. So he logically felt that Missionaries must abandon their hope of conversion.

The two questions that Ambedkar raised forty years ago

have more relevance today than earlier. 'The mentality of the convert has not changed and neither has it discarded Caste. There are Brahman Christians and Non-Brahman Christians.' The social condition of the converts is unchanged. Even now, they want 'safeguard of their civil liberties and ways and means for their economic uplift'.

Inspite of all his misgivings,doubts, personal distaste for Christianity a dispassionate assessment of the Indian Christian community was that it 'is undoubtedly the most educated and enlightened community in India.' Ambedkar wrote that his comments are those of a friend.... See great dangers for them ahead. They have to reckon with militant Hinduism masquerading as Indian Nationalism'. In this respect too, Ambedkar perceived the divisive policies of the majority community, their inherent biases, their closed minds and their attitudes of derision which to him was inflexible. He used Christian analogy like 'I am a shepherd .... If you follow me, you will shed your ignorance'. Gail Omvedt had commented that 'Ambedkar was above all a man of strategy .....'

Christophe Jaffrelot observed that P.G. Solanki an elected member of the Legistative Council of Bombay who had converted to Christanity returned to Hinduism after discovering that the condition of the Untouchable was the same all over. (Michael Madhusadhan Dutt from Bengal also reverted to his old religion for other reasons.) The 'Old Christians'—Syrians were similar to the Brahmans in resisting 'the inflow of lower orders'.[13] The Missionaries had highlighted that the Caste-system was an insult to human dignity. The egalitarian ideas spread by them, had encouraged the lower Castes to raise themselves.

Eventually, after grappling and understanding the religions of India, in relation to social conditions as well as in the context of hierarchical setup to which India have succumbed to, centuries ago, Ambekar concluded that the only solution '.....that which promises equal opportunity to all is the true religion'. (Ambedkar's speech of Jan. 14, 1955 in Bombay cited in M.S. Gore *The Social Context of an Ideology*) The link between discrimination and fundamental rights was also comprehended by him.[14] Ambedkar failed to amalgamate/recognize Indian Christians in Indian Nationalism of his times only holding their religion against them. What he did not see was that Christianity went from the East to the West.

REFERENCES

1. Dr. Babasaheb Ambedkar, *Writings and Speeches,* Vol. 5, Education Department. Government of Maharashtra, 1979. Compiled by Vasant Moon. Chapter 30- The Condition of the Convert pp 446-476.
2. James Massey. *Dr.B.R. Ambedkar: A Study in Just Society.* Centre for Dalit/Subaltern Studies. Manthar.p 51.
3. Dr. I.S. Vidyasagar. *Concept of Humanism of Dr. Ambedkar,* ABD Publishers, Jaipur, p. 66.
4. *The Bible,* New Testament. Mathew.Chapter 5.Verses 5-7.
5. *The Bible,* Old Testament. Book of Ruth.
6. Dr. Babasaheb Ambedkar. *Writings and Speeches,* Vol. 7, Bombay, Education Department, Government of Maharashtra, 1990, p. 45.
7. James Massey. *Dr. B.R. Ambedkar: A study in Just Society.* Centre for Dalit/Subaltern Studies. Manthar, p. 61.
8. *Ibid.,* p. 51.
9. *B.R. Ambedkar* (Political thinkers of Modern India-16) edited byVirender Grover. From Chapter 'Ambedkar's Concept of Religion', by F.H. Bennus. Deep & Deep Publication, 1998 New Delhi, p. 413.
10. D.R. Jatava, *Ambedkar's Philosophy of Religion,* Published by INA SHREE Publishers, Jaipur, p.66.
11. Dr. Babasaheb Ambedkar. *Writings and Speeches,* Vol. 1, Education Department, Government of Maharashtra 1979. Compiled by Vasant Moon. 15.3.47 p. 10.
12. Dr. Babasaheb Ambedkar. *Unpublished Writings.* 1989 Chapter 29 Christianizing the Untouchables.
13. Christophe Jaffrelot. *Analysing and Fighting Caste: Dr. Ambedkar and Untouchability,* Permanent Black, 2005, p. 123.
14. B.R. Ambedkar. *His Relevance Today,* Edited by Narayan Rao, A., Soma Sekhar, K., Audiseshaiah, Gyan. Essay. Dr. Ambedkar and Minorities by Prof. Mumtaz Ali Khan, New Delhi, p. 11.

14

Dalits and Human Development: A Human Rights Perspective

Mr. Shashi Kumar

Human development and Human rights are closely inter-related. The development of human being cannot be accomplished if all the aspects of human rights, such as civil, political, socio-economic and culture rights are recognised and protected. Actually the human rights are essential for over all development of the personality of the individual in a society.

Human rights are inalienable and inherent rights of human being and primarily it consists of civil-political, socio-economic and cultural rights of human being as an individual or group. The individual need a conducive environment for complete development of self. In this respect, the state plays a vital role. In fact, it is political obligation of the state to create such an infrastructure and provide necessary arrangements where individual can grow its potentialities in developing its personality in every aspect.

In the contemporary human right discourse, the importance of human development cannot be overlooked. Earlier the progress of the country was determined by the national income only. At present the human development of any country is accessed on the Para meters of human rights also. In the UNDP standard of Human Development index the health, education are important component of development indicators.

In the context of our country, the same Para meter of human development is applied. The country has vast percentage of human resource as growing population. Out of this dalits (scheduled caste and Scheduled tribes) constitute one-third population of the country. They are marginalized and exploited section of the Indian society. If human rights of dalits are not protected and promoted then they are not regarded as developed human being. Dalits are the marginalized section of the Indian society and they are at the bottom of all human development indicators, as the data churned out every year by the Human Development Report of the country amplify the reality.

Under this background, the paper makes a modest attempt in understanding the problem of human development of dalits in human rights perspective. In reference to Indian society it deals with the nature of discrimination and exploitation pertaining to dalits community. It discusses the various constitutional safe guards and measures provided by the state in ameliorating the condition of the dalits.

Dalits in Indian Society

Indian society has a multi-cultural identity. It poses several differences on the basis of caste, creed, language and ethnic identities. One of the distinguish feature of the Indian society is caste hierarchy. In the ladder of this social hierarchy the forward caste exists at top and the dalits at the bottom. The upper strata of the Indian society, which are also known as forward caste or swarn people, are developed community. Since centuries the forward caste have been enjoying rights of development. They have access to education; freedom to poses land and was wealthy and dominant over the society. Therefore, they are remained developed and have been enjoying all fruits of development, whereas the condition of dalits is contrary to the forward caste. Dalits, for centuries have suffered inequality, exploitation and denial of opportunities. They could not enjoy the basic values of human rights. They were living in indignity life. They were socially segregated and economically discriminated. The worst stigma of Dalits was the problem of Untouchability, which was by product of Hindu caste system. It was not only a form of social discrimination but also a source of economic exploitation. Dalits were not allowed to enter in village during daytime or to use the public utilities such as roads, well, tanks and their entry was ban in public places like temples. They were made to live on the outskirts of the village and were forced to serve the forward caste people. They were assigned such works only, which were unclean and filthy. B.R. Ambedkar understood the untouchability not only evil of religious system but as a kind of economic discrimination worst than slavery. Dalits were denied right to develop themselves. They remained primarily illiterate, poor, and exploitative (Ambedkar).

From the human rights point of view the Hindu Social system has conflicting relation with universal human rights norms. In the Hindu social order the life of human being is regulated by religion. The Hindu social system of social and religious governance is founded not on the principle of liberty, equality and fraternity and the democratic values, which formed the basis of universal human rights, but the principle of inequality in every sphere of life.

The inequality in social or civil sphere of Hindu society can be observed between different castes, law of marriages and rule of law, including rule of punishment. In economic sphere there exists unequal distribution of economic rights related to ownerships of property, trade, employment, wages, education etc., among the caste groups (Thorat, 2000). Hence, Thorat argues that " Hindu Social order is based on three interrelated elements namely predetermination of social, religious and economic rights of each caste based on birth; the unequal and hierarchical (grade) division of these rights among the caste; and provision of strong social, religious and economic ostracism supported by religious ideology to maintain order (Thorat, 2000).

Even after the sixty years of independence in the contemporary Indian society, these disparities and inequalities in the context of dalits are still prevailing. The unjust social order of Hindu society obstructs in the fulfilment of universal respect for human rights.

After independence in 1950, the Indian state set forth two major objectives to fulfil. Firstly, the creation of egalitarian civil society based on the democratic value structure. Another, task was to introduce the rapid economic growth. For accomplishing both the objectives, the Indian state resorted to a strategy of planned economic development. The main motto was of having economic development with social justice. However, the trust of economic development was such that the social service sector continued to lag behind and accentuated social economic disparities in the country. The hiatus between rich and poor has become more widen. Still the Indian state is striving to provide basic amenities to poor and the socially disabled groups. There exits a contradiction in Indian social order. One could surprise that despite of immense natural, cultural and human resources a vast majority of the population are denied access to development benefits. Dalits are placed in last in enjoyment of benefit of development process. The fruits of development have not been tricked to them.

Constitutional Rights of Dalits

Our Constitution adheres to the principles of Universal Declaration of Human Rights, which reads, "All human being are born free and equal in dignity and rights. They are endowed with reason and conscience and should act towards one another in a spirit of brotherhood." Keeping view of these universal principles of human rights the Indian Constitution has incorporated several provisions under its set of articles, which protect and promotes human rights of each citizen of this country. In the context of development of people of the country in general and dalits in particular are concern, the Indian state has provided protective, development and preferential treatment for upliftment of dalits. The basic human rights of dalits are not only material needs but also non-material needs such as the right to live with freedom, human dignity and self-respect.

Though the dalit word is not reflected in the Constitution of India. But the reference of Scheduled Caste and Scheduled Tribe connotes its synonym.

Under the Article 14, in Indian Constitution, all the citizens of our country are equal before law and they are treated equal irrespective of their difference on caste, creed, language and regions.

Under the Article 17 the untouchability has been abolished. To provide effect to this article, the Untouchability (Offences) Act, 1955 and later this act was made more stringent through amendment and also renamed as the Protection of Civil Rights Act, 1955 (Govt 1977). The PCR Act provides for penalties for refusing admission to hospitals, educational institutions, hostels, or temples etc., for refusing to sell goods or vendor services, for preventing the exercise of any rights under article 17. This includes access to shops, public restaurants and places of public entertainment or wells, tanks, bathing ghats (or places), roads, and places of public resort. Under this act such works are illegal like scavenging, sweeping and removal of carcasses, flaying animals etc.

In 1989, The Parliament of India also enacted the Scheduled caste and the Scheduled tribes (Prevention of Atrocities) Act for taking measures to prevent the atrocities on SC/STs people. The 1989 Act specifies some forms of atrocities for making penalty: forcing the eating of obnoxious substances; dumping waste matter on land; intimidation during voting; mischievous litigation; false information; public humiliation; denudation; wrongful occupation of land; dispossession; bonded labour; outrage of modesty; sexual exploitation; fouling of water resources; obstruction of entry to a place of public resort; eviction of habitation; mischief with explosive; destruction of building; and suppression of evidence.

Article 23 of the Indian Constituion prohibits traffic in human beings and bonded labour *(begar)* and other similar forms of forced labour and provides that any contravention of these provisions shall be an offence punishable in accordance with law. Though the article does not mention specifically SC/Sts but as majority of bonded labours belong to SC/STs, therefore this Article has a special significance for dalits.

Educational and Cultural Rights of Dalits

Article 15(4) under the Indian Constitution empowers the

state to make any special provision for the advancement of any socially and educationally backward classes of citizens or for SC and ST. This provision has enabled the state to reserve seats for SCs and STs in educational institutions including technical, engineering and medical colleges and in Scientific and Specialised courses. Article 330 provides for reservation of seats for SC/STs in the Lok Sabha. Article 332 provides for reservation of seats for SC/STs in the State Vidhan Sabhas (Legislative Assemblies).

The Constitution of India also provides directive principles to Indian State under the Article 46 for safeguarding the educational and economic interests of the weaker sections of the people, and in particular, of the SC/STs. The Indian state has to protect them from social injustice and all forms of exploitation.

Education is tool of empowerment for dalits. The education of the dalits makes them to enjoy the benefit of employment reservation. Education is not only a means for betterment of their own life but it also indicative of their socio-economic status. The government has introduced many scholarship and incentive measures for educational empowerment of dalits. However, dalits are denied of right to education. They have biggest challenge in access to education is that of Drop Outs tendency, which is more than 80% in the school going dalit students. While several factors are responsible for higher rate of dropouts among the students belonging to dalits families, the problem of acute poverty can be held as the most decisive factor. These dropouts' dalit children are hired as a child labour. Moreover, the severity of poverty compels the dalit families to send their children to factories for earning. These dalits children work at hazardous industries, serve as servant in restaurants and domestic places at the cost of their childhood and educational rights.

Socio-Economic Condition of Dalits

Despite various measures to ameliorate the socio-economic condition of dalits, Dalits remain vulnerable. They are denied number of human rights. They are subjected to various offences, indignities, humiliations and harassment. They have, in several brutal incidents, been deprived of their life and property. Serious crimes are committed against them for various historical, social and economic reasons.

The main root of atrocities on the dalits over the centuries is the caste system. Caste is the bane of Indian society and the worst enemy of the dalits. Though the abolition of untouchability was a key constitutional provision for securing human dignity to dalits, yet its practice continues to be widely prevalent in the society. There has been several micro-level studies conducted which provided grime reality of untochability prevailing in the Indian society (Thorat). It also indicated that untouchability has acquired different dimensions and still prevalent in rural areas widely. It was observed in several micro level studies that untochability mainly exits in public place, where social interaction takes place much. Hotels are still barred for dalits, if allowed they have to sit in last rows and use separate cups and utensils for serving. They cannot take water from Public tanks. They are not allowed to participate in religious procession or they can n't take out marriage procession through lanes of high caste colonies. The dalits are not allowed for inter-caste marriage or dinning together.

The dehumanising practice of manual scavenging is yet going on. Almost all those scavenging carrying human night soil on their head are belong to dalit community. Even someplace the government has officially employed the scavenging communities in cleaning and filthy jobs. Though Employment of Manual Scavengers and Construction of Dry Latrines (Prohibitions) Act 1993 was enacted and enforced from 1997, the inhuman practice of such activities still carrying out in different parts of the country. The National Commission for Safai karamcharis has been set up in 1994 to monitor over eradication programme of scavenging and for safeguarding the interest of Safai karamcharies. Despite the government initiatives for prohibiting the inhuman practice the Indian society still suffer with it.

Economic Discrimination of Dalits

Dalits are economically discriminated and deprived from benefits of economic development. The state government introduced land reform laws for imposing ceiling on landholdings so that surplus land may be distributed among the landless. Possession of land makes economically empowered and provide prestige in his personality. It also provides independent source of income. In Indian agriculture the dalits are land less people and this is a major cause of their poverty and under-development. The dalits are denied the right of owing land. Whatever little lands are owned by the dalits are either unfertile lands or the lands are given far from irrigation facilities etc. They are also denied the right to bargaining wages and whatever they are given as wage they have to accept it. Generally dalits work as bonded labour and get fewer wages. The landlord exploits them and when they take money than the moneylenders also exploit them.

Inadequate access to agricultural land and capital leaves no option to dalits to divert towards urban areas. Large numbers of dalits are being migrated from rural to urban regions. In urban regions dalits have to work as unskilled worker. They resort to manual wage labours. They are also subjected to discrimination and exploitation in wage labour market.

Disparities in Employment: Violation of Right to Work

More than sixty per cent of dalits are workers in rural areas and more than 30 percent are in urban region depending upon wage employment, for earnings livelihood. The level of employment and wage rates determines their earnings. Dalits are suffered from discrimination in employment and wages distribution. In the white-collar jobs most of the positions or employment vacancies are gained by the upper caste. The serving vacancies of posts of menial work are mostly filled with dalits workers. The Government has introduced the reservation system for providing adequate employment in service sectors. Despite this the reservation quota of dalits are not fully achieved. The unemployment rates are much higher in dalits.

Exploitation of Dalit Women

Dalit women suffer more from harassment, oppression and exploitation than their upper caste counterparts. The literacy rate among dalit women is very low. Dalit women continue to suffer sexual exploitation of dominant caste. They are most vulnerable community in the society. The women in general are having thirty per cent reservation in Panchayat and local administrative bodies. If any dalit women become representative of the people or she has contested election than she has to face wrath of untouchability and exploitation to large extent. The incidences of parading naked dalit women by the dominant caste are common feature in rural areas. Sexual exploitation and rape of dalit women by men folk of dominant caste for taking revenge against dalit rivalry are much common in villages. A large number of such cases have been reported from Bihar, Rajasthan and Maharashtra states (Gopalaguru, 1995).

Human Rights Watch (1999) has reported that use of sexual abuse and other forms of violence against dalit women as mean of subjugation by the dominant caste. Even the Police exploits the dalit women to inflict suppression or for curbing protest movement of dalits. Dalit women have been beaten, arrested and sexually exploited during violent search and raids operation by the police forces. Dalit women have also been arrested and raped in police custody generally in anguish of punishing the male culprits. In southern states, for the religion sake the dalit women are forced into prostitution in Devdasi system. On the deplorable condition of dalit women, a Dalit human right activist rightly observed that

> "Dalit women are at the bottom in our community. Within the Women's movement, Dalit issues have not been taken seriously. Within the dalit movement, women have been ignored. Dalit women have contributed to this discourse... Women's labour is already undervalued; when she is a Dalit, it is nil...the atrocities are also much more vulgar (Human rights Watch 1999).

Atrocities and Crime Against the Dalits

In our society dalits being a weakest and vulnerable section continue to suffer from exploitation and atrocities. Despite the presence of constitutional safeguards and legal measures for the protection of dalit rights, the incidence of atrocities and crime against dalits continues to be reported from different parts of the country.

In the recent years the crime against the dalits has been increased manifold. In rural areas the violence against the rural Dalits continued unabated. Atrocities like murder, rape, kidnapping, abduction, dacoity and robbery are common form of crimes that are committed against the dalits. In the below a table is given which projects the incidence of crimes against scheduled castes in India from period 1992 to 2005. Table provides number of reported cases of various types of crimes being committed against the dalits. It indicates that criminal offence like murder and rape of dalit women have been increasing. The incidence of kidnapping, robbery and arson have also increased in past one decade. Moreover the many cases have been registered under the Protection of Civil Rights Act and SC/ST (prevention of Atrocities) Act, which are mainly related to practice of untouchability, discrimination and atrocities against the dalits.

Conclusion

In the contemporary human rights discourse the human development constitute an important part. Human rights that has its origin from the period of Magna Carta in 12th century as a demand of legal rights of citizen against the Monarchy regime and later in twentieth century it was developed and internationally recognised as universal rights of human being in the form of Universal Declaration of Human Rights in 1948. In the modern usage, human rights is understood as basic entitlements of the human being for the accomplishing complete human development of human personality. The state has political obligation not only for recognising the human rights of its citizens and providing them legal protection but also to ensure the socio-economic arrangement for development of individual. The protection and promotion of all aspect of

Table 14.1: Crime Head-wise Incidence of Crimes Against Scheduled Castes in India

Crime Head	*1995*	*1996*	*1997*	*1998*	*1999*	*2000*	*2001*	*2002*	*2003*	*2004*	*2005*
Murder	571	543	513	516	506	526	763	739	581	654	669
Rape	873	949	1037	923	1000	1083	1316	1331	1089	1157	1172
Kidnapping/Abduction	276	281	243	253	228	268	400	319	232	253	258
Dacoity	70	90	58	49	36	38	41	29	24	26	26
Robbery	218	213	162	150	109	108	133	105	70	72	80
Arson	500	464	389	346	337	290	354	322	204	211	210
Hurt	4544	4585	3860	3809	3241	3497	4547	4491	3969	3824	3847
PCR Act	1528	1417	1216	724	678	672	633	1018	634	364	291
SC/ST (P O A)Act	13925	9620	8070	7443	7301	7386	13113	10770	8048	8891	8497
Others	10492	13278	12396	11425	11657	11587	12201	14383	11401	11435	11077
Total	32996	31440	27944	25638	25093	25455	33501	33507	26252	26887	26127

Source: Ministry of Home Affairs, Government of India.

human rights such as civil-political, socio-cultural and economic rights of individual is necessary for over all development of human being.

Under the above hypothesis a brief attempt has been made in the above discussion to understand the condition of dalits of the Indian society. We have discussed that whether the basic Human rights of dalits are protected or not. Whether their educational rights are protected. How they are economically benefited. What is the condition of dalit women in the society?

It is concluded through above discussions that after sixty years of independence the condition of dalits are not much improved. Though the dalits have special concern as protection of their rights in the Indian constitution and many legislative and administrative measures have also been taken by the Indian state for protection of dalit rights and for upliftment of social condition of dalits, yet they are treated discriminately and exploited widely in different parts of the country. They are still lag behind the dominant forward castes and not able to enjoy the fruits of economic development. Of course due to affirmative action of reservation by the state in education and employment, the dalits are able to get education and employment. Consequently their living standard little bit improved and their social mobility rose upward. This transformation is also visualised in the political sphere of the state where the dalit ideological based political parties are bargaining for political power and share in the economic development.

From the human rights point of view, the dalits are facing obstacles in access of education and employment avenues. They are economically discriminated in the labour market. They are deprived of benefits of development process. Large numbers of dalits are still landless, bonded labours, child labours in the country that indicates sheer violation of all norms and principles of human rights. Literacy rate are much low among the dalits and they are poverty stricken populace of the country. Though untouchability has been legally banned but we can still witness large cases of practice of untouchability being reported in the country. Dalits are most vulnerable community as far as infliction of crime against them. They suffered large number of atrocities and humiliation in the society.

I felt that protection and promotion of human rights of dalits cannot be materialised without a sensitisation of the society. There is greater need for effective state intervention in the form of rigorous implementation of various legislative and development measures for the dalits.

REFERENCES

1. B.R. Ambedkar, *Castes in India: their Mechanism, Genesis and Development* (Bheem Patrika Publication, Jalandhar, 1977).
2. Sukhadeo Thorat, "Human Rights of Ex-Untouchables in India: violations and enforcement" in *Indian Journal of Human Rights*, Vol. IV, No. 1 & 2, 2000.
3. *Ibid.*, p. 90.
4. The Government also notified the Rules i.e., the PCR Rules, 1977 to carry out the provisions of this Act. For giving effect to this Act the Bonded labour System (Abolition) Act, 1976 was enacted.
5. Sukhdeo Thorat, "Human Rights of Ex-Untouchables in India: violations and enforcement" in *Indian Journal of Human Rights*, Vol. IV, No. 1& 2, 2000.

Bibliography

Planning Commission (1962), 'Perspective of Development 1961-1976: Implications of Planning for a Minimum Level of Living. A Decade of Development', Perspective Planning Division, reproduced in *Poverty and Income Distribution in India,* edited by T.N. Srinivasan & P.K. Bardhan (1974).

Dandekar, V.M. & N. Rath (1971): *Poverty in India* (Poona, Indian School of Political Economy).

Planning Commission (1979) , "Report of the Task Force on Projections of Minimum Needs and Effective Consumption", Government of India.

Panikkar, P.G.K. (1972), "Economies of Nutrition", *EPW,* Annual Number 1972.

Jain, L.R. & B.S. Minhas (1991). Rural and Urban Consumer Price indices by commodity Groups (States and all India: 1970-71 to 1983). *Sarvekshana,* Vol. XV, No.1, July-Sept. 1991, (Issue No. 49).

Sudip Kumar Mohapatra (1997) : "Poverty alleviation Anathema of the Indian experience". Reserve Bank of India Occasional papers, Vol. 18, Nos.2&3, special issue (June and Sept.)

Hanumantha Rao, C.H. (1985); "Agricultural Growth and Rural Poverty; Some lessons from past Experience", *EPW,* Vol. XII, Nos. 33 & 34, Special Number, August.

Vaidyanathan (1986), *Agricultural Development of Rural Poverty,* Institute of Development Studies, Madras (Mimeo).

Ahluwalia, M. (1978), "Rural Poverty & agricultural Performance in India", *Journal of Development Studies,* Vol. 14, April 1978, pp. 298-323.

Radhakrishna, R., S.A.R. Sastry and S. Sudhakar Reddy (1983):

"Determinants and Dimensions of Rural Poverty, some Implications for Development". CESS, Hyderabad, Nov. 1983.

Parthasarthay, G. (1987): "Changes in the Incidence of Rural Poverty and Recent Trends in some aspects of Agrarian Economy", *Indian Journal of Agricultural Economics,* Vo1. 42, No. 1, Jan.-March: 1987.

Srinivasan T.N. (1979): "Trends in Agriculture in India 1949-50 to 1977-78", *EPW,* Vol. XIV, Nos. 30, 31 and 32. Special Number, August 1979.

Hanumantha Rao, G. (1977): *Caste & Poverty: A Case Study of SC in A Delta Village,* Savitri Publication, Malikipuram.

Bardhan, P.K.(1984): *Land, Labour and Rural Poverty: Essays in Development Economics,* Oxford University Press, Delhi: 1984.

Brahmananda, P.R. (1982): *Productivity in the Indian Economy,* Himalaya Publishing House, Bombay 1982.

Visaria, P. (1980): "Poverty and Unemployment in India", *Indian Journal of Agricultural Economics,* Vol. XXXV, No. 3, July.-Sept.

Krishnamurthy, J. (1984: "Changes in the Indian Work Force", *EPW,* Vol. XIX, No. 50, Dec. 15.

Thorat, S.K. (1996): "The impact of New Economic Policy on the Scheduled Castes". *The Fourth World: Journal of the Marginalised People,* NISWASS.

Nancharaiah, G. (1988): *Land & Caste,* New Himalaya Publishers, Bombay.

Hanumantha Rao, G. (1985), *Op. Cit.*

Chakravarthy, B. (1977) : Constitutional Safe Guards and Development Programs for Weaker Sections, Planning and Management of Development Projects for SCs and STs, NIRD, Hyderabad.

Satyandra Tripathi (1987): *Development of Rural Poor,* Rawat Publications, Jaipur.

Harikumar (1984) : "Has Integrated Rural Development Program Succeeded", *Yojana,* Vol. 28, September 1-15, 1984.

Perumal Rao and Natarajan (1988): Integrated Rural Development Programme Assistance in AndhraPradesh : An Evaluation, *Kurukshetra,* Vol. 36, No. 6, March 1988.

Rakesh Upadyaya : *Integrated Rural Development in India: A Basic Approach in Policy,* Himalaya Publishing House, Bombay.

Prakash Mehata and Bhardwaja (1987): *Integrated Rural Development Program : A Case Study in Himachal Pardesh,* B.R. Publishing Corporation, Delhi.

Harikumar (1984) : "Has Integrated Rural Development Program Succeeded", *Yojana,* Vol. 28, September 1-15, 1984.

Chiranjeevi (1992): Impact of Integrated Rural Development Program on SCs and STs: A Case Study, Unpublished M.Phil. Dissertation submitted to University of Hyderabad.

Rural Development Statistics Report 1998, Published by NIRD, Hyderabad.

Rural Development Statistics Report 1994 and 1995, published by NIRD, Hyderabad.

8th Five Year Plan Documents, Planning Commission, Government of India.

Population Census Report 1981 & 1991, Directorate of Census, Hyderabad, Government of India,

Rural Development Statistics Report 2003 and 2004, published by NIRD, Hyderabad.

Bagchi, A.K. (1988), *Economy Society and Polity,* Oxford University Press.

Das, Sukumar (2000), "A Critical Evaluation of Land Reforms in India", in Sinha B.K. and Pushpendra (eds.), *Land Reforms in India,* Vol.5, Sage Publications, New Delhi.

De Silva, G.V.S., et al (1988): *Towards Theorisation of Rural Development.*

Dharmakumar (1982), *The Cambridge Economic History of India,* Vol. II, Orient Longmans.

Diwakar, D.M., (2000): "Agrarian Transformation in Uttar Pradesh", *Journal of Social and Economic Development,* Vol. III, No. 1, January-June.

_______ (2000a): "Purvi Uttar Pradesh ke Kheti mein Poonji ka Vikas", *Lokyuddha,* November-December.

Dorner, P. (1972), *Land Reforms and Economic Development,* Penguin, Harmondsworth.

Government of India (1980): Report on the Backward Class Commission, Vol. I.

Government of India (1973): Approach to the Fifth Five Year Plan 1974-79, Planning Commission.

Joshi, P.C. (1982), *Land Reforms in India,* Allied Publishers, New Delhi.

Mishra, G.P. (1996), *Distribution of Surplus Land and Rural Poor,* APH Publishing Corporation, New Delhi.

Mishra, G.P. & D.M. Diwakar, (2005): *Land Reforms and Human Development,* Manak Publications, Pvt. Ltd. New Delhi.

Neale, W.C. (1962), *Economic Change in Rural India: Land Tenure and Reforms in Uttar Pradesh: 1800-1955,* Kennikat Press, London.

Prasad, P.H., (1980): "Rising Middle Peasantry in North India", *Economic and Political Weekly,* Annual Number.

Radhakrishnan, P. (1989), *Peasant Struggles Land Reforms and Social Change,* Sage Publications, New Delhi.

Raychoudhuri, R.C. and I. Habib (1982), *The Cambridge Economic History of India,* Vol. I, Orient Longmans.

Sampurnanand, B. (1936), *Agrarian Enquiry Committee Report,* Note of Ch.VI, p. XV.

Singh, B. and Shridhar Mishra (1964), *A Study of Land Reforms in Uttar Pradesh,* Oxford Book Company, Calcutta.

Tandon, P.D. et al, (1936), *Congress Agrarian Enquiry Committee Report, 1936,* Prabhu Publications, Gurgaon (Haryana).

Thorner, D. (1976), *The Agrarian Prospects in India,* Allied Publishers Ltd., New Delhi.

Dharma Kumar, *Land and Caste in South India,* Manohar publications, New Delhi, 1992.

Radha Krishna, Agricultural growth, employment and poverty, 43rd conference of Indian Society of Labour Economics, Bangalore, 2004.

Nancharaiah, *Agrarian Reforms and Agrarian Change,* Atlantic Publishers, New Delhi, 2000.

Directorate of Economics & Statistics, Govt. of A.P, Statistical Abstract of Andhra Pradesh, 2003, Hyderabad.

Ahmad, A., and J. Morduch, 1993. Identifying sex bias in the allocation of household resources: Evidence from linked household surveys from Bangladesh. Harvard Institute of Economic Research Working Paper 1636. Cambridge, Mass., U.S.A.: Harvard University.

Behrman, J. 1988a. "Nutrition, health birth order, and seasonality: Intrahousehold allocationamong children in rural India", *Journal of Development Economics* 28 (1):43-62.

Buvinic, M., and G. Gupta. 1992. Targeting woman-headed households and woman-maintainedfamilies in developing countries: Views on a policy dilemma.International Center for Research on Women, Washington, D.C.Mimeo.

Christian, P., R. Abbi, S. Gujral, and T. Gopaldas. 1989. "Socioeconomic determinants of childnutritional status in rural and tribal India". *Ecology of Food and Nutrition* 23(1): 31-38.

Cornia, G., and F. Stewart. 1992. Two errors of targeting. Paper presented at the World Bank Conference on Public Expenditures and the Poor: Incidence and Targeting, June 17-19,Washington, D.C.

Das Gupta, M. 1987. "Selective discrimination against female children in rural Punjab, India", *Population and Development Review* 13(1):77-100.

Fauveau, V., A. Briend, J. Chakraborty, and A.M. Sardar. 1990. "The contribution of severe malnutrition to child mortality in rural Bangladesh: Implications for targeting nutritional interventions", *Food and Nutrition Bulletin* 12(3) : 215-219.

Haddad, L., and R. Kanbur. 1990. "How serious is the neglect of intrahousehold inequality?", *Economic Journal* 100 (402): 866-881.

Harbert, L., and P. L. Scandizzo. 1982. Food distribution and nutrition intervention. The case of Chile. World Bank Staff Working Paper 512. Washington, D.C.: World Bank.

Miller, B. 1981. *The Endangered Sex: Neglect of Female Children in Rural North India*. Ithaca, N.Y., U.S.A.: Cornell University Press.

Miller, B.D. 1992. Gender discrimination in intrahousehold food allocation in South Asia: Debates and dilemmas. Paper presented at 1992 Meetings of American Anthropological Association, San Francisco, November 2-6. George Washington University, Washington, D.C.

Pettigrew, J. 1986. "Child neglect in rural Punjabi families", *Journal of Comparative Family Studies* 17(1): 63-85.

Warrier, S. 1992. Patriarchy and daughter disfavor in West Bengal, India. Ph.D. dissertation draft. Syracuse University, Syracuse, N.Y., U.S.A.

Dhawan, B.D. (1995), *Groundwater Depletion, Land Degradation and Irrigated Agriculture in India,* Commonwealth Publishers, New Delhi.

Gulati A.; Ruth Meinzen-Dick; K.V. Raju (2005), *Institutional Reforms in Indian Irrigation,* Sage Publication, New Delhi.

Janakiraman, (1993), "In Search of Hidden Tanks: Some Hidden Facts", *Economic and Political Weekly,* Vol. 28, No. 26.

Nayak, Sanatan (2006), "Land Degradation in Uttar Pradesh: Causes, Extent and Intensity", in Jodha. N.S.; Pushpam Kumar; Sudhakar Reddy (eds.), *Ecology and Human Well-Being,* Oxford Publications, Forthcoming Issue.

Palanisami et al. (1996), Management of Tank Irrigation by Government and Community: An Analysis of Tank Irrigation Performance in Tamil Nadu, A Report on Water Technology Centre of Tamil Nadu Agricultural University, Coimbatore.

Pant, N. (2004), "Trends in Groundwater Irrigation in Eastern and Western Uttar Pradesh", *Economic and Political Weekly,* Vol. 39, No. 31, July 31.

Pant, N. (2005), "Control of and Access to Groundwater in Uttar Pradesh", *Economic and Political Weekly,* Vol. XL, No. 26, June 25.

Raju, K.V. (2005), "Sustainable Water Use in India: A Way Forward", in Proceedings of Seminar on Statistical Accounting of Water Resources, CSO, Government of India.

Rao, C. H. Hanumatha (2005), *Agriculture, Food Security, Poverty and Environment: Essays on Post-Reform India,* Oxford University Press, New Delhi.

Saleth, M. (1996), *Water Institutions in India, Economics, Law and Policy,* Institute of Economic Growth Studies in Economic Development and Planning, No. 63, Commonwealth Publishers, New Delhi.

Shah, Tusar (1993), *Ground Water Markets and Irrigation Development: Political Economy and Practical Policy,* Oxford University Press, Mumbai.

Singh, Kartar (1994), *Managing Common Pool Resources Principles and Case Studies,* Oxford University Press, Delhi.

Sivasubramaniyan, K. (1997), "Irrigation Institutions under Two Major Tanks in Tamil Nadu", *Review of Development and Change,* Vol. 2, No. 3, July-December.

Vaidyanathan, A. (1994), "Impact of Irrigation on Productivity of Land", *Journal of Indian School of Political Economy,* Vol. 6, No. 4.

Vaidyanathan, A. (2001), "Irrigation Subsidies", Paper Presented In The World Bank Conference On Economic Reforms, New Delhi, 21-22, May.

Sen, Amartya. 2004. *Social Exclusion: Concept, Application and Scrutiny,* New Delhi, Critical Quest.

Silver, Hillary. 1995. "Reconceptualizing Social Disadvantage: Three paradigms of Social Exclusion", in *Social Exclusion: Rhetoric, Reality, Responses,* edited by Gerry Rodgers, et al. Geneva: International Institute for Labour Studies.

Lella Karunyakara, *Modernisation of Buddhism: Contributions of Amedkar and Dalai Lama XIV,* Gyan Publishers, New Delhi, 2002.

Economic Survey 2000-2001, Government of India.

"Labouring under a Misconception". *Outlook Magazine,* 2006.

National Planning Commission Reports, 1991 to 1999.

National Sample Survey Report, 1993-94.

Centre for Monitoring of Indian Economy (CMIE), Public Finance, March 2000.

Samuel, I. & Prakasam, G (1998). "Withering of Welfare State: Liberalised Market and Development Delusion", *Social Watch Country Report.*

Bernstein, H., Crow. B. & Johnson. H. (eds). *Rural Livelihoods: Crises and Responses*, 1992, Oxford University Press, United Kingdonm, at 10.

Deaton, A. & Dreze, J.: "Poverty & Inequality in India: A Rexamination", *Economic and Political Weekly*, 2002, p. 3731.

State Finances: The Factual Position. Finance and Planning Department, June. 1996 & Strategy Paper on Fiscal Problems, Finance Department, 2001, Government of Andhra Pradesh.

<<www.aplivelihoods.org».

Chambers, R. & Conway, G. R., Sustainable Rural Livelihoods: Practical Concepts for the 21st Century, IDS Discussion Paper 296. 1991, p. 1.

Rodgers, G., "What is so Special About a Social Exclusion Approach", in Rodgers, G., Gore, C. and Figueiredo, J.B. (eds), *Social Exclusion: Rhetoric, Reality, Responses*, 1995, IILS/UNDP, Geneva, pp. 253-282.

Figuerora, A., Altamariano, T. and Sulmont, D., Social Exclusion and Inequality in Peru, 1996, IILS/UNDP, Geneva.

Bhalla, A. and Lapeyre. F., "Social Exclusion: Towards an Analytical and Operational Framework", *Development and Change*, Vol. 28 (1997), Institute of Social Studies. 1997, Blackwell Publishers Ltd, Oxford, at p. 419.

Thorat, S.K., "Inequality and Caste Based Discrimination: Reflection on Theory and Empirical Facts with Respect to Scheduled Caste Wage Labour in India", keynote address. Workshop on Economic Development of the Scheduled Castes with special reference to Agricultural Labourers, Gokhale Institute of Politics and Economics, 2002, Pune and Thorat, S.K. & Deshpande, R., "Caste and Labour Market Discrimination". *ILJE*, Vol. 2, No. 4, Oct.-Nov. 1999.

Strategy Paper on Welfare of SCs and STs, Government of Andhra Pradesh, Hyderabad.

Rural Labour Inquiry, Report of General Characteristics of Rural Labour Households, 1983-84, 1987-88. 1993-94, Labour Bureau. Ministry of Labour, Shimla.

National Sample Survey 55th round, July 1999 - June 2000, table no. A-168. 27. Directorate of Economics and Statistics, Government ofAndhra Pradesh, 1990.

Directorate of Economics and Statistics. Government of Andhra Pradesh. 1999 & 1994.

Ellis, F. & Seeley, J. Globalisation and Sustainable Livelihoods: An Initial, Background Briefing Note, 2000, U.K., p. 2.

Rassumssen, L. "Economic Inequality, Human Rights and Labor Markets", *Netherlands Quarterly of Human Rights*, Vol. 15/2, 1997.

Rural Labour Enquiry Report 1994, Labour Bureau, Government of India.

Quarterly Progressive Report on Implementation of Land Ceiling Laws, 1996, Government of India.

Census Reports 1981 and 1991 and 2001.

Agricultural Census, DES, Government of AP.

Educational Statistics, 1998-99, Directorate of School Education, Government of AP.

National Family Health Survey 1999.

S. Mahendra Dev. Base line Survey Reports CESS, 2002.

Dr. Babasaheb Bhimrao Ambedkar: *Writings and Speeches*, Bombay, Government of Maharashtra, Department of Education.

Robbin, Jeanette, *Dr. Ambedkar and His Movement*, Hyderabad, Dr. Ambedkar Publication Society, 1964.

V. Chandra Mowli, B.R., *Ambedkar: Man and His Mission*, New Delhi, Sterling.

Madhu Limaye, "B.R. Ambedkar: A Social Revolutionary", in *Prime Movers: Role of Individuals in History*, New Delhi, Radiant, 1985.

D.R. Jatava, *The Social Philosophy of B.R. Ambedkar*, Agra, Phoenix Publication, 1965.

Aggarwal, Yash, *Education and Human Resource Development*, (New Delhi: Commonwealth, 1988).

APEID, Towards equality of Educational Opportunities, (Bangkok: UNESCO, 1985).

Haq, Mahbub Ul and Khadija Haq, *Human Development in South Asia*, (Islamabad: HDC, 1998).

MHRD, Selected Educational Statistics, 1997-98, (New Delhi: MHRD, 1998).

National Plan of Action, India, Education for All, (New Delhi: Department of Elementary Education and Literacy, MHRD,2006), (first published in 2003).

Oakes, J., "What Educational Indicators? The Case for Assessing the School Context", Educational Evaluation and Policy Analysis, Vol. 11, (1989).

Tyagi, P.N., Education For All: A Graphic Presentation, (New Delhi: NIEPA, 1993).

Ram, Nandu, 1988, *The Mobile Scheduled Castes: Rise of a New Middle Class*, Hindustan Publishing Corporation, New Delhi.

Srinivas, G., 2004, Ideology and Identity: A Study of the Dalit Middle Class in Hyderabad, (Ph.D Dissertation, Mimeo, University of Hyderabad).

Vishwanathan, G. and K. Narasimha Reddy, 1985, *Scheduled Castes: A Study in Educational Achievement*, Scientific Services, Hyderabad.

Farrington, J., Priya Deshinkar, Crig Johnson and Daniel Start (2006), *Policy Windows and Livelihood Futures: Prospects for Poverty Reduction in Rural India*, OUP, New Delhi.

UNDP, (1999), Human development Report prepared by United Nations Development Programme.

Bardhan, Pranab, (1996), "Decentralized Development", *Indian Economic Review*, Vol. XXXI, No. 2, pp. 139-156.

Hobbley, Mary (1996), "Institutional Change within the Forestry Sector: Centralized Decentralization", Working Paper 92, ODI.

Harries, J., (2000), *De-politicizing development: The World Bank and Social Capital*, Left Word, New Delhi.

Manor, James (1999), *The Political Economy of Democratic Decentralization*, Washington, DC, The World Bank.

Sharma, C.H. (2006). 'Decentralization Dilemma: Measuring the Degree and Evaluating the Outcomes', *The Indian Journal of Political Science*, Vol. LXVII, No. 1, Jan.-Mar., 2006, 49-64.

Baumann, Pari, Rajesh Ramakrishnan, Manish Dubey, Rajiv K. Raman, and John Farrington, (2003), Institutional Alternatives and Options for Decentralized Natural Resource Management in India, ODI, Working Paper 230.

Castern Tukka, (2005), "Ownership and Incentives in Joint Forest Management: A Survey", *Development Policy Review*, Vol. 23, pp. 78-104.

Sunderline, W., Angelsen, A., Brian and others (2005), "Livelihoods, Forests and Conservation in Developing Countries: An Overview", *World Development*, special issue, Vol. 33, No. 9, pp. 1383-14302.

Solesbury, Willam, (2003), "Sustainable Livelihoods: A Case Study of the Evolution of DFID Policy", Working Paper 217, Overseas Development Institute.

Desai, M., (2000), *Development and Nationhood: Essays in the Political Economy of South Asia*, OUP, New Delhi.

Kaviraj, S., (ed), (1998), *Politics in India*, OUP.

Chatterjee, P., (1999), *State and Politics in India*, Oxford University Press (OUP), New Delhi.

Blair W. Mary, (1996), 'Democracy, Equity and Common Property

Resources Management in the Indian Subcontinent', *Development and Change,* Vol. 27, pp. 475-499.

Adhikari Bhim, (2005), 'Poverty, Property rights and collective action: Understating the distributive aspects of common property resource management', *Environment and Development Economics,* Vol. 10, pp. 7-31.

Agrawal, Arun and Gupta, Krishna (2005), 'Decentralization and Participation: The Governance of Common Pool Resources in Nepal's Terai', *World Development,* Vol. 33, pp. 1101-1114.

Baumann, Pari, Rajesh Ramakrishnan, Manish Dubey, Rajiv K. Raman, and John Farrington, (2003), Institutional Alternatives and Options for Decentralized Natural Resource Management in India, ODI, Working Paper 230.

Samatha (2005), Andhra Pradesh Community Forest Management Project: A Preliminary independent evaluation of a World Bank Forestry Project, Hyderabad.

Kumaran, K.P, (ed), (2000), Impact of Economic Reforms on SC&STs, National Institute of Rural Development, Hyderabad.

Government of Andhra Pradesh, (2002), Community Forest Management Report, Vol. I, prepared by Project Monitoring Unit.

James Massey. *Dr. B.R. Ambedkar: A study in Just Society,* Centre for Dalit/Subaltern Studies, Manthar, p. 51.

Dr. I.S Vidyasagar. *Concept of Humanism of Dr. Ambedkar,* ABD Publishers, Jaipur, p. 66.

The Bible. New Testament.Mathew.Chapter 5.Verses 5-7.

The Bible.. Old Testament. Book of Ruth.

B.R. Ambedkar (Political thinkers of Modern India-16) edited by Virender Grover. From Chapter 'Ambedkar's Concept of Religion' by F.H. Bennus. Deep & Deep Publication, 1998 New Delhi, p.413

D.R. Jatava, *Ambedkar's Philosophy of Religion,* published by INA SHREE Publishers, Jaipur, p. 66.

Dr. Babasaheb Ambedkar. *Unpublished Writings.* 1989. Chapter 29 Christianizing the Untouchables.

Christophe Jaffrelot. *Analysing and Fighting Caste: Dr. Ambedkar and Untouchability,* Permanent Black, 2005, p. 123.

B.R. Ambedkar: His Relevance Today. Edited by Narayan Rao, A., Soma Sekhar, K., Audiseshaiah, Gyan. Essay. Dr. Ambedkar and Minorities by Prof. Mumtaz Ali Khan. New Delhi, p. 11.

List of Contributors

Prof. D.M. Diwakar, Professor in Economics, Giri Institute of Development Studies, Lucknow.

Dr. L.C. Mallaiah, Faculty in Economics, Department of Economics, Babasaheb Bhimrao Ambedkar Central University, Lucknow.

Dr. K.B. Ratna Kumari, Faculty in Economics, Department of Economics, University of Hyderabad.

Prof. K.Nageswara Rao, Dean & Professor in Economics, Department of Economics, Sri Kridshna Deveraya University, Anantapur, A.P.

Dr. G. Sridevi, Faculty in Economics, Department of Economics, Mount Carmel Management Institute, Banglore.

Dr. Y. Chinnarao, Associate Professor in History, Centre for Study of Exclusion and Inclusive Policy, Jawaharlal Nehru University, New Delhi.

Prof. L. Karunyakara, Director, Ambedkar Center for Dalit and Tribal Studies, Mahtmagandhi International Hindi University. Wardha.

Dr. G. Srinivas, Assistant Professor in Sociology, Jawaharlal Nehru University, New Delhi.

Dr. V.M. Ravikumar, Assistant Professor in History, Babasaheb Bhimrao Ambedkar Central University, Lucknow.

Mr. G. Ravi, Research Scholar, Department of Economics, University of Hyderabad, Hyderabad.

Dr. Sanatan Nayak, Assistant Professor in Economics, Giri Institute of Development Studies, Lucknow.

Nina David, Associate Professor in History, Department of Western History, University of Lucknow, Lucknow.

Mr. Shashi Kumar, Faculty in Human Rights, Department of Human Rights, Babasaheb Bhimrao Ambedkar Central University, Lucknow.

Index